Welfare States in a Turbulent Era

IN A TURBULENT ERA SERIES

These are turbulent and changing times. The longer-term effects of phenomena such as Covid-19, climate change, the rise of China and Brexit as well as populist politics on businesses, the economy and geo-politics are still unknown. Given these rapidly changing economic and social norms, businesses, organisations and institutions must be nimble to thrive. Focusing on one area at a time, this series seeks to investigate best practice, cutting-edge research and new ways of operating in this turbulent era.

For a full list of Edward Elgar published titles, including the titles in this series, visit our website at www.e-elgar.com.

Welfare States in a Turbulent Era

Edited by

Bent Greve

Professor in Social Science, Department of Social Sciences and Business, University of Roskilde, Denmark

IN A TURBULENT ERA SERIES

Cheltenham, UK • Northampton, MA, USA

© Editor and Contributors Severally 2023

Cover image: elCarito on Unsplash

With the exception of any material published open access under a Creative Commons licence (see www.elgaronline.com), all rights are reserved and no part of this publication may be reproduced, stored in a retrieval system or transmitted in any form or by any means, electronic, mechanical or photocopying, recording, or otherwise without the prior permission of the publisher.

Chapter 5 is available for free as Open Access from the individual product page at www.elgaronline.com under a Creative Commons Attribution NonCommercial-NoDerivatives 4.0 International (https://creativecommons.org/licenses/by-nc-nd/4.0/) license.

Published by
Edward Elgar Publishing Limited
The Lypiatts
15 Lansdown Road
Cheltenham
Glos GL50 2JA
UK

Edward Elgar Publishing, Inc.
William Pratt House
9 Dewey Court
Northampton
Massachusetts 01060
USA

A catalogue record for this book
is available from the British Library

Library of Congress Control Number: 2023937049

This book is available electronically in the Elgaronline
Sociology, Social Policy and Education subject collection
http://dx.doi.org/10.4337/9781803926841

Printed on elemental chlorine free (ECF)
recycled paper containing 30% Post-Consumer Waste

ISBN 978 1 80392 683 4 (cased)
ISBN 978 1 80392 684 1 (eBook)

Printed and bound in the USA

Contents

List of figures		vii
List of tables		ix
List of contributors		x
Preface		xiv
1	Welfare states in turbulent times Bent Greve	1
2	Demography – once again and still challenging the welfare states Cristiano Gori and Matteo Luppi	10
3	Self-employment and technology: different models of labor relations Ferry Koster	28
4	The perceived dilemma between debt reduction and a fair society: saving for a rainy day without increasing poverty? Jakub Sowula and Martin Seeleib-Kaiser	48
5	The evolution of welfare attitudes in Europe over the past four decades Gianna Maria Eick	71
6	Climate change and its effect on welfare states Ian Greener	84
7	Keynesian economics steering is back – end of liberal economic policy? Mogens Ove Madsen	98
8	The welfare state and handling health challenges Caroline Rudisill	112
9	Welfare states, growth regimes, and the emergence of the knowledge economy: social policy in turbulent times Julian L. Garritzmann and Bruno Palier	127

10	Allies or enemies of the welfare state? Welfare support and critiques from (left-wing) protesters in Europe *Femke Roosma*	142
11	Conflicting demands and financial abilities? *Bent Greve*	167
12	Effective and fair labour markets: more and focused active labour market policy? *Henri Haapanala*	180
13	Mass migration due to climate change? A critique of the security focus on climate mobilities *Meltem Yilmaz Sener*	195
14	The welfare state in turbulent times: a perspective from the United States *Alex Waddan*	210
15	The way welfare states can develop in turbulent times *Bent Greve*	226

Index 232

Figures

2.1	Projection of the beneficiaries' evolution of pension systems and LTC sectors in selected EU countries: incidence of the retired population over labour force (A), and relative 2019–2070 growth of the dependent population (B)	16
2.2	Cost of ageing in selected EU countries. Projection of the cost of ageing as % of GDP 2019–2070 and relative change (labels) (A). Composition of the cost of ageing by welfare area against peaking years, and relative change (B)	19
3.1	Share of self-employed and union density, 2019	33
3.2	Share of solo self-employed and union density, 2019	34
3.3	Work hours of self-employed and union density, 2019	34
3.4	Digitalization and union density, 2019	35
3.5	Platformization and union density, 2019	35
3.6	Digitalization and share of self-employed, 2019	36
3.7	Digitalization and share of solo self-employed, 2019	37
3.8	Digitalization and work hours of self-employed, 2019	37
3.9	Platformization and share of self-employed, 2019	38
3.10	Platformization and share of solo self-employed, 2019	38
3.11	Platformization and work hours of self-employed, 2019	39
4.1	Necessity analysis	57
5.1	"Government should reduce differences in income levels" (mean) in European regions, 2002–2018	74

5.2	Convergence and divergence of "Government should reduce differences in income levels" (mean) across socioeconomic groups (2002–2018)	76
5.3	Different government areas where spending should be increased/decreased (mean) in Europe, 1985–2015	78
9.1	Enrollment rates in primary, secondary, and tertiary education (regional averages are weighted by country-population size)	130
9.2	Occupational change across countries	133
9.3	Two-dimensional welfare legacies	136
10.1	Support for redistribution and participation in protest (average country means of 2008 and 2016)	151
10.2	Perceived 'bad' standard of living of the unemployed and participation in protest (average country means of 2008 and 2016)	152
10.3	Perceived underuse of benefits and participation in protest (average country means of 2008 and 2016)	152
11.1	Core important national issues for EU citizens since 2014	168

Tables

3.1	Overview of dataset, measures, and period	32
3.2	Panel analysis of union density (2016–2019)	39
3.3	Analyses of country clusters based on work hours of self-employed and DPEI	44
4.1	Sufficiency analysis	60
10.1	Percentage of respondents involved in any type of protest in 2008 and 2016 overall, per type and per country	150
10.2	Multilevel regression analyses on three outcome variables	154
10.3a	Multilevel regression models – moderation effects of country groupings on support for redistribution	157
10.3b	Multilevel regression models – moderation effects of country groupings on the perceived bad standard of living of the unemployed	159
10.3c	Multilevel regression models – moderation effects of country groupings on the perceived underuse of benefits	161
11.1	Percentages in each country who want to spend more or much more on one or more areas, given this could influence level of taxes and benefits in EU countries and the OECD average	170

Contributors

Gianna Maria Eick is an Assistant Professor of Political Science in the Faculty of Social and Behavioural Sciences at the University of Amsterdam and she is part of the Amsterdam Institute for Social Science Research (AISSR). Before, she worked as a Postdoctoral Researcher and Lecturer in Political Science at the University of Konstanz. She obtained a PhD in Social Policy from the University of Kent and a BA/MA in Sociology from the University of Hamburg. Her research interests include welfare states, welfare chauvinism and Social Europe. She currently works on several cross-national research projects on these topics, including the Horizon 2020 project 'The Future of European Social Citizenship' (EUSOCIALCIT).

Julian L. Garritzmann is Professor of Political Science at the Goethe University Frankfurt. He works at the intersection of comparative political economy, public policy, party politics, and public opinion, with a special focus on education and social policy. His previous books include *The World Politics of Social Investments* (two volumes with Silja Häusermann and Bruno Palier, Oxford University Press 2022), *A Loud, But Noisy Signal? Public Opinion, Parties, and Interest Groups in the Politics of Education Reform in Western Europe* (with Marius Busemeyer and Erik Neimanns, Cambridge University Press 2020), and *The Political Economy of Higher Education Finance* (Palgrave 2016).

Cristiano Gori is Full Professor in Social Policy in the Department of Sociology and Social Research at the University of Trento. He holds a PhD in Social Policy at the London School of Economics and Political Science (LSE). His research interest has always been in social policy, looking at both the overall topic and several specific areas. Over the recent years, his work has focused mostly on two subjects: long-term care policies for elderly people and policies against poverty and social exclusion.

Ian Greener is Head of Social Science at the University of Aberdeen. He is extremely concerned about the tendency of those who lead us to be preoccupied with other, short-term challenges, while our planet is driven to become uninhabitable through the lack of serious action to address climate change. Ian's two most recent books examine the great societal challenges we face (*Welfare States in the 21st Century*, Edward Elgar 2021) and how well health systems work (*Comparing Health Systems*, Policy Press 2020). He is proud to live in Scotland with his wife and spaniel Archie, but wishes his adopted country was a bit better at sport.

Bent Greve is Professor in Social Science with an emphasis on welfare state analysis at the University of Roskilde, Denmark. His research interest focuses on the welfare state, and social and labour market policy, often from a comparative perspective. He has published extensively on social and labour market policy, social security, tax expenditures, public sector expenditures and financing of the welfare state. He is editor of *Social Policy & Administration*. Recent books includes *Myths, Narratives and the Welfare State* (Edward Elgar 2021), *Austerity, Retrenchment and the Welfare State* (Edward Elgar 2020), *Poverty: The Basics* (Routledge 2020), *Routledge International Handbook of Poverty* (ed., Routledge 2020), *Welfare, Populism and Welfare Chauvinism* (Policy Press 2019), *Routledge Handbook of the Welfare State* (ed., 2nd edition, Routledge 2019), *Multidimensional Inequalities* (De Gruyter, 2021), and *Rethinking Welfare and the Welfare States* (Edward Elgar 2022).

Henri Haapanala is a PhD candidate in social and economic sciences at the Herman Deleeck Centre for Social Policy, University of Antwerp. His research project studies the effect of organised labour and civil society on social inequality in the advanced democracies. Specifically, he focuses on the effects of trade unions and collective bargaining on labour market inequalities in a comparative European perspective. He holds an MSc in Comparative Social Policy from the University of Oxford.

Ferry Koster is Full Professor of Work and Institutions at the Department of Public Administration and Sociology of Erasmus University Rotterdam. He investigates labour markets and welfare states from an employer perspective. Recent research focuses on the knowledge economy, the platform economy, organisational innovation, and the consequences for institutions.

Matteo Luppi works at the National Institute for the Analysis of Public Policies (INAPP) in Rome. He holds a European PhD in Socio-Economic and Statistical Studies and worked in several research institutes and universities such as Collegio Carlo Alberto, Utrecht University and Politecnico di Milano. His main research interests concern the integrational inequalities and ageing population process, with special attention to comparative studies of welfare states. His works appear in international peer reviewed journals such as *Work, Employment and Society*, *European Sociological Review*, *Current Sociology* and *Social Policy & Administration*.

Mogens Ove Madsen, PhD, Macroeconomic Methodology, Theory and Economic Policy (MaMTEP) research group, Aalborg University, is Associate

Professor in Economics at the Business School. His research is focused on didactics, theory of science and Keynesianism and his empirical work is about economic policy and the EMU. He currently works as Head of the Board of Studies.

Bruno Palier is CNRS Research Director at Sciences Po, Centre d'études européennes et de politique comparée. He works on the comparative political economy of welfare state reforms. He has published numerous articles in international journals and various books, among others *The World Politics of Social Investments* (two volumes with Julian L. Garritzmann and Silja Häusermann, Oxford University Press 2022), *Growth and Capitalism in Advanced Capitalist Economies* (with Anke Hassel, Oxford University Press 2020) and *Welfare Democracies and Party Politics* (with Philip Manow and Hanna Schwander, Oxford University Press 2018).

Femke Roosma is an Assistant Professor at the Department of Sociology at Tilburg University. Her research focuses on (the legitimacy of) social policies and welfare states. She studies multiple dimensions of support for the welfare state, solidarity and deservingness perceptions and (support for) universal basic income.

Caroline Rudisill, MSc, PhD is an Associate Professor and Director of Population Health Sciences Greenville at the Arnold School of Public Health, University of South Carolina. She is a health economist and conducts research on the economics of health behaviours and decision-making about health-related risks. She is also interested in how economic evaluation can play a role in coverage decisions in health systems worldwide particularly when it comes to diabetes and obesity-related interventions such as bariatric surgery and weight loss programmes. She has previously held faculty positions at the London School of Economics and Political Science and Kings College London.

Martin Seeleib-Kaiser is Professor of Comparative Public Policy at the Eberhard Karls University Tübingen (Germany). Prior to his appointment in Tübingen, he held appointments at the University of Oxford (2004–2017), Duke University (1999–2002) and Bremen University (1993–1999; 2002–2004). He was a visiting scholar/guest professor at George Washington University (USA, 1996), Shizuoka University (Japan, 1997), Bielefeld University (Germany, 2003/04), Aalborg University (Denmark, 2008), and the WZB Berlin Social Science Centre (Germany, 2016/17). From 2011 to 2015 he served as Head of the Social Policy Department at the University of Oxford and since 2022 he is the Director of the Institute of Political Science at Tübingen University. Since 2018, he is editor of the *Journal of European Social Policy*. His research focuses on the politics of social policy and comparative social policy analysis.

Areas of research interest are: the relationship between globalisation and welfare systems, political parties and the welfare state, the interplay between 'public' and 'private' social protection policies and associated processes of dualisation, welfare state change and continuity, and social rights of EU citizens. He has published widely, amongst others in: *American Sociological Review*, *British Journal of Industrial Relations*, *Comparative Political Studies*, *European Journal of Social Security*, *Journal of Common Market Studies*, *Journal of European Social Policy*, *Social Policy and Administration*, *Social Politics*, and *West European Politics*.

Jakub Sowula studied Political Science, Economics and Mathematics (First State Examination Degree 2018) at the Eberhard Karls University Tübingen (Germany). He finished his second state examination degree with distinction at the seminar for teacher education and training Rottweil (Gym, 2020). Currently, he is a PhD candidate at Tübingen (Germany) investigating the relationship between welfare-state-related knowledge, welfare deservingness and welfare attitudes with a focus on youth. He is also a researcher at the University of Teacher Education Berne (Switzerland). His research interests are welfare attitudes and welfare deservingness, welfare state change and continuity from a comparative perspective, welfare regimes, public policy analysis, political and civic education, and intuitive explanatory patterns in education. His thesis on welfare state change in Germany, Sweden, Italy and the US received the Polis e.V. award for an outstanding thesis in political science.

Alex Waddan is Associate Professor in American Politics at the University of Leicester specialising in the study of US social policy, especially in the fields of health and social welfare. He is the author or co-author of six books including *The Politics of Policy Change* (Georgetown University Press 2012) and *Obamacare Wars: Federalism, State Politics and the Affordable Care Act* (University of Kansas 2016), as well as numerous peer reviewed journal articles.

Meltem Yilmaz Sener, PhD, is a Senior Researcher at the Center for Intercultural Communication at VID Specialized University, Norway. She got her PhD degree in Sociology from the University of Illinois, Urbana-Champaign in the USA in 2010. Previously, she also worked at Nord University as an associate professor and Istanbul Bilgi University as an assistant professor, in addition to holding visiting positions in the US and Norway. Her research interests are in migration, transnational studies, development, social inequality, social policy, and gender.

Preface

Welfare states are seemingly in a constant flux and changes. This as a consequence of many and varied circumstances from external factors to national changes in preferences. Thanks to all contributors to this book in ensuring high quality chapters for the book. This also implies that many and varied viewpoints and from different disciplinary approaches are presented within the book.

I hope the book overall will stimulate academics and others across disciplines interested in understanding the course of developments for the welfare states in continuing turbulence.

Bagsværd and Roskilde
October 2022
Bent Greve

1. Welfare states in turbulent times
Bent Greve

1.1 INTRODUCTION

Welfare states have for a long time been argued to be in crisis (OECD 1981). This could be due to exogenous shocks, or perhaps conflicting perspectives on what to prioritize in the different welfare states. There have also been variations in the types of national crisis as well as the ever-present issue of whether the ambition, goals and citizens' expectations of what should be delivered by the welfare states has been reached. There have been discussions on the dismantling, restructuring and/or cutting back of the welfare states. Recent years seem to indicate that different kinds of crises have emerged, and which are often very unpredictable, such as the COVID-19 pandemic and the Ukrainian crisis, and earlier in this century the financial crisis. At the same time there is the climate crisis, which also can influence quality of life as well as being a pressure on the resources available for welfare states more generally. Spending on how to reduce the impact of climate change might thus be in competition with money for the financing of the welfare states. Changes in technology causing a huge impact on jobs also implies turbulence. This is not just due to changes in the number of available jobs, but also changes in the quality hereof that are on the way, including a possible squeezing of the middle class (OECD 2019). Increasing levels of economic inequality have raised issues not only on the degree of redistribution the welfare state shall try to reach, but also the legitimacy of the welfare states if inequality continues to be very high, implying that the welfare state will redress fewer of the consequences caused by market forces. Demographic transitions such as an increasing elderly population are still and have for a long time been considered a challenge, with pressure on especially the health and long-term care systems, but also on how to finance pensions in the years to come. Health and long-term care are, at the same time, welfare state services with a high degree of public support.

For decades, inflation has not in reality been important to be aware of, but with the Ukraine crisis and difficulties in trade due to the COVID-19 pandemic, it has once again come onto the agenda for future development. The COVID-19 and Ukrainian crises have thus not only increased the pressure on spending for existing as well as possible new purposes, but have also brought back the issue of the impact of inflation on welfare states, including how it influences the buying power of social security benefits and the economic distribution among different groups in society. Thereby, the crises have also raised the issue of what is the best economic policy to steer societies in the wanted direction.

It is with the background of these examples that this book tries to analyse and discuss the development of mainly rich Western welfare states and tries to integrate into the presentation the very difficult issue of how to prioritize the scarce resources between the many competing needs. This is because, even if being aware of a number of challenges, this does not inform about how to tackle the challenges. As an illustrative example, moving towards lower economic growth might help with the climate crisis, but it would also imply fewer options to fulfil the demand for more welfare state service and income transfers. Lower economic growth can further increase the conflict between, and options for, change in public and private consumption in societies. There can even, and often will, be a number of contradictions with winners and losers of different types of change. The use of new technology in welfare states, beside the possible strong consequences for those in the labour market, for example, could make part of the administration of benefits and services better and more efficient. However, the use hereof can also imply bias in monitoring users' welfare benefits and services, such as by profiling who is at risk of becoming long-term unemployed and in need of specific support in the unemployment benefit system.

Frustrations and conflicts between different social groups, sometimes labelled 'them and us' in different countries, often related to migration or possibly the divide between rich and poor or those with a feeling of being included and those feeling excluded, is also an issue that needs to be tackled in the years to come. However, not only is a more traditional Robin Hood-type debate emerging, but also the intergenerational perspectives are at the front of debates, combined with where to spend available resources and for which purposes. Some instruments that might help to alleviate one problem can, at the same time, increase others. This is part of the conflict on how to make decisions and argue the case for why this is seen as the best possible solution. The balance between state, market and civil society is therefore also once again a battle zone filled with conflicting perspectives on who should do what and under what conditions.

It is with this background that this book, through chapters by authors with diverse backgrounds (theoretically, geographically, gender and age) as well as topics covered, presents the pressures and possible ways forward for welfare states in the years to come. The concluding chapter brings the contributions together, with an emphasis on how to interpret and understand how turbulent times pose options for new directions and developments hereof, as well as implying risks for the welfare states.

1.2 CONFLICTING PERSPECTIVES

Individuals, interest groups, generations, ideology are labels we can use to understand that there are many different interested parties who want to have a say in how a given society should develop in the years to come and how to prioritize the existing resources. Interest groups can be more or less well articulated as interest, and thereby be more or less argued not as self-interest, but as either a necessary politics or what is argued to be in the best interest for overall societal development. This includes strands of research to understand perspectives on welfare state development related to issues of austerity, populism, welfare chauvinism, economic policy, technology, etc., and the literature is large (but for a number of publications see Pierson 2001; Starke 2006; Norris and Inglehart 2019; Greve 2021; Furedi 2018; Peralta-Alva and Roitman 2018; Starke, Kaasch, and van Hooren 2013). There are also conflicting perspectives as to what, if anything, shall be done with regards to inequality and poverty (see Sen 1973; Atkinson 2015; Stiglitz 2012; Alvaredo et al. 2018).

Solving the different demands for having a larger part of the cake in a society is not a new issue, but with seemingly more and varied ambitions for the role of the state this can be exaggerated. This is even more so if some have the feeling of being left behind when the train is moving, which is part of the more populist approach, but also part of the broader divisions of the availability of options for some but not all in many societies (see for example Isenberg 2017; McGarvey 2018; Hochschild 2016). This is also no longer just a rich/poor divide, but also a squeezing of the middle class (OECD 2019). Included herein is also, for some, the perception that not all who get benefits should have them, e.g. a classical debate on deservingness (Laenen 2020). We also do not have a scientific way of arguing whether some are more deserving than others, and perhaps this can only be done by looking into and defining how we understand a poverty line and arguing for what a decent and just society is, although theories of justice risk being normative perceptions of what the good society is without good instruments to ensure the best decisions. Still, social sciences need to inform about the consequences of different choices as best and most effectively as possible, including the varying impacts on individuals as well as on societies. The average information on impacts is often not sufficient enough in order to grasp the impact on various groups in societies. These types of conflicts on who gets and who does not are amplified when an unforeseen crisis arises, not only because this implies an economic pressure on the individual and society, but also because it might imply the need to move resources from one part of the welfare state to another, such as when demographic composition changes.

However, not only is there a conflict on where to use resources. There can and will be, as has been the case for as long as rulers have wanted to have income for the state (Keen and Slemrod 2021), conflicting perspectives on where and how best to finance welfare states with as few distortions as possible, as well as the system being just. This also includes that support for welfare interventions can be less when and if connected with how it is paid for. So, in relation not only to the discussion on where to spend the money, but also who shall spend it, a constant topic for debates is how the money shall be financed. This is all while discussions often seem to be in camps of supporting either the public or the private sector, with the exception of pure public goods, when in reality the public and private sector are in fact strongly dependent on each other (Greve 2022).

It is therefore overall a question not only of where and how to spend money, but also for what purpose, including – given the environmental challenges – how to keep the welfare states' generational contract (Birnbaum et al. 2017) active while trying to reduce the climate crisis. Furthermore, this is, which is only to a very limited extent touched upon in this book, also a conflict between different countries around the globe. This is because, for example, the zero growth approach might be fine for already rich countries, but not for low-income countries with a high degree of poverty and lack of economic resources. Low growth might also in individual countries be fine for those already enjoying a good standard of living, but not necessarily for those without one. This is a conflict between the haves and the have nots (Ben-Ami 2012).

This does not imply the situation is the same and with the same core issues in all types of countries, it is however a challenge for all welfare states to steer the boat in turbulent weather. The rest of this chapter gives a snapshot of what to expect in the individual chapters and a few concluding remarks.

1.3   OVERVIEW OF THE BOOK

The book is divided into two separate but interlinked parts. The chapters are ordered so there are some presenting the core challenges now and those expected in the years to come (Part 1 – Chapters 2 to 7) and then a section analysing pathways for welfare states' future development and how to cope with the challenges ahead for the welfare states, as well as a focus outside Europe and a concluding chapter.

After this introductory chapter follows Chapter 2 by Gori and Luppi who present one of the strong challenges for welfare states – the change in demographic composition with an ageing population implying a new balance between those in the labour market and those outside it. This questions the generational contract, but also how to steer and manage these changes in different welfare states given that strong increases in expenditures on health and long-term care as well as pensions might be underway.

Technology is a challenge, and this is the focus of Chapter 3 by Koster. The focus is on understanding how new technology and work are related by looking at the connections between digitalization, the use of platforms for jobs, self-employment and labour relations. Besides the possible risk for those losing their jobs as a consequence of new technology, other risks are a lower degree of union members, as well as a lower degree of social security especially for those who become solely self-employed. New cleavages thereby arise in welfare states, presumably also implying a need for new types of social security.

In Chapter 4 Sowula and Seeleib-Kaiser discuss how to combine debt reduction and fiscal consolidation, including saving for a rainy day, such as a financial crisis. They use fuzzy-set qualitative comparative analysis (fsQCA) for a large number of European countries to show that not only export-driven approaches are a possible pathway, but also that a strong focus on full employment would be a way to tackle the issue. At the same time, they show the dilemma that high levels of economic growth can, for environmental reasons, be difficult and thereby reduce the strategic options available for governments in modern welfare states.

The attitudes of voters, as is the focus of Chapter 5 by Eick, are central in order to understand what influences decision makers when prioritizing in welfare states. The overall level of support to welfare states seems to be stable, while at the same time there is support for social investment policies such as education, but still also strong support for classical welfare states services such as health and long-term care. This is while at the same time at least part of income transfers, such as unemployment benefit and social assistance, do receive less support. This can influence how welfare states continue to develop.

The climate crisis is a strong challenge, as is the focus in Chapter 6 by Greener, including how it influences the options for other purposes in welfare states. How to find a way to mitigate the consequences of climate changes is important, and it is pointed out that one might need a new social contract implying a more equitable distribution of resources making the transition to a more green economy possible.

What type of economic policy to pursue in a number of the Western world countries has been discussed for quite some time. As discussed in Chapter 7 by Madsen, the question is whether Keynesian economic policy is back. In the 1970s, Keynesian economic policy became discredited and was replaced in most countries by a stronger focus on the role of the market. The financial crisis and especially the COVID-19 crisis were clear indications of the need for state support to ensure the overall level of demand. In this way this might have implied that support for the role of the state in economic policy has again become stronger.

Chapter 7 is the last chapter in Part 1 and is followed in Part 2 by a number of chapters focusing on the options and possibilities for welfare state development.

Health is one of the strongest challenges for the welfare states due to, among other things, demographic changes, and this is the focus of Chapter 8 by Rudisill. This includes the economic pressure due to the ageing societies, but also the continuous new, better and more expensive options for treatment and also the high degree of inequalities in health, including access to treatment. Whether new ways of influencing behaviour, such as nudging, can be part of relieving the pressure on the welfare states is still an open question. Technology seems also likely to be part of the answers to the question of solving the increasing need with the available economic resources.

The knowledge economy also poses new challenges for welfare states, as presented by Garritzmann and Palier in Chapter 9, including variations in educational attainment level and – as also discussed in other parts of the book – new technology. The consequences vary across different countries and types of welfare states. They show four potential welfare reform scenarios to cope with these challenges. These include social investments, social protectionism, market liberalism or basic income strategies. They will all have different distributional and societal consequences for the welfare states' development.

Chapter 10 by Roosma looks into the legitimacy of the welfare states, especially by focusing on those who participate in social movements and protest about the changes in a number of welfare states. They raise the important question: Are people who participate in protest more or less supportive of the welfare state compared to the general public and are they more or less critical of the welfare state? The chapter's conclusion is that those criticizing the policies are often those who are most in favour of and support the welfare states. Thus, left-wing supporters of the welfare states, even by supporting the welfare states, also risk reducing the support for the welfare states by the protests about, and critiques of, their development.

There are conflicting demands and scarce resources, and as discussed in Chapter 11 by Greve, this raises the need for using evidence as part of the decision-making process, but also in order to be able to manage economic crises and ensure a stable public sector economy. Those countries with a stable public sector economy have thus been better able to cope with bubbles as well as other unexpected crises than others. At the same time, this does not reduce the need for international cooperation in order to ensure reduce tax evasion, the use of loopholes, etc. in order to achieve the necessary tax income to finance welfare states.

Active labour market policy (ALMP) has, in a number of countries, been seen as important for a well-functioning labour market, which is the core issue for Chapter 12 by Haapanala. The chapter shows that despite not all ALMPs being effective, the policy has an important function, albeit also the risk that part of the policies (i.e. ALMPs) are mainly used by those who have the best chance to return to the labour market and therefore get the most help. However, the chapter also shows that human capital development has again become more of a focus within the ALMP.

Climate change is covered in several chapters in the book. In Chapter 13 by Yilmaz Sener the focus is on whether this will imply growing migration and thereby implying an increased pressure on welfare states, such as also witnessed earlier in this century as a consequence of civil wars. This has been seen by some as a security threat and implied a risk of more closed societies. The chapter analyses this and points also to other reasons for migration, as well as the situation whereby people will not be able to migrate and will have to live with the dire consequences of the strong impact on living conditions in countries most exposed to climate change.

Chapter 14, by Waddan, takes a look at the US welfare state as a contrasting case to many European countries' approach to welfare. It shows that even if there have been changes, such as the Affordable Care Act, and some changes towards supporting more vulnerable families and groups during the COVID-19 crisis, the US is still a clear example of a liberal welfare state with a number of hidden elements, implying that inequality is high and many continue to live in poverty.

Lastly, Chapter 15 sums up and concludes the book.

1.4 CONCLUDING REMARKS

We are living in turbulent times, and recent years have seen stronger turbulence than we have been used to for many years. Before the financial crisis in this century, especially the oil-price crisis in the 1970s could be mentioned as a time which presented a strong challenge to welfare states and their future development. Turbulence in weather can change the direction of the wind, but also the level of sun, rain, storms, etc., all of which influence overall development. This is also the case for the welfare states. One implication is, presumably, that there is a stronger need today for having money available for a rainy day, and this needs to be balanced with the ongoing needs and expectations from the voters, the impact of changes in technology and demography, and the need for higher spending in relation to climate change.

At the same time, the welfare state can be the institution that can help in making the transitions and changes to the possible ways to live for those hit by the strong changes. The welfare state can reduce possible market failures, as well as functioning as a so-called 'Piggy Bank' (Barr 2001). It can also help in the redistribution of resources over the life cycle, including between rich and poor, and thereby take into consideration that we do not all have the same capabilities (Nussbaum 2005), and then this can support the option that if most people are to have a chance of a good life, then societal intervention is needed. Which form this takes can be discussed, as well as the size hereof, but it does not question the need for a strong welfare state to ensure the overall best options for a number of people. How to balance the different options given the scarce resources available – which, if low economic growth is a target, will be even stronger – implies the need for coherent and transparent information on how and in what way priorities are done.

LITERATURE

Alvaredo, Facundo, Lucas Chancel, Thomas Piketty, Emmanuel Saez, and Gabriel Zucman. 2018. *World Inequality Report 2018*. Cambridge, MA: Belknap Press.

Atkinson, Tony. 2015. 'What Can Be Done about Inequality?'. *Juncture* 22 (1): 32–41. https://doi.org/10.1111/j.2050-5876.2015.00834.x.

Barr, Nicholas. 2001. *The Welfare State as Piggy Bank: Information, Risk, Uncertainty, and the Role of the State*. Oxford: Oxford University Press.

Ben-Ami, Daniel. 2012. *Ferraris for All: In Defence of Economic Progress*. Bristol: Policy Press.

Birnbaum, Simon, Tommy Ferrarini, Kenneth Nelson, and Joakim Palme. 2017. *The Generational Welfare Contract: Justice, Institutions and Outcomes*. Cheltenham, UK and Northampton, MA, USA: Edward Elgar Publishing.

Furedi, Frank. 2018. *Populism and the European Culture Wars: The Conflict of Values between Hungary and the EU*. Abingdon: Routledge.

Greve, Bent. 2021. *Research Handbook of Austerity, Retrenchment and Populism*. Cheltenham, UK and Northampton, MA, USA: Edward Elgar Publishing.

Greve, Bent. 2022. *The Role of the Public Sector: Economics and Society*. Cheltenham, UK and Northampton, MA, USA: Edward Elgar Publishing.

Hochschild, Arlie Russell. 2016. *Strangers in Their Own Land: Anger and Mourning on the American Right*. New York: The New Press.

Isenberg, Nancy. 2017. *White Trash: The 400-Year Untold History of Class in America*. New York: Penguin.

Keen, Michael, and Joel Slemrod. 2021. *Rebellion, Rascals, and Revenue: Tax Follies and Wisdom through the Ages*. Princeton, NJ: Princeton University Press.

Laenen, Tijs. 2020. *Welfare Deservingness and Welfare Policy: Popular Deservingness Opinions and Their Interaction with Welfare State Policies*. Cheltenham, UK and Northampton, MA, USA: Edward Elgar Publishing.

McGarvey, Darren. 2018. *Poverty Safari: Understanding the Anger of Britain's Underclass*. London: Picador.

Norris, Pippa, and Ronald Inglehart. 2019. *Cultural Backlash: Trump, Brexit, and Authoritarian Populism*. Cambridge: Cambridge University Press.

Nussbaum, Martha C. 2005. 'Capabilities as Fundamental Entitlements: Sen and Social Justice'. In Alexander Kaufman (Ed.), *Capabilities Equality: Basic*

Issues and Problems (pp. 44–70). Abingdon: Routledge. https://doi.org/10.4324/9780203799444.
OECD. 1981. *The Welfare State in Crisis*. Paris: OECD.
OECD. 2019. *Under Pressure: The Squeezed Middle Class*. Paris: OECD.
Peralta-Alva, Adrian, and Augustin Roitman. 2018. 'Technology and the Future of Work'. WP/18/207. IMF Working Paper.
Pierson, Paul. 2001. 'Coping With Permanent Austerity: Welfare State Restructuring in Affluent Democracies'. In Paul Pierson (Ed.), *The New Politics of the Welfare State* (pp. 410–456). Oxford: Oxford University Press. https://doi.org/10.1109/TELSKS.2011.6143211.
Sen, Amartya. 1973. *On Economic Inequality*. New York: Norton.
Starke, Peter. 2006. 'The Politics of Welfare State Retrenchment: A Literature Review'. *Social Policy and Administration* 40 (1): 104–120. https://doi.org/10.1111/j.1467-9515.2006.00479.x.
Starke, Peter, Alexandra Kaasch, and Franca van Hooren. 2013. *The Welfare State as Crisis Manager: Explaining the Diversity of Policy Responses to Economic Crisis*. Basingstoke: Palgrave Macmillan.
Stiglitz, Joseph E. 2012. *The Price of Inequality: How Today's Divided Society Endangers Our Future*. New York: W.W. Norton & Company.

2. Demography – once again and still challenging the welfare states
Cristiano Gori and Matteo Luppi

2.1 INTRODUCTION

European and developed countries have been experiencing ageing pressure for quite a long time now. More than 20 years have passed since 2001, when the European Council in Stockholm highlighted the need to 'regularly review the long-term sustainability of public finances, including the expected strains caused by the demographic changes ahead'. Today, ageing populations represent an overall societal risk and pose crucial challenges to national economies and societies, and especially to the sustainability of national welfare states (Gusmano and Okma, 2018).

A Eurostat demographic projection of the expected changes in the European population between 2019 and 2070 indicates that, while the size of the young population – those aged under 14[1] – will decrease by around 15%, the size of very old population – those aged over 85 – will grow by 170%. This growth will vary across countries. However, the ageing process is a widespread phenomenon in Europe, as is shown by the fact that 19 of the 20 countries with the oldest populations in the world are European Member States. Indeed, in Europe a steady total fertility rate below the natural replacement rate of 2.1, a progressive increase in life expectancy and the recent entry into retirement age of the baby boom generation represent the leading causes of the expected ageing process (European Commission, 2018). This process will result in a progressive reduction in the ratio between those of working age and those of non-working age in the population in the coming years.

In general terms, the number of dependent people, especially the elderly, that each worker or adult will have to directly or indirectly and formally or informally support will increase (European Commission, 2021a). This will undoubtedly impact the welfare state. On the one hand, it poses a sustainability issue: even without considering a potential increase in population needs, national governments have to, and will have to, face the welfare demands of the dependent population with, in relative terms, reduced resources (Meier and Werding, 2010). On the other hand, it poses a feasibility issue: national systems have to and will have to (re-)organise their welfare sectors to be able to respond to greater demand, not only in absolute and relative terms but also in terms of its internal composition concerning population needs (European Commission, 2020a), especially regarding the distribution of (new and old) social risks over the life cycle.

In particular, the effects generated by the ageing process can be understood by looking at three main areas: demand-side pressures; supply-side effects; and financial and economic needs.

Demand-side pressures refer to the modification of the demographic structure in terms of absolute and relative ageing, its internal composition regarding cohorts and genders, and also family composition. These pressures result in a variation in the amount of welfare benefits needed by the population in the coming decades. These pressures are mainly driven by structural variation in the demographic composition, but also by modification of other welfare agencies, among which include the role played by households. Concerning this, although the role that the family plays in the overarching architecture of the welfare system varies among European countries, it has a crucial redistributive role in European welfare states as it provides family members with financial and non-financial resources before the welfare state is called on to jump in (Frericks et al., 2021).

As is better explained in the next section, evidence indicates that welfare state redistributive mechanisms move along the line of demographic cohorts rather than between different socio-economic status groups (Esping-Andersen and Myles, 2009; Gàl and Medgyesi, 2017; Vanhuysse et al., 2021). In other words, the more polarised (or aged) a population structure is, the more consumption of welfare benefits there tends to be and the more pressure there is on the working-age population, who mainly sustain the feasibility of the welfare system (Vanhuysse et al., 2021). Similarly, the thinner family structures are, the less support they can provide along intergenerational lines (Saraceno and Keck, 2010).

Supply-side effects are the efforts that welfare sectors have to make to react to these demand-side pressures. In particular, assuming a constant level of the quality and intensity of services provided, they indicate the potential gaps between different scenarios and actual system capacity. European welfare states diverge in a plurality of ways (Esping-Andersen, 1990; Greve, 2019) such as generosity, accessibility, development, orientation toward kinds of benefits (in-kind vs monetary measures), familialism (Ferrera, 1996) and financial mechanisms (Sinfield, 2019). The same applies to single welfare sectors such as pensions (Bonoli and Natali, 2012), long-term care (Gori et al., 2016a) and healthcare (Gevers et al., 2000). Even assuming similar welfare benefit consumption generated by the demand-side pressures, the response required for national systems to satisfy it would differ concerning the specific characteristics of their welfare sectors. Reasoning regarding future welfare state sustainability and assuming a no-policy-change scenario indicates that a mild increase in the *quantity* of welfare benefits in a comprehensive and generous welfare state will potentially result in more considerable pressure than a more significant expansion in a marginal welfare state.

Financial and economic needs constitute the cost attached to these different scenarios. In this chapter we assume this area is the outcome of our exercise. Various aspects of welfare state outcomes can be measured, such as their capacity for inequality reduction (Korpi and Palme, 1998). However, welfare state expenditure in GDP terms is commonly conceived as a proxy for welfare state generosity and comprehensiveness (Jacques and Noël, 2018). Furthermore, system sustainability is closely linked with the fiscal pressure generated and the relative variation needed to account for the ageing process, as the recent wave of retrenchment that interested various European welfare states suggests (Levy, 2021). To understand the impact of the ageing process on the sustainability of welfare systems it is essential to monitor and carefully read the evolution of demand-side pressures, their interaction with specific supply-side characteristics of national systems and how their joint effects translate into variations in financial and economic needs.

Specific elements can mitigate these envisaged impacts of ageing on welfare sustainability. Besides direct policy interventions, which are likely to happen in the future but the effects of which are complex to estimate, other elements are at stake. The expected lengthening of the healthy stage in later life could result in more extended and differentiated forms of lengthening of the active phase, positively impacting the working-age/non-working-age ratio. Technological transitions could also support this, particularly the introduction of new technologies which on the one hand can help the economy amid a shrinking working force and on the other support and ease the raising of the working age. Furthermore, welfare sustainability can also be influenced by the potential outsourcing role played by private welfare pillars.

This chapter focuses on how the three areas related to ageing processes can potentially affect the sustainability of European welfare systems in the long run. It concentrates mainly on areas more exposed to the ageing of the population (pensions, health and long-term care) in a limited set of EU countries selected because they have different welfare state orientations and are subject to diverging demographic pressures. Using aggregated data from Eurostat and recent European Commission reports the chapter analyses how European countries are characterised regarding the three areas identified. A further section deals with the drivers that can potentially mitigate the impacts generated by the intersection between demand-side pressures and supply-side effects. This descriptive overview allows an understanding of how diverging demographic pressures will impact different welfare sector systems.

2.2 DEMAND-SIDE PRESSURES

In social science debates in recent decades high importance has been attached to welfare state redistribution mechanisms and capacity. Regarding the topic of this chapter, the issue is not which redistributive approach is more important or efficient but instead that of contextualising these redistributive mechanisms within the context of ageing populations.

In a recent work based on a sample of over 400,000 Europeans in 22 EU countries, Vanhuysse et al. (2021, 11) clearly show that '[European] welfare states serve as a channel through which working-age people of higher status support people of inactive age across all socio-economic status groups'. The authors indicate that even after controlling for the progressive role of financing contributions (taxes) and the – less progressive – role of welfare benefits (in terms of both cash and in-kind measures), redistribution between age groups is the primary redistribution mechanism in European welfare states (ibid.).

This finding highlights the centrality of the ageing population concerning the sustainability of welfare state systems. Furthermore, it indicates that the ratio between those of working age and those of non-working age in the population – the total-age-dependency ratio[2] – constitutes a helpful demographic index to read the internal age composition of a given population and that it can be seen as a potential proxy for the demographic pressure on the welfare system. In particular, it represents an important tool concerning the welfare pillars more exposed to ageing pressure, such as pensions, healthcare and the long-term care system.

A Eurostat demographic projection[3] (baseline scenario) indicates that in the next five decades in the 27 EU Member States the ratio between those of working age and those of non-working age will grow by a factor slightly higher than 1.4, passing from 54.9% in 2019 to an estimated 78.4% (+23.5 percentage points) in 2070. In the same period, while the overall European population is expected to decrease from 447.7 million to 424.3 million, a reduction of around 5%, the dependent population (the young and older adults) will grow by about 8 percentage points. Furthermore, while European countries differ in their demographic structures and related ageing processes, the long-run horizon seems to level out these differences, with the majority showing growth similar to the EU27 factor (1.4). In contrast, France, Finland and Sweden perform slightly better (1.2/1.3) whereas three Central-Eastern European countries (Poland, Lithuania and Slovakia) plus Malta and Luxembourg turn out to be more exposed with a factor higher than 1.6.

In recent decades migratory inflows have helped offset the shrinking of the working-age population (European Commission, 2021a). Both direct – using expected net migratory inflows – and indirect – adding a correction equal to 10% of the projected decline in the working-age population to the net migratory inflows – Eurostat projections account for the variation in the active population related to migration. However, it should be considered that due to high historical volatility over time and between countries, assumptions in migration projections are methodologically challenging. Bearing this in mind, Eurostat data indicate that in the EU as a whole net inflows are projected to decrease from about 0.3% of the EU population in 2019 to around 0.2% from the mid-2020s onwards. Although net migration is assumed to become positive in all EU Member States between 2019 and 2070, potentially reducing the impact of ageing populations, in some countries the situation differs. In Central-Eastern European countries such as Latvia, Lithuania and Romania cumulative net migration – the relation between emigrants and immigrants in the period considered – will be negative, making migration a further element fuelling the ageing population.

The increase of 23.5 percentage points (pps) in the proportion of the overall EU population that is non-working from 2019 to 2070 has little to do with the youngest cohorts. The proportion of Europeans aged below 14 in the working-age population will remain more or less stable in this period, only increasing by about 0.8 pps from 23.5% to 24.3% (corresponding to a relative increase of 3.4%). In contrast, the 'weight' of the older adult population on the working-age population follows a different pattern. An old-age-dependency ratio projection indicates an increase of 72% in the next five decades, growing from 34.1% in 2019 to 54% in 2070. According to this projection, across the 27 EU Member States in 2070, while there will be one child for every four adults, there will be around 0.6 older people for each adult.

Of course, these patterns vary among the EU countries. In Poland, the demographic structure will significantly turn toward ageing no earlier than 2040, indicating significant room for manoeuvre. On the contrary, in other countries such as Italy and France, like the overall EU27 area, and with a milder intensity in the Netherlands, Germany and Denmark, the ageing process is already entirely in place. It will steadily grow until around 2045 and then slow down. However, even in countries with a better outlook the demographic structure will significantly change in the long run. In the period considered, the proportion of the overall non-working-age population will grow by 19.3 pps in Denmark, 20.6 pps in Germany and 22.0 pps in the Netherlands, values not so far from the expected overall proportion in the EU 27 (23.5 pps) and that in Italy (25 pps).

Besides demographic structural changes, a further worrying element concerns the modification of the demographic composition in terms of household size. These two elements – demographic structure and family composition – are significantly connected concerning welfare sustainability. Even in more defamilialised welfare sectors families have central agency in the welfare diamond (Evers et al., 1994). In the life cycle, families are crucial in producing welfare for their members, both in economic (i.e. as a safety net system) and non-financial (i.e. caring and education) terms, integrating the formal provision offered by the welfare state and the market.

In the last decade, while the absolute number of households in Europe has risen, the average size has declined. Between 2010 and 2019, average household composition slowly reduced from 2.4 to 2.3 members. Notably, in 2019 around a third of all households in Europe consisted of a single person, a 19% increase since 2010. Furthermore, the share of households without children has steadily grown, contrasting with a stable trend for those with children (European Commission, 2020b).

2.3 SUPPLY-SIDE EFFECTS

How do these household and demographic structural modifications translate into the expected supply of welfare benefits? A recent Ageing Report (European Commission, 2021a) provides valuable tools for a preliminary understanding of the potential magnitude of this 'ageing wave' that the European welfare states will face in the coming years.[4]

In line with demographic projections, in the EU total labour supply is set to decline in the long term. Although the expected total participation rate for those aged 20–64 is projected to rise from 78.2% in 2019 to 80.7% in 2070, mainly driven by higher female participation and the expected results of legislated pension reforms implemented in various countries which will raise the retirement age (see below), the labour supply in the EU by those aged 20 to 64 is projected to fall by 15.5% in the period 2019–2070.

In contrast, the three welfare pillars more exposed to ageing pressure – pensions, long-term care and healthcare systems – present an opposite trend. While the average age at which people exit the labour market in the EU is expected to increase by 1.6 years for men and by 1.8 years for women by 2070, in the same period the estimated duration of retirement extends by around four years – 4.2 years for men and 3.6 years for women.

The double effect of retirement extension and the relative reduction in the size of the working-age group compared to those in retirement severely impacts the relationship between workers and pensioners. At the EU level in the period 2019–2070, the estimated increase of 28 million (public) pensioners and the expected reduction in the labour force population (14–64 years) of almost 32 million translates into an increase of 25 pps in the ratio of pensioners to the labour force, passing from 57% to 83% (Figure 2.1, panel A).

This trend varies among the EU countries. Although all the countries in Figure 2.1 have an increase in the ratio of pensioners to workers, its magnitude differs widely. While the Netherlands and Denmark are expected to respectively experience a slight increase and a stable trend in this ratio and Italy and Germany will behave similarly to the European trend, estimations for Poland and France indicate that pensioners will slightly outnumber the labour force.

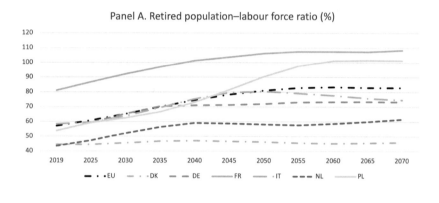

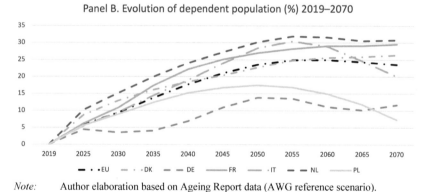

Note: Author elaboration based on Ageing Report data (AWG reference scenario).

Figure 2.1 *Projection of the beneficiaries' evolution of pension systems and LTC sectors in selected EU countries: incidence of the retired population over labour force (A), and relative 2019–2070 growth of the dependent population (B)*

Estimations of the potential beneficiaries of long-term care (LTC) in the period considered lead to similar concerns regarding growing pressure on the capacity of the system. At the EU level, the dependent population potentially needing both in-kind and cash LTC benefits will grow almost linearly with an increase of 3.5 pps every five years until 2040, with a slowly reducing trend in the following 15 years and then a reversal in the trend during the decade before 2070. However, even accounting for a decrease in the size of the European dependent population after 2060, European Ageing Working Group (AWG) projections (European Commission, 2021a) indicate a relative rise of 23.5% between 2019 and 2070 (Figure 2.1, panel A).

This overall trend and also the national ones are not only affected by the evolution of the demographic structure, even if the effect of the baby boom generation entering the older segment of the population in the period 2019–2040 is clear. Given the relative institutionalisation of the LTC sector in the welfare area (Gori et al., 2016a), they are also affected by the evolution and the characteristics of LTC systems themselves – for instance the degree of recourse to informal care provision or to the private market – and also the overall national health level, which depends on future developments in the quality of life in each country (see below).

Figure 2.1 takes 2019 as the reference year and indicates how national LTC sectors will need to expand their capacity – or find alternatively solutions – to meet the evolution of the potential need for LTC in the next 50 years. At the EU level, the lion's share of this expansion is expected in the next 20 to 30 years with a peak in 2050 at an estimated 25% growth in LTC needs. Denmark, France and the Netherlands are in line with the average EU estimation, but the latter two countries show a slightly larger increase in demand for services over the period analysed, also as a consequence of the high level of development and generosity of their LTC sectors (Gori et al., 2016b). Italy follows a similar pattern but with a significant drop after 2050. Germany and Poland show less worrying scenarios with more modest increases, probably for different reasons: significant reforms implemented in Germany and residual sector development in Poland.

Despite being targeted at a larger population than LTC, healthcare services are also conditioned by demographic structure. Needs for healthcare goods and services depend not only on the size of the population but also on its overall health level, which is linked to its age and gender structure, particularly the share of older people. Besides high expenditure on young people and during maternity, age-related expenditure profiles of healthcare provision indicate that public spending on healthcare generally increases at age 60 and peaks at age 90 (European Commission, 2016).

This pattern is due to the higher incidence of multi-morbidity conditions in older people. Consequently, population structure, and ageing in particular, is one of the drivers of increasing healthcare expenditure (European Commission, 2021a). Increased longevity without an improvement in health status leads to increased demand for services over a more extended period and so increases overall healthcare needs (Zweifel et al., 2005).

However, while the potential impact of the demographic component can be defined precisely, estimation of the evolution of the future development of a population's health status is subject to high uncertainty. Recent empirical evidence points to mixed scenarios (Salomon et al., 2012; Heger and Kolodziej, 2016) and the progressive improvement of health can be threatened by prominent rises in some causes of disability. Furthermore, while new medical technologies have successfully reduced the impact of a growing number of fatal diseases, technological progress can paradoxically result in greater health goods needs (see below).

2.4   FINANCIAL AND ECONOMIC NEEDS

The demand-side and supply-side projections suggest that European welfare states will come under pressure in the coming decades. The financial and economic costs of ageing allow understanding of the magnitude of this pressure and how it will change over time. As in the previous section, the following projections, which are derived from the recent Ageing Report (European Commission, 2021a), refer to the AWG reference scenario. They must be considered as possible educated guesses rather than exact forecasts. This caution is related to the long horizon and assumptions in the reference scenario, which mainly estimates demographic effects while limiting the potential positive impacts of other counterfactual elements (such as significant welfare reforms).

The total cost of ageing in the EU, which stood at 24% of GDP in 2019, is projected to rise by 1.9 pps of GDP by 2070, reaching 25.9% (Figure 2.2, panel A). The peak in age-related expenditure as a share of GDP takes place around the middle of the projection period (Figure 2.2, panel B), and for the majority of EU countries the highest value is reached before the end of the projection horizon (European Commission, 2021a). However, among the Member States observed (Figure 2.2) four of the six will experience the maximum increase close to 2070. This late effect indicates that their demographic structure has only recently started to age and the impact is postponed compared to, for example, Italy and France.

The relative variation in the cost of ageing in the period 2019–2070 GDP, which is driven by when the peak year occurs, indicates that among the countries observed, and in the whole EU (European Commission, 2021a), three different profiles of long-term spending trends emerge: (i) in Italy and France, falls in total age-related expenditure relative to GDP are expected of respectively −0.1 pps and −0.8 pps; (ii) in Denmark and in the EU as a whole the age-related expenditure ratio is expected to moderately rise with an increase below 3 pps; and (iii) in Germany, Poland and especially the Netherlands, projections indicate significant impacts of the cost of ageing between 3.3 pps and 5.4 pps.

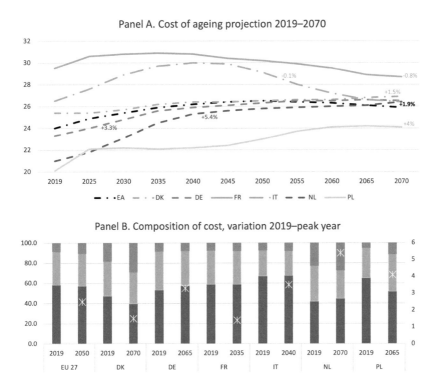

Note: Author elaboration based on Ageing Report data (AWG reference scenario). In the estimation presented in panel A the (always positive) effect of the cost attached to education system is included.

Figure 2.2   Cost of ageing in selected EU countries. Projection of the cost of ageing as % of GDP 2019–2070 and relative change (labels) (A). Composition of the cost of ageing by welfare area against peaking years, and relative change (B)

However, the overall variation in the total cost of ageing (in the period 2019–2070) hides potential significant impacts on the financial sustainability of welfare states and how the three welfare areas considered drive the growing cost attached to ageing. Focusing on the magnitude (and composition) of age-related expenditure in the estimated peak year significantly reduces the variation among countries (Figure 2.2).

Indeed, even though France in comparative terms still presents a positive outlook, in 15 years it is expected to experience a 1.4 pp increase in overall expenditure, which is significantly more than the −0.8 pps of the 2019–2070 variation. Furthermore, under this lens, the Italian scenario completely changes. Before the drop in overall expenditure estimated after 2045, Italy will face considerable pressure on the sustainability of its welfare system. In 2040 the country is expected to register a 3.3 pp increase and around a third of its GDP will be drained by the social security system. Due to the stable trend, the situation slightly varies in the EU as a whole, with the maximum increase of 2.5 pps in 2050. In contrast, the scenario remains unchanged in the other Member States considered due to the late peak year.

The choice of period, 2019 to 2070 or 2019 to the peak year, considerably changes the effect of the welfare area on the variation in age-related expenditure. The increase up to 2070 is mainly driven by long-term care and healthcare spending, with the two items combined projected to rise by two pps of GDP in the EU (European Commission, 2021a). Among the countries considered, at the peak year (Figure 2.2, panel B) the pressure of ageing cost is primarily driven by projections of pension expenditure, which, except in Denmark, has the highest increase in the period considered.

Indeed, while the public pension benefit ratio (average pensions in relation to average wages) is projected to decline in almost all the Member States by 2070 and public pension expenditure is set to return to close to its 2019 level in the second part of the period considered, healthcare and LTC expenditure are more directly affected by demographic ageing. In other words, the higher intrinsic complexity of the healthcare and LTC sectors in controlling public spending through balancing mechanisms as in the pension system (for instance, pay-as-you-go pension systems) results in these sectors being more exposed in the long run to the combined effect of demand-side and supply-side pressures.

2.5 INTERVENING MITIGATING DRIVERS

Demographic ageing constitutes an almost unalterable process that can only be slightly modified by an unexpected rise in fertility and with the related effects only visible after decades. However, unlike demand-side pressures, the supply-side effects on welfare state sustainability can be mitigated using specific adjustments and adopting recent positive interventions and best practice in various fields.

In this regard, the primary area of intervention concerns the need to boost employment rates among older workers (Martin, 2018) and in parallel to extend what it means for older workers by introducing innovative mechanisms that enable public pension systems to adjust dynamically to the growth in longevity (Duval, 2004; Gruber and Wise, 2004).

The consecutive waves of public pension reforms directed at adjusting systems to population ageing that have interested most developed countries since the mid-1990s have addressed the longevity risk mainly by using 'static' solutions (Carone et al., 2016; OECD, 2019). The 2006 pioneering reform of the Danish retirement system, which aimed to ensure that longer lives would result in longer working lives through a (semi-) 'automatic' adaptation of the pensionable age linked to developments in the life expectancy of 60-year-olds, represents an essential milestone in this direction (von Nordheim and Kvist, 2022). Indeed, following this reform, the European Commission and European Council pension reform advice, which from 2011 was provided to the Member States in annual country-specific recommendations, was hinged on linking life expectancy and the pensionable age (European Commission, 2012, 2015). The Danish path was soon followed by the other Nordic countries, which reformed their pension systems by linking the pensionable age to life expectancy in the last decade (von Nordheim and Kvist, 2022). This orientation was supported by evidence indicating that individual economic incentives to help later retirement alone are unable to make a sufficiently large share of people work longer, potentially producing opposite results and increasing labour market structural inequalities (ibid.). On the contrary, indexing pensionable ages to longevity may provide a promising approach to regulating retirement and raising the pensionable age, thus ensuring the financial sustainability of public pension systems in the future.

Besides pension system characteristics, retirement behaviour is influenced by the industrial relations system and its impact on late-career labour markets and well-established social norms regarding retirement and the pensionable age. Similarly, the not-so-recent trend of working longer in developed countries has institutional and statutory aspects not only related to pension systems as the rising average educational attainments of older cohorts suggests, but also has social and cultural elements such as female labour market attachment and reciprocal influence within couples, better health status and the possibility of higher financial availability in later life (Martin, 2018). However, evidence indicates that the increase in older worker (55–74 years) employment rates registered in the OECD area in the last three decades is mainly driven by higher retention rates within firms – i.e. older workers staying on longer with the same firm – rather than willingness on the part of employers to hire older workers (ibid.). In general terms, this phenomenon results from a combination of, on the one hand, rights and status earned by older workers, such as seniority wage premiums and employment protection legislation which disincentivises the hiring of older workers, and on the other hand age discrimination and a perceived lack of digital skills related to productivity acting as barriers to hiring older workers (Martin, 2018; Age Platform Europe, 2021). Two primary solutions to boost the labour market for older workers relate to the calibration between active labour market policy (ALMPs) and investment in lifelong learning (Martin, 2018). As is highlighted in a meta-analysis of ALMPs in a large set of countries, older workers do not represent a separate target group for these interventions, which mainly focus on gender and younger workers (Card et al., 2018). Similarly, (older) adults are less involved in lifelong learning compared to other groups of workers. Furthermore, among these groups those who are more exposed to labour market risks – poorly educated adults – do not participate much in such programmes and also registered a more significant drop in attendance during the COVID-19 pandemic (OECD, 2021).

Further labour market developments might help. Encouraging part-time work or flexible arrangements for older workers, especially males late in their careers, would help achieve the aim of working longer (Martin, 2018). In this regard, the gig economy, which ensures greater flexibility in working arrangements in the late-career phase could constitute a potential positive element for older workers (Cook et al., 2019). However, some feasibility issues weaken this solution. The fact that compensation in the gig economy is based on productivity can be a challenge for older workers, especially those who benefited from increasing age/earnings profiles due to implicit contracts in traditional jobs (ibid.). This requires institutional interventions in (semi-)retirement measures to encourage working continuity.

Beyond longer working lives, a healthier working population is a mitigating driver of the impact of ageing (European Commission, 2021a). Indeed, ageing population-generated pressures are directly related to how individuals and societies age. Therefore, healthy ageing is a central issue. A recent book *Ageing and Health* (Greer et al., 2021) indicates from a life-course perspective a possible route to reach the goal of healthy ageing. Policy initiatives must encourage the healthy development of individuals in all stages of their lives so that human capital can be accumulated and maintained over the course of one's life. This indicates that besides advances in healthcare and cures, prevention and healthy living education will have to be the aims of future policymakers.

A further element to consider which is potentially crucial for future welfare sustainability concerns the willingness of the population to pay (WTP) taxes to finance these services. Indeed, as private insurance, especially in the LTC field, is scarcely developed in European countries (Bucher-Koenen et al., 2015), willingness to pay for collective services is an essential element in understanding the future evolution of national welfare states. Evidence in this regard is still quite limited but for the case of Denmark it indicates positive WTP for improvements in LTC services for older citizens (Amilon et al., 2020). Although encouraging, this result is scarcely generalisable and indicates a need for more research to understand the 'room for manoeuvre' that policymakers will have in the future.

2.6 CONCLUSION

This contribution has highlighted how the ageing population can potentially harm the sustainability of European welfare systems by focusing mainly on pressures generated related to the demand side, the supply side and their combined effects in terms of economic and financial needs, and also focusing on potential mitigating drivers.

In addition to confirming that ageing is among the primary future challenges to welfare systems, the evidence reported indicates that, besides the different magnitudes at the national level, it is essential to consider the specific timing and composition of age-related expenditure. In particular, while the pension system, which will represent the lion's share of the expected ageing pressure on the sustainability of European welfare systems, can be considered an age-related redistributive mechanism able to balance – for a quite extended period and with adequate reforms – costs and revenue, the healthcare and LTC sectors are more exposed to demographic structural modifications.

This is particularly true regarding the role of technological progress and service quality. Besides demographic drivers, the faster growth of healthcare compared to GDP per capita is mainly explained by technological improvements (OECD, 2006). Indeed, innovations in medical technology are generally believed to be the primary drivers of healthcare spending. The positive substitution effect of technological innovation – more cost-efficient treatment of previously treated medical conditions – is offset by the expansion mechanism effect, namely the possibility of treating diseases that were not treated previously (European Commission, 2021a). On the other hand, service quality, especially in the LTC sector, is receiving growing recognition and importance (European Commission, 2021b). However, due to its high associated costs, reducing the quality of services is one of the main cost-containment strategies that policymakers adopt to control growing LTC budgets (Gori and Luppi, 2022). Further advances in both directions can therefore improve and expand the quality of life of the older population at the expense of additional pressure on welfare sustainability.

NOTES

1. In this chapter, we rely on the first variant of the total-age-dependency ratio, which identifies the young population as those aged between 0 and 14 years and the older population as those aged 65 and over. Unlike the second variant – in which the young population threshold is set at 19 years and that of the old popu-

lation remains at 65 years – this indicator could miss accounting for current and future rises in the average years of schooling. However, we prefer the first variant since not considering later entry in the labour market could in part compensate for the potential and already in place dual effect related to, on the one hand, rises in the pension age (European Commission, 2020a) and, on the other hand, longer life expectancy (European Commission, 2021a).
2. The total-age-dependency ratio is a measure of the population's age structure. It relates the number of individuals who are likely to be dependent on the support of others for their daily living – the young and the elderly – to the number of those capable of providing this support. The total-age-dependency ratio, or age-dependency ratio, is the ratio of the sum of the number of young people aged 14 and below and the number of elderly people aged 65 years and over to the number of people of working age. This ratio can be further decomposed into other indicators related to the relative incidence of each type of dependent population. The young-age-dependency ratio indicates the incidence of those aged 14 years and below in the active population (15–64 years). In contrast, the old-age-dependency ratio adopts the same method and is the ratio between people aged over 65 and the active population.
3. The figures presented in this section are derived (if not specified elsewhere) from the recent Eurostat (2021) demographic balances and indicators projection adopting the baseline projection scenario.
4. A necessary disclaimer. Given the very long time span over which the Ageing Report's projections presented here are made, they must be interpreted as an indication of future trends rather than exact and reliable figures. Furthermore, to avoid excessive recourse to potentially misleading rather than clarifying projection data, we focus exclusively on projections estimated in the AWG reference scenario. This scenario is built with a 'no-policy-change' assumption (i.e. the projections are defined assuming that current policies remain unchanged), highlighting the evolution of the welfare states in terms of need and expenditure related to demographic pressure.

REFERENCES

Age Platform Europe. (2021). *The Right to Work in Old Age*. Brussels. https://www.age-platform.eu/publications/right-work-old-age

Amilon A., Ladenburg J., Siren A. and Vernstrøm Østergaard S. (2020). Willingness to pay for long-term home care services: Evidence from a stated preferences analysis. *Journal of the Economics of Ageing*, 17, 100238. doi.org/10.1016/j.jeoa.2020.100238.

Bonoli G. and Natali D. (2012). Europe's transformations towards a renewed pension system. In Bonoli G. and Natali D. (eds.) *The Politics of the New Welfare State* (pp. 182–205). Oxford: Oxford University Press.

Bucher-Koenen T., Schütz J. and Spindler M. (2015). Long-term care insurance across Europe. In Börsch-Supan A., Kneip T., Litwin H., Myck M. and Weber G. (eds.) *Ageing in Europe: Supporting Policies for an Inclusive Society* (pp. 353–368). Berlin: De Gruyter.

Card D., Kluve J. and Weber A. (2018). What works? A meta-analysis of recent active labor market program evaluations. *Journal of the European Economic Association*, 16(3), 894–931. https://doi.org/10.1093/jeea/jvx028

Carone G., Giamboni L., Laine V. and Pamies S. (2016). *Pension Reforms in the EU since the Early 2000s: Achievements and Challenges Ahead*. European Economy Discussion Paper 042. DG ECFIN. European Commission.

Cook C., Diamond R. and Oyer P. (2019). Older workers and the gig economy. *AEA Papers and Proceedings*, 109, 372–376.

Duval R. (2004). *Retirement Behaviour in OECD Countries: Impact of Old-age Pension Schemes and Other Social Transfer Programmes*. OECD Economic Studies, No. 37. OECD.

Esping-Andersen G. (1990). *The Three Worlds of Welfare Capitalism*. Princeton, NJ: Princeton University Press.

Esping-Andersen G. and Myles J. (2009). Economic inequality and the welfare state. In Nolan B., Salverda W. and Smeeding T. M. (eds.) *The Oxford Handbook of Economic Inequality* (pp. 639–664). Oxford: Oxford University Press.

European Commission. (2012). *White Paper: An Agenda for Adequate, Safe and Sustainable Pensions*. COM (2012) 55 final. European Commission.

European Commission. (2015). *The 2015 Pension Adequacy Report* (Vol. I). European Commission.

European Commission. (2016). *Joint Report on Health Care and Long-Term Care Systems & Fiscal Sustainability*. Volume 1, Institutional Paper 037. Brussels. doi:10.2765/680422

European Commission. (2018). *The 2018 Ageing Report: Economic & Budgetary Projections for the EU Member States (2016–2070)*. Institutional Paper 079. Brussels. doi:10.2765/615631

European Commission. (2020a). *Ageing Europe: Looking at the Lives of Older People in the EU*, 2020 Edition. Publications Office of the European Union, Luxembourg. doi:10.2785/628105

European Commission. (2020b). *Report on the Impact of Demographic Change*. Brussels. https://ec.europa.eu/info/sites/info/files/demography_report_2020_n.pdf

European Commission. (2021a). *The 2021 Ageing Report: Economic & Budgetary Projections for the EU Member States (2019–2070)*. Institutional Paper 148. Brussels. doi:10.2765/84455

European Commission. (2021b). *Long-term Care Report: Trends, Challenges and Opportunities in an Ageing Society*. Volume II, Publications Office. https://data.europa.eu/doi/10.2767/183997

Eurostat. (2021). *Population Projections in the EU*. https://ec.europa.eu/eurostat/statistics-explained/index.php?oldid=497115#Population_projections

Evers A., Pijl M. and Ungerson C. (eds.) (1994). *Payments for Care: A Comparative Overview*. Aldershot, UK: Avebury.

Ferrera M. (1996). The 'Southern Model' of welfare in social Europe. *Journal of European Social Policy*, 6(1), 17–37. doi:10.1177/095892879600600102

Frericks P., Gurín M. and Höppner, J. (2021). Family as a redistributive principle of the welfare state: The case of Germany. *Journal of Social Policy*, 1–21. doi:10.1017/S0047279421000787

Gàl R. I. and Medgyesi M. (2017). *Financing the Lifecycle or Mitigating Poverty: Redistribution in the Hungarian Welfare System by Age and Income*. NTA Working Paper No. 20.

Gevers J., Gelissen J., Arts W. and Muffels R. (2000). Public health care in the balance: Exploring popular support for health care systems in the European Union. *International Journal of Social Welfare*, 9, 301–321. https://doi.org/10.1111/1468-2397.00141

Gori C., Fernandez J. L. and Wittenberg R. (eds.) (2016a). *Long-term Care Reforms in OECD Countries*. London: Policy Press.

Gori C., Barbabella F., Campbell J., Ikegami N., D'Amico F., Holder H., Ishibashi T., Johansson, L., Komisar H. and Theobald H. (2016b). How different countries allocate long-term care resources to older users: A comparative snapshot. In Gori C., Fernandez J. L. and Wittenberg R. (eds.) *Long-term Care Reforms in OECD Countries* (pp. 77–116). London: Policy Press.

Gori C. and Luppi M. (2022). Cost-containment policies in long-term care for older people across the OECD: A scoping review. *Ageing & Society*, 1–24.

Greer, S., Lynch, J., Reeves, A., Falkenbach, M., Gingrich, J., Cylus, J. and Bambra, C. (2021). *Ageing and Health: The Politics of Better Policies* (European Observatory on Health Systems and Policies). Cambridge: Cambridge University Press. doi:10.1017/9781108973236

Greve B. (ed.) (2019). *Routledge Handbook of the Welfare State*. Abingdon and New York: Routledge.

Gruber J. and Wise D. (eds.). (2004). *Social Security Programs and Retirement Around the World: Micro-estimation*. Chicago, IL: University of Chicago Press.

Gusmano M. K. and Okma K. G. H. (2018). Population aging and the sustainability of the welfare state: What makes a good life in late life? Citizenship and justice in aging societies, special report. *Hastings Center Report*, 48(5), S57–S61. doi:10.1002/hast.915

Heger D. and Kolodziej I. W. K. (2016). *Changes in Morbidity Over Time: Evidence from Europe*. Ruhr Economic Papers 640, RWI – Leibniz-Institut für Wirtschaftsforschung, Ruhr-University Bochum, TU Dortmund University, University of Duisburg-Essen.

Jacques O. and Noël A. (2018). The case for welfare state universalism, or the lasting relevance of the paradox of redistribution. *Journal of European Social Policy*, 28(1), 70–85. doi:10.1177/0958928717700564

Korpi W. and Palme J. (1998). The paradox of redistribution and strategies of equality: Welfare state institutions, inequality and poverty in the Western countries. *American Sociological Review*, 63, 661–687.

Levy J. D. (2021). Welfare retrenchment. In Béland D., Morgan K. J., Obinger H. and Pierson C. (eds.) *The Oxford Handbook of the Welfare State* (2nd edn, pp. 552–567). Oxford: Oxford University Press.

Martin P. J. (2018). *Live Longer, Work Longer: The Changing Nature of the Labour Market for Older Workers in OECD Countries*. IZA Discussion Paper Series No. 11510.

Meier V. and Werding M. (2010). Ageing and the welfare state: Securing sustainability. *Oxford Review of Economic Policy*, 26(4), 655–673. http://www.jstor.org/stable/43664649

OECD. (2006). *Projecting OECD Health and Long-Term Care Expenditures: What are the Main Drivers?* Economics Department Working Paper No. 477. OECD Publishing, Paris.

OECD. (2019). *Pensions at a Glance 2019: OECD and G20 Indicators*. OECD Publishing, Paris.

OECD. (2021). *OECD Skills Outlook 2021: Learning for Life*. OECD Publishing, Paris, https://doi.org/10.1787/0ae365b4-en.

Salomon J.A. et al. (2012). Healthy life expectancy for 187 countries, 1990–2010: A systematic analysis for the Global Burden Disease Study 2010. *Lancet*, 380(9859), 2144–2162. doi: 10.1016/S0140-6736(12)61690-0.

Saraceno C. and Keck W. (2010). Can we identify intergenerational policy regimes in Europe? *European Societies*, 12(5), 675–696. doi:10.1080/14616696.2010.483006.

Sinfield A. (2019). Fiscal welfare. In Greve B. (ed.) *Routledge Handbook of the Welfare State* (2nd edn, pp. 23–33). Abingdon and New York: Routledge.

Vanhuysse P., Medgyesi M. and Gal R. I. (2021). Welfare states as lifecycle redistribution machines: Decomposing the roles of age and socio-economic status shows that European tax-and-benefit systems primarily redistribute across age groups. *PLoS ONE*, 16(8), e0255760. https://doi.org/10.1371/journal.pone.0255760

von Nordheim F. and Kvist J. (2022). Regulating the retirement age: Lessons from Nordic pension policy approaches. *Regulation & Governance*, early online view. https://doi.org/10.1111/rego.12475

Zweifel P., Steinmann L. and Eugster P. (2005). The Sisyphus syndrome in health revisited. *International Journal of Health Care Finance and Economics*, 5(2), 127–145.

3. Self-employment and technology: different models of labor relations

Ferry Koster

INTRODUCTION

The link between technology and work has received a lot of attention recently. Much of the current debates, both in public and academic spheres, relate to issues such as the replacement of work, increasing complexity of work, and a further inequality in the labor market between lower and higher skilled workers (Mitchell & Brynjolfsson, 2017; Van Roy et al., 2018). While these discussions are indeed recent, they also resonate with the downskilling and upskilling debates of the past (Braverman, 1974; Gallie, 1991; Burris, 1998). To date, the analyses underlying these debates have generated interesting and relevant insights concerning which jobs are at risk and what the future of work may look like (Lund et al., 2021). Clearly, the changes that occurred during the COVID pandemic are closely connected to this as policymakers, employers, and employees figure out whether the economy is moving towards a "new" normal (Chandrasekaran, 2021; Malhotra, 2021).

Prior research can be summarized as follows. First, there are studies focusing on the impact of new technology on work. In these studies, most attention is paid to the direct relationship between technology and work. Hence, they show how work and tasks are affected by new technologies such as robots and artificial intelligence (Mitchell & Brynjolfsson, 2017; Frank et al., 2019). Second, there are studies zooming in on a particular type of work that has developed recently, namely jobs that are provided via online platforms. Here the emphasis is for example on the contractual relations of these workers, the quality of their jobs, as well as the impact of platforms on collective action. Hence, these studies provide information about the jobs of platform workers and their tendency to form or join unions (Nissim & Simon, 2021). Third, with regard to collective action, there are several studies examining how collective action (with an emphasis on union density) is affected by such factors as technological change, globalization, financialization, and economic integration (Vachon et al., 2016; Meyer, 2019).

However, prior work also misses some aspects that may be necessary to get a full integrated picture of new technologies (in particular, digitalization of the economy), quality of work, and collective action. Two aspects requiring further attention are the following. To date, insights rely on partial analyses. First, the impact of new technology is extensively studied in relation to work (for example, if the focus is on the displacement of jobs). Where this culminates into social risks, these studies also address the impact of technology on collective action (Rovny, 2014). A particular field of study aims at understanding the connection between platform workers, the job quality they experience, and their relationship with labor unions. However, less is known about how digitalization of the wider economy plays out for collective action. In addition to that, the organizational/employer perspective is largely absent from the analyses. Not much is known about the considerations of employers regarding job design and labor relations in relation to digitalization. Therefore, less is known about the strategies and preferences of employers regarding the use of technology, as well as their preferences regarding labor relations. In the following, both issues are addressed; the labor side of collective action is investigated through union density and in addition to that, the employer perspective is examined regarding their preferences towards labor relations and consultation of employees. As a result, information is available for different subthemes that are central to today's economy, but an integrative view or analysis is currently not available.

This chapter aims to discuss the relationship between three labor-related topics, namely digitalization of the economy (and as a subdimension of that namely the platform economy, which will be referred to as platformization), self-employment, and labor relations. It does so, empirically, by integrating different data sources, each of which focus on one of these topics. Bringing them together allows us to investigate their interrelations. Special attention is given to the organizational perspective, by means of investigating strategies and preferences of employers concerning work and labor relations. Of these three topics, the latter (labor relations) are believed to be affected by the first two (technological change and self-employment). Besides that, it is also believed that technological change and digitalization are among the drivers of self-employment. This would for example hold if the platform economy reflects the rise of a gig economy in which workers no longer are attached to one organization but move from gig to gig (Vallas & Schor, 2020). Gig work implies that platform workers are on-call workers that do not have an employment relationship with the contracting organization and hence this means that self-employment rises.

What the analyses provided in this chapter test is what may be called the *standard argumentation* linking technology and the use of platforms with employment relations and labor relations which runs as follows: as economies become more reliant on technology, the number of self-employed increases, and since the tendency among the self-employed to join labor unions is lower, this will negatively impact the position of these unions. The present chapter weighs the different aspects of this argumentation. It does so in two different ways. The first part of the analysis focuses on the macro level by investigating how technology, self-employment, and labor relations are related at the national level. To the extent that data allow, trends are investigated. It is possible to do this for the more general trend of digitalization but not for platformization of the economy. The second part of the analysis focuses on organizational strategies across different countries. This part of the analysis enables us to investigate whether technology and self-employment have an impact on organizational decisions and preferences regarding labor relations and employment contracts.

Theoretically, this chapter relies on the idea that organizations are embedded in an institutional and economic environment, which in turn affects their strategies, structures, and preferences (Dacin et al., 1999; Geary & Signoretti, 2021; Koster, 2022). The environment is conceptualized with macro-level conditions (the extent to which an economy relies on the self-employed and the levels of digitalization and platformization). These conditions are investigated in relation to organizations, reflecting the choices of employees. To understand how these macro conditions are related to these choices, the chapter also uses insights from institutional regime-type theories (e.g. Powell et al., 2020).

DATA SOURCES AND MEASURES

Several datasets are combined to conduct the analyses. These datasets provide information about the different subthemes investigated here. It is intended that the analyses are performed on a comparable set of countries. As such, each of these datasets limits the countries that can be included in the analyses. Countries for which there is no complete data are dropped from the analyses (there is one exception here: the United Kingdom is included in all analyses except the ones in which digitalization is investigated, because of missing data). Since the organizational data are collected across European countries, this provides the first major selection. In addition to that, national-level data about digitalization, self-employment, and labor relations further limit the number of countries that could be included. For a large part, the analyses include information about the largest share of European countries.

Indicators of Self-employed in the Economy and Labor Relations

Eurostat provides information about the total number of self-employed per country. These numbers are divided by the total number of employed persons to calculate the *share of self-employed* per country and year (measured as the number of self-employed relative to the total working populations). Since this is a very general indicator of the share of self-employed, leading to an overlooking of underlying variations in the group of self-employed, several additional indicators are included. It was considered to add a variable indicating that the self-employed position is combined with another one. However, that turns out to show very little variation, both between countries and over time. Therefore, two other variables are included to capture the self-employed, namely the *share of solo self-employed* and the *working hours of the self-employed*. The share of solo self-employed specifically focuses on the self-employed without personnel as a subpopulation of the self-employed (this variable is also measured relative to the total working population in a country). The working hours variable indicates the average number of hours that the self-employed work in a country and can be interpreted as an additional indicator of the size or importance of self-employment in a country. *Labor relations* are indicated by union density. This measure is available through the International Labour Organization (ILO).

Platformization: DPEI

The *Digital Platform Economy Index* (DPEI) assesses the extent to which a national economy reflects a digital ecosystem (Acs et al., 2021; Szerb et al., 2022). The DPEI is a composite index containing four sub-indices (digital technology infrastructure, digital user citizenship, digital multi-sided platform, and digital technology entrepreneurship). Each of these indices is measured with three "pillars," which are then measured with 61 variables. For the variables and the construction of the index, see Acs et al. (2021). These data are available for 116 countries.

Control Variable: Industrialization

As prior research shows that the structure of the economy, in terms of production and services, impacts on union density, the level of *industrialization* is added to the models as a control variable.

Digitalization: DESI

The *Digital Economy and Society Index* (DESI) is constructed by the European Commission (2021) and consists of four dimensions and nine subdimensions (for the construction of the composite indicator, see European Commission, 2021). These data are available for 27 European countries for 2016–2021 (the

United Kingdom is not included in this measure, but available in the other datasets).

Organizational Characteristics and Preferences: ECS

The last round of the European Company Survey (ECS; see Van Houten & Russo, 2020) was used to assess the *strategies and preferences of employers*. The ECS contains information about a representative sample of organizations across 30 European countries. Indicators that are investigated here include the share of employees with an open-ended contract (measured from 1 to 7), the share of employees receiving formal training (measured from 1 to 7), and preferences regarding consultation (with employee representatives, with employees directly, both or none). Next to that, the ECS is used to take into account digitalization and technology factors (e.g. the use of robots and technology to monitor production quality and employee performance), as well as several controls (like organizational size and economic sector).

Table 3.1   Overview of dataset, measures, and period

Dataset	Measures	Time period
Eurostat	Self-employed (share of total employment)	2016–2020
Eurostat	Self-employment as second job	2016–2020
Eurostat	Work hours of self-employed	2016–2020
ICTWSS	Union density	2016–2019
DESI	Digitalization of the economy	2016–2020
DPEI	Platformization of the economy	2019
ECS	Organizational strategies and preferences	2019
Worldbank	Industralization	2016–2020

As Table 3.1 shows, the analyses are constrained by the availability of the data. While data on digitalization is available for several years (2016–2020) the indicators for platformization are only known for 2019. The data are investigated in three parts. First, a cross-national (static) comparison of countries at the macro level is conducted. This part relies on correlations and serves as a starting point. Clearly, it is possible that these outcomes also reflect other country differences. Therefore, in the second step, the focus is on trends as well as other factors that may be of influence. Third, a cross-national comparison of companies (combining the macro level with the organizational level) is provided.

NATIONAL-LEVEL ANALYSES

Cross-sectional Outcomes

The first question this chapter aims to answer is whether and how labor relations are related to self-employment, digitalization of the economy, and platformization. As an indicator of labor relations, the focus is on union density (UD), which is widely applied in prior studies (e.g. Vachon et al., 2016). Figures 3.1–3.5 provide an overview of how union density relates to the percentage of self-employed in the country, the level of digitalization of the economy (DESI), and the usage of platforms (DPEI) for 2019.

Based on Figures 3.1, 3.2, and 3.3, the following results stand out. First, the correlation between self-employment is close to zero for all the indicators. Second, if there were a relation between the two, it is not completely sure in which direction it goes, as the first two indicators lean towards a negative relationship and the third is positive.

Figures 3.4 and 3.5 show that the connection between digitalization and platformization of the economy have a different relation with labor unionization than the self-employment indicators; there is a positive association between digitalization and platformization and union density. Nevertheless, an important difference between the outcomes is that the relationship of union density and digitalization is more pronounced than the one between union density and platformization. This suggests that there is a more direct connection between

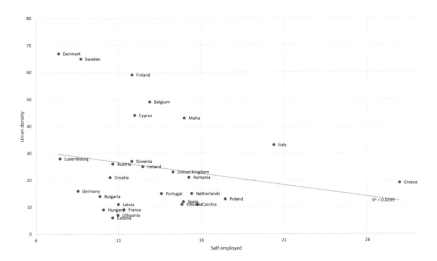

Figure 3.1   Share of self-employed and union density, 2019

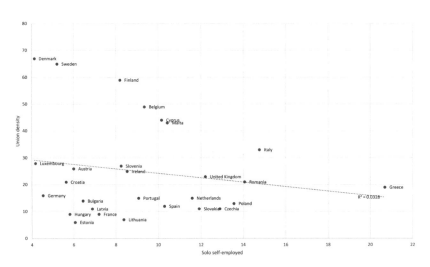

Figure 3.2   Share of solo self-employed and union density, 2019

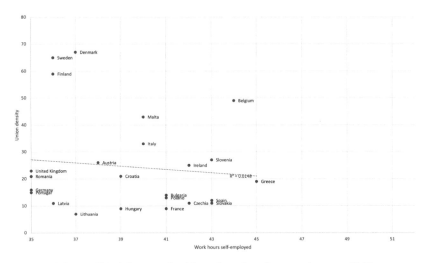

Figure 3.3   Work hours of self-employed and union density, 2019

digitalization and labor relations than between platformization and the unions. This leads to a preliminary idea about platformization, namely that it may make sense to think in terms of country clusters: Denmark, Sweden, and Finland combine unionization with platformization, and the United Kingdom and the Netherlands are examples of countries with less unionization and extensive platformization. Lower levels of platformization are combined with more unionized labor in Malta and Cyprus and combined with lower levels of union density in Hungary, Latvia, and Bulgaria. This idea of country clusters is explored in more detail below.

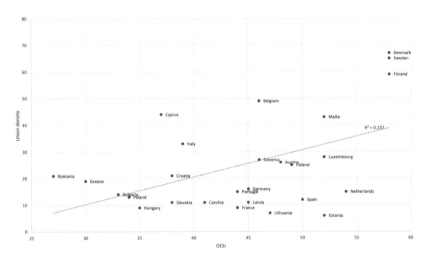

Figure 3.4   Digitalization and union density, 2019

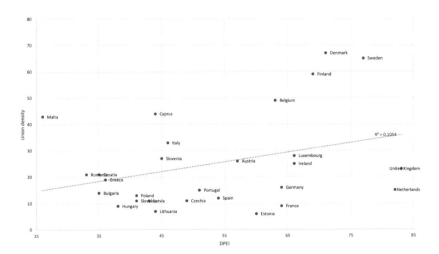

Figure 3.5   Platformization and union density, 2019

The previous figures suggest that the relationship between union density and the presence of self-employed in an economy on the one hand and technology on the other, differ. Therefore, it is also worthwhile to look further into how technology and the indicators of the self-employed are related (the next step: whether other factors come into play is analyzed in the next section). As Figures 3.6–3.11 show, most correlations are very weak, except for the ones between digitalization of the economy and the share of self-employed in the economy (both total and solo self-employed). To start with the latter: this relationship is negative; on average, in more digitalized economies, the lower is the share of self-employed. This also holds for platformization of the economy, but these outcomes are less strong. Furthermore, there is no connection between digitalization and platformization on the one hand and the number of working hours of self-employed on the other.

Longitudinal Analyses

So far, the presented graphs provide cross-sections of the economy. It is possible to investigate changes in union density, the share of self-employed, and digitalization of the economy, controlled for industrialization. Platformization of the economy cannot be investigated as longitudinal data for platformization are not available. It should be noted that the time frame is relatively small. At the maximum, there are only five years that can be analyzed. This is further restricted as there are no union density data for 2020. Models are investigated in which union density numbers were imputed, but since this did

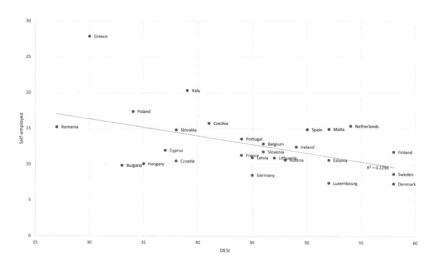

Figure 3.6   Digitalization and share of self-employed, 2019

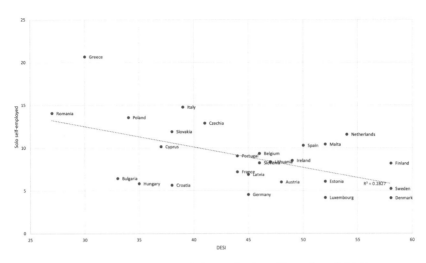

Figure 3.7   Digitalization and share of solo self-employed, 2019

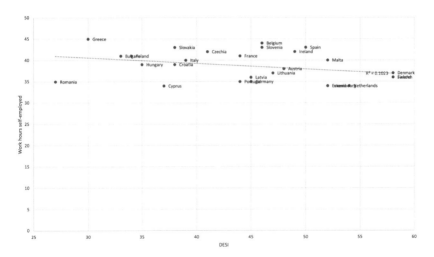

Figure 3.8   Digitalization and work hours of self-employed, 2019

not affect the outcomes, the results with the known data are presented below. Furthermore, models are examined in which each of the independent variables of self-employment were added separately. Since this did not alter the results, the complete models are reported.

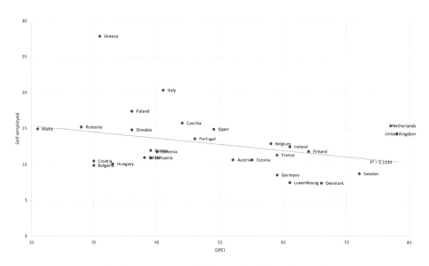

Figure 3.9   Platformization and share of self-employed, 2019

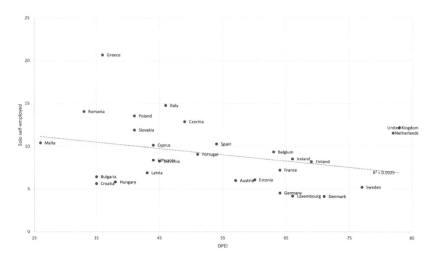

Figure 3.10   Platformization and share of solo self-employed, 2019

Table 3.2 presents the results of the longitudinal analyses. Model (1) shows that the self-employment indicators as well as industrialization are not significantly associated with union density. Adding these variables to the model does not lead to an improvement of the model. These outcomes remain the same if digitalization of the economy is added in model (2). Model (2) shows that dig-

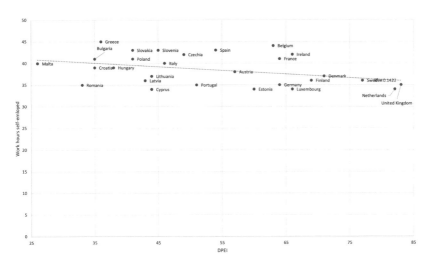

Figure 3.11   Platformization and work hours of self-employed, 2019

italization of the economy is positively related to union density. Overall, these longitudinal analyses confirm what was found in the cross-sectional analyses presented in the previous section.

Table 3.2   Panel analysis of union density (2016–2019)

	(1) b	s.e.	p	(2) b	s.e.	p
Intercept	24.63	2.86	0.00	24.89	2.60	0.00
Year	−0.40	2.77	0.89	−1.77	2.56	0.49
Self-employed	−0.23	0.30	0.46	0.05	0.34	0.89
Solo self-employed	0.06	0.08	0.48	0.06	0.08	0.45
# Work hours self-employed	0.12	0.26	0.63	0.22	0.27	0.43
DESI				0.52	0.20	0.01
Industrialization	0.00	0.00	0.19	0.00	0.00	0.29
Deviance (from the empty model)		1.33	0.245		5.64	0.02

Note: n = 74.

These national-level analyses lead to several preliminary conclusions about the connection between digitalization, platformization, self-employment, and labor relations. Some of them confirm the standard argumentation, but there are also some notable deviations. Regarding the confirmation of existing ideas: there is some evidence that self-employment works out negatively for labor unions, at least, when looking at the total share of self-employed. This picture is nuanced once other indicators are taken into the analyses. Then, when the indicators are analyzed simultaneously over time, there is no connection with the overall share of self-employed, while the share of solo self-employed and work hours of self-employed are positively related to union density.

Furthermore, there are other outcomes which are less in line with the argumentation found in the literature. Most of all, the shift towards self-employment is not related to levels of digitalization and platformization or increasing digitalization. On the contrary, the opposite is found; if anything, self-employment is negatively related to digitalization and platformization of the economy. This is noteworthy, since discussions concerning platformization usually directly link this to self-employment, with the idea that platform workers do not have employment contracts and instead belong to the gig economy. Formally, platforms do not employ workers, and by definition, these workers are independent contractors (Cunningham-Parmeter, 2018; Hastie, 2020). This idea is not so much refuted here as such. It is not argued that platform workers are not gig workers, but the outcomes show that this is not the whole story. There are different ways of interpreting the outcomes. While it may be the case that platform workers are (solo) self-employed, the argumentation does not work the other way around: in economies based on self-employment it is not the case that these economies are digitalized or make extensive use of platforms.

What is more, and this is evidenced by the longitudinal data, both digitalization and self-employment do not undermine unionization. Notably, it is suggested that digitalization goes along with more unionization. Finally, it should be noted that the outcomes need to be handled with caution as one may argue that the number of self-employed reflects the official numbers, whereas the gig economy may in fact consist of workers that are not visible in these statistics. In that case, there should be a growth of the informal economy due to platformization, which may not be taken up completely in the present analysis.

Apart from that criticism on the data, the analyses lead to a deviation from the standard argumentation as well as a new insight regarding platformization and self-employment. Rather than thinking in terms of relationships between them, it seems to make sense to focus on country clusters; self-employment and digitalization are found to come in different combinations.

ORGANIZATIONAL ANALYSES

Next, it is investigated whether the patterns found at the national level are also evident at the level of the organization. While prior analyses tend to focus on the national level (for example to explain union density), on the job or task level (to explain the impact of technology on work), or on the specific case of platform workers (to assess their job quality and preference regarding representation), here, in contrast, attention is paid to the question of whether self-employment, digitalization, and platformization matter for organizational strategies and preferences. The focus is not solely on platform organizations, but on organizations in general.

The analyses are conducted in three steps. First, the national-level indicators of self-employment, digitalization, and platformization are related to the organizational-level outcomes (representation, quality of work, and investments). Second, it is explored to what extent organizational indicators of digitalization relate to the organizational outcomes. Third, the suggestion made earlier that clusters of countries may be identified that matter for understanding the organizational outcomes is explored.

Before presenting the models, it is necessary to make some notes about the tables. These tables only include the parameters of the associations that are discussed. Hence, these provide selections of the outcomes, as these analyses also include control variables at the organizational and the national level, but which are not shown in the table to save space. These are organizational size, economic sector, three digitalization indicators (the use of robots, and systems for monitoring employee performance and production quality), GDP, and ageing of the population. These control variables are not reported and discussed, apart from the digitalization indicators, which are further explored in a separate section (the complete tables are available upon request).

Relation with National Level

The question of whether self-employment (both in terms of the share of self-employed and the average working hours), digitalization, and platformization at the national level have consequences for organization is answered with different indicators. First, attention is paid to how organizations deal with their labor relations. The ECS contains information about the type of employee representation and nine options are provided, including no representation present. Respondents could pick one of the options.

Self-employed, labor relations, and employee relations
Overall, the conclusion of these analyses is that there are some notable outcomes if the indicators of the self-employed are related to the preferences of employers regarding labor relations.

First, if there are relatively more self-employed present in the economy, employees prefer to consult with employees directly (or in combination with representatives), compared to not consulting employees at all or consulting with employee representatives. Employees do prefer to consult employees, but not through formal bodies, which may indicate that the position of unions is weakened by the relative size of the self-employed.

Second, focusing on the work hours of the self-employed, the outcomes are somewhat stronger, as employers have a weaker preference for consulting with employee representatives compared to not negotiating at all. There is even some evidence in the direction of preferring not to consult employees at all. Since this is not too strong, it can also be interpreted as being indecisive regarding the consultation of employees in the organizations, which again may signal the weakening of union power.

Then, turning to the direct relation between employers and employees, it turns out that the indicators of self-employment are not directly associated with the use of permanent contracts and training investments of organizations.

Digitalization, platformization, labor relations, and employee relations
Digitalization and platformization have the same impact on labor relations. Overall, representation of employees is stronger if the economy is more digitalized or platformized. Nevertheless, this does not hold for labor unions; this is one of the bodies that is less often present in organizations. Hence, organizations tend to consult with other bodies rather than (traditional) unions.

At the same time, there is a stronger preference for consulting with employee representation and with employees directly among organizations, if digitalization and platformization are more present in the economy. Again, this provides support for the idea that employers seek more direct ways of consulting with employees rather than through labor unions.

Finally, employee contracts are not affected by digitalization and platformization. However, formal training is. Digitalization and platformization are positively related to the number of employees receiving formal training.

Organizational-level Outcomes

Finally, the analyses also shed light on the question whether organizational factors matter for the outcomes discussed above in relation to digitalization, platformization, and self-employment. Proxies for the use of platforms and the share of self-employed at the company level are not available in the ECS. However, there are some indicators for the use of digitalization, namely whether the organization uses robots, information systems for product quality, and information systems for employee monitoring (all measured dichotomously).

The use of the kinds of technology have mixed outcomes for the organizational strategies and preferences. The use of information systems to monitor product quality is associated with a stronger preference for consulting with the representatives of employees and directly with employees. Moreover, the tendency to consult with workers is stronger if organizations make use of robots. Another clear-cut outcome at the organizational level is that the number of workers with an open-ended contract is not affected by these three digitalization indicators. The number of employees participating in formal training is higher if organizations use these kinds of digitalization.

Country Clusters

The previous analyses show that organizations seem to be affected more by digitalization and platformization and less by self-employment within the economy. The different graphs presented earlier in this chapter suggest that it may be worthwhile thinking in terms of clusters rather than an association between digitalization, platformization, and self-employment. Table 3.3 presents an example of this. In this table four clusters of countries are distinguished based on two dimensions: platformization and work hours of self-employed (with four fixed clusters). By doing so, this leads to a good-quality classification of countries, indicating that they can be grouped together in clusters that are distinguishable.

The resulting classifications deviate from existing ones. For example, the Varieties of Capitalism (Hall & Soskice, 2001; Boschma & Capone, 2015) classification distinguishes between liberal market economies (LMEs) and coordinated market economies (CMEs), in which the Netherlands belong to the latter group of countries and the United Kingdom to the first. Other institutional models also do not directly fit the country classification found here (Powell et al., 2020; Ferragina & Filetti, 2022). One reasons for this difference is that the indicators are less "institutional" and more "economical." Nevertheless, it is difficult to regard digitalization and self-employment as completely separated from the institutional structure of a country, as there are both policy and cultural factors that are affecting these dimensions (Marenco & Seidl, 2021).

The next question is whether these clusters matter for the organizational strategies and preferences. As Table 3.3 shows, there are some differences between the clusters as well as similarities. Both shed a new light on the previous analyses. Most of all, the clusters differ in terms of union density. The countries scoring high on work hours and platformization have the highest union density. Union density is comparatively low in countries with high levels of platformization and where the self-employed work fewer hours.

This finding is further corroborated if one looks at the preferences concerning the consultation of employees and employee representatives. In the countries combining digitalization with self-employment these preferences are markedly stronger than in the countries in which the self-employed work

Table 3.3 Analyses of country clusters based on work hours of self-employed and DPEI

Cluster	1	2	3	4
Countries	Bulgaria	Netherlands	Austria	Denmark
	Croatia	United Kingdom	Belgium	Estonia
	Greece		Czechia	Finland
	Hungary		Ireland	France
	Latvia		Italy	Germany
	Lithuania		Poland	Luxembourg
	Malta		Portugal	Sweden
	Romania		Slovakia	
			Spain	
Work hours self-employed	Low	Low	High	High
DPEI	Low	High	Low	High
Union density	++	0	+	+++
Consult with…				
Representation	-	--	0	Ref
Directly	-	--	0	Ref
Both	-	--	-	Ref
None	Ref	Ref	Ref	Ref
Paid training	0	++	0	Ref
Permanent	+	0	++	Ref

fewer hours. However, in this latter cluster, organizations tend to spend more on formal training.

This exploration of country clusters leads to some novel insights about platformization, self-employment, and labor relations. Instead of thinking in terms of direct relations, the focus on country clusters means that different paths become evident. The clearest difference in that regard is found between countries combining platformization of the economy with low levels of self-employment (in this example number of work hours) with higher levels. In the first cluster, union density as well as the tendency of employers to consult employees is lower than in the countries belonging to the other cluster.

DISCUSSION AND CONCLUSION

The analyses presented in this chapter aim to further understand how new technology and work are related by focusing on the connections between digitalization, platformization, self-employment, and labor relations, both at the national and at the organizational level. Oftentimes, it is believed that these trends are moving in one direction, namely of increasing digitalization, increasing self-employment, and a weakening position of labor unions. The results of this chapter show that this is not the whole story.

First, the technology dimension (that is: digitalization and platformization) of the economy and the self-employment dimension differ in their outcomes. While there are some indications that economies relying more strongly on self-employment are less unionized and employee representation in organizations in these countries is weaker, this does not hold for all indicators of self-employment. Furthermore, the opposite holds for digitalization and platformization. The two technology factors investigated here go along with more unionization, employee representation, and organizational outcomes that may benefit workers, such as autonomy and training. What is more, the analyses suggest that technology and self-employment are negatively related as well. Apart from the cross-sectional analysis, this was further evidenced by a negative relationship over time, showing that increasing digitalization explains decreases in the share of the self-employed in the economy.

Second, the analysis also shows that it may be that the connections between technology, self-employment, and labor relations are not so much direct, but need to be approached from a regime perspective. In fact, countries may follow different pathways despite similar levels of technology and technological change. Notably, while in several countries, technology-intensity is combined with less self-employment and more union density (e.g. Sweden and Denmark), others have an opposite profile and combine technology with self-employment and weaker unions (the Netherlands and the United Kingdom). While the separate dimensions explain outcomes at the organizational level, technology-intensity is associated with a stronger emphasis on autonomy and learning, it is the combination of technology with the share of self-employed that explains why organizations choose to enter into long-term relations with their employees. It makes sense to view this latter observation in combination with the weaker unions in these countries.

In short, there is little support for the view that self-employment undermines unionization and, even if this was found, this relationship is not due to the use of technology. What is more, technology is a better predictor of unionization than the share of self-employed. Overall, technology-intensity is associated with stronger unions and workplace collaboration. However, the example combining platformization with the work hours of the self-employed (as a proxy for the importance of the self-employed in the economy) leads to additional insights.

Given that the use of technology will intensify in the future, which can be assumed as digitalization trends are evident in all countries included in the sample, the question is how union density, self-employment, and organizational outcomes will develop. From the direct relationships the following future is foreseen: less self-employment, more unionization, and more worker autonomy and employee training. Nevertheless, the analyses also point towards the direction of a different future, namely one consisting of increasing differences between countries, with on the one hand countries applying a model in which technology-intensification is combined with unionization and workplace collaboration and on the other hand countries in which technology-intensification is combined with a weaker position of unions, increasing worker autonomy, and declining levels of worker security.

REFERENCES

Acs, Z. J., Szerb, L., Song, A., Komlosi, E., & Lafuente, E. (2021). *The Digital Platform Economy Index 2020*. Global Entrepreneurship and Development Institute. www.thegedi.org

Boschma, R., & Capone, G. (2015). Institutions and diversification: Related versus unrelated diversification in a varieties of capitalism framework. *Research Policy*, *44*(10), 1902–1914.

Braverman, H. (1974). *Labor and Monopoly Capital: The Degradation of Work in the Twentieth Century*. New York: Monthly Review Press.

Burris, B. H. (1998). Computerization of the workplace. *Annual Review of Sociology*, *24*(1), 141–157.

Chandrasekaran, R. (2021). The future of work: How HR drives digital transformation in the new normal. *Strategic HR Review*, *20*(3), 84–87.

Cunningham-Parmeter, K. (2018). Gig-dependence: Finding the real independent contractors of platform work. *North Illinois University Law Review*, *39*(3), 379–427.

Dacin, M. T., Beal, B. D., & Ventresca, M. J. (1999). The embeddedness of organizations: Dialogue and directions. *Journal of Management*, *25*(3), 317–356.

European Commission. (2021). *Digital Economy and Society Index (DESI) 2021: DESI Methodological Note*. Brussels: European Commission.

Ferragina, E., & Filetti, F. D. (2022). Labour market protection across space and time: A revised typology and a taxonomy of countries' trajectories of change. *Journal of European Social Policy*, 09589287211056222.

Frank, M. R., Autor, D., Bessen, J. E., Brynjolfsson, E., Cebrian, M., Deming, D. J., Feldman, M., Groh, M., Lobo, J., Moro, E., Wang, D., Youn, H., & Rahwan, I. (2019). Toward understanding the impact of artificial intelligence on labor. *Proceedings of the National Academy of Sciences*, *116*(14), 6531–6539.

Gallie, D. (1991). Patterns of skill change: Upskilling, deskilling or the polarization of skills? *Work, Employment and Society*, *5*(3), 319–351.

Geary, J., & Signoretti, A. (2021). The role of socio-economic embeddedness in promoting cooperation in the workplace: Evidence from family-owned Italian firms. *Economic and Industrial Democracy*, 0143831X211039012.

Hall, P. A., & Soskice, D. (eds) (2001). *Varieties of Capitalism: The Institutional Foundations of Comparative Advantage*. Oxford: Oxford University Press.

Hastie, B. (2020). Platform workers and collective labour action in the modern economy. *University of New Brunswick Law Journal*, *71*, 40–60.

Koster, F. (2022). Organizations in the knowledge economy. An investigation of knowledge-intensive work practices across 28 European countries. *Journal of Advances in Management Research*, ahead-of-print.

Lund, S., Madgavkar, A., Manyika, J., Smit, S., Ellingrud, K., Meaney, M., & Robinson, O. (2021). *The Future of Work after COVID-19*. McKinsey Global Institute No. 18.

Malhotra, A. (2021). The postpandemic future of work. *Journal of Management*, *47*(5), 1091–1102.

Marenco, M., & Seidl, T. (2021). The discursive construction of digitalization: A comparative analysis of national discourses on the digital future of work. *European Political Science Review*, *13*(3), 391–409.

Meyer, B. (2019). Financialization, technological change, and trade union decline. *Socio-Economic Review*, *17*(3), 477–502.

Mitchell, T., & Brynjolfsson, E. (2017). Track how technology is transforming work. *Nature*, *544*(7650), 290–292.

Nissim, G., & Simon, T. (2021). The future of labor unions in the age of automation and at the dawn of AI. *Technology in Society*, *67*, 101732.

Powell, M., Yörük, E., & Bargu, A. (2020). Thirty years of the *Three Worlds of Welfare Capitalism*: A review of reviews. *Social Policy & Administration*, *54*(1), 60–87.

Rovny, A. E. (2014). The capacity of social policies to combat poverty among new social risk groups. *Journal of European Social Policy*, *24*(5), 405–423.

Szerb, L., Komlosi, E. S., Acs, Z. J., Lafuente, E., & Song, A. K. (2022). *The Digital Platform Economy Index 2020*. Cham: SpringerBriefs in Economics.

Vachon, T. E., Wallace, M., & Hyde, A. (2016). Union decline in a neoliberal age: Globalization, financialization, European integration, and union density in 18 affluent democracies. *Socius*, *2*, 2378023116656847.

Vallas, S., & Schor, J. B. (2020). What do platforms do? Understanding the gig economy. *Annual Review of Sociology*, *46*(1), 273–294.

Van Houten, G., & Russo, G. (2020). *European Company Survey 2019: Workplace Practices Unlocking Employee Potential*. Dublin: Eurofound.

Van Roy, V., Vértesy, D., & Vivarelli, M. (2018). Technology and employment: Mass unemployment or job creation? Empirical evidence from European patenting firms. *Research Policy*, *47*(9), 1762–1776.

4. The perceived dilemma between debt reduction and a fair society: saving for a rainy day without increasing poverty?

Jakub Sowula and Martin Seeleib-Kaiser

INTRODUCTION

Austerity policies were perceived by many political actors as *the* strategy to deal with the aftermath of the financial and the European sovereign debt crises. It was argued that deficit and debt reduction had become the ultimate goal and social policies had to be subordinated accordingly (Blyth, 2013). Countries should pursue strategies to reduce debt and "save for a rainy day" in prosperous economic times to enable them to react with expansionary fiscal policies in hard times without relying on ever higher debt levels that could have serious economic consequences (Reinhart et al., 2012). Whereas in the past high debt could be reduced through high economic growth, such a strategy of a "'free lunch' that raises welfare at the same time as it erodes the debt burden" (Best et al., 2019: 240) no longer seems possible in times of moderate growth. As debt reduction via (hyper)inflation also seems not to be an option, fiscal consolidation has become a "necessity" during good economic times (e.g., Abbas et al., 2013; Alesina and Ardagna, 2010), as already suggested by Keynes.

Although the policy paradigm of austerity started to be questioned in light of an abating scholarly debate and some politicians propagating the end of austerity, this seems to be an illusion, as increases in spending do not automatically mark a new policy paradigm, especially if those do not match pre-austerity levels or are not adjusted to demographics and inflation (Bell, 2018; Inman, 2019). Moreover, the political will and obligation to reduce deficits and balance budgets are increasingly institutionalised, evident by the growing number of fiscal rules (Gootjes et al., 2021). Taking into account the weakening of organised labour and the continued challenges for the welfare state, the "legacy of austerity" is far from over (Irving, 2021), all of which places fiscal consolidation prominently on the policy agenda.

Fiscal consolidation is possible via two main mechanisms: expenditure reductions or revenue increases. Both can be accompanied by negative side effects. Tax-based consolidation can negatively impact short-term economic growth and be less promising in sustainably reducing deficits and debt (Alesina et al., 1998; Alesina and Ardagna, 2010, 2013; Guichard et al., 2007), whilst spending-based consolidation can lead to sharp increases in inequality and poverty (e.g., Agnello and Sousa, 2014; Ball et al., 2013; Ciminelli et al., 2019; Furcerci et al., 2015; McManus et al., 2021). Accordingly, states face – in analogy to Okun's (2015) famous trade-off between efficiency and equality – a perceived dilemma between a fair society and successful debt and deficit reduction.

To what extent governments are able to pursue successful and fair fiscal consolidation policies remains an open empirical question, as electorates tend to oppose welfare-state retrenchment and tax increases (Pierson, 2001). In this paper, we address the question under which conditions and causal pathways countries can accomplish the seemingly impossible, i.e., achieve deficit and debt reduction in economic good times without increasing poverty. Or, to put it differently: *how is it possible to save for a rainy day without taking away the people's umbrellas?* To answer this question, we apply a fuzzy-set qualitative comparative analysis (fsQCA) among the countries of the European Economic Area (EEA) plus Switzerland between 1994 and 2019, excluding "the rainy day" (2008–2013) of the financial and sovereign debt crisis. The outcome of interest is *fair* fiscal consolidation, for which we investigate budget consolidation efforts (depicted by the debt-ratio and primary budget balance, cf. Wagschal and Wenzelburger, 2008) and poverty developments. We include socio-economic (GDP growth, output gap, employment, trade balance), institutional (budget balance rule, Eurozone membership) and party-political factors (left parties in government) as potential causal conditions (Wagschal and Jäkel, 2010).

The paper contributes to the existing literature by investigating fair fiscal consolidation from a novel methodological angle via set-theoretic relations instead of net effects, enabling the study of the complex interplay of several potentially causal pathways for debt and poverty reductions. In the following sections, we present the set-theoretical expectations for the configurations of causal conditions and the outcome, the results of the fsQCA analysis and its implications for *when*, *how* and *by whom* it is possible to solve the perceived dilemma.

SET-THEORETICAL EXPECTATIONS FOR HOW TO ACHIEVE FAIR FISCAL CONSOLIDATION

The literature on fiscal consolidation points to numerous conditions potentially enabling positive debt and deficit developments while simultaneously preventing poverty increases. Most straightforwardly, this could be achieved through (high) economic growth (Abbas et al., 2013; Best et al., 2019; Hagemann, 2012; Molnar, 2012), which – if distributed properly – also could lead to the poorest getting their fair share (Dollar et al., 2013). In a high growth scenario, debt reduction is possible directly via increases in the denominator of the debt-to-GDP ratio and indirectly through improvements in the primary balance, i.e., higher revenues (through taxes) without having higher expenditures. The same is true if a country is in a good position in the economic cycle (positive output gap), resulting in lower unemployment and higher inflation. Ideally, countries could then act counter-cyclically by increasing taxes and reducing expenditure, which could help reduce debt.

Severe fiscal consolidation during economic downturns or low economic growth could have adverse effects. Not only are the mechanisms described above reversed, but larger fiscal consolidation could result in even higher debt-ratios due to fiscal multiplier effects on economic growth (Best et al., 2019; Blanchard and Leigh, 2013). In short, the economic situation of a country matters (cf. von Hagen and Strauch, 2001). This could be true not only for the success of fiscal consolidation but even more so for its effects on income distribution, with inequality and poverty rising strongly when consolidating in times of low growth and economic downturns (Agnello and Sousa, 2014; McManus et al., 2021). Translated into set-theoretic expectations, the presence of low economic growth and large negative output gaps could stand in the way of solving the dilemma.

To tackle debt and deficits, growth needs to be complemented by further conditions: one way is high employment, as high labour force participation fosters long-term economic growth (Best et al., 2019) and potentially reduces poverty. Moreover, this could directly improve the primary balance as having many people employed could mean higher tax revenues and lower costs for unemployment protection. Another way is to focus on export surpluses, which could pay for fiscal consolidation (cf. Perotti, 2011). However, there is disagreement about the causal direction between trade (or current account) and fiscal balances (Barro, 1974; Darrat, 1988; Feldstein and Horioka, 1980; Summers, 1988). Empirical studies regarding this issue have provided mixed conclusions for different countries and years (e.g., Algieri, 2013; Rault and Afonso, 2009; Siničáková et al., 2017; Xie and Chen, 2014). Since fair fiscal consolidation is the outcome of interest, we include trade balance as a potential causal condition. Furthermore, we include trade balance and not current account deficits in our analysis, as countries can have long-standing current account deficits but still be able to pay off their debt if simultaneously having a trade surplus. Overall, a trade surplus could help repay debt and lead to economic growth.

In addition to socio-economic conditions, institutional and party-political factors can play a role.[1] First, it could make a difference whether countries are members of the Eurozone. Although the Stability and Growth Pact applies to all EU Member States, specific regulations and sanctioning mechanisms exclusively affect Eurozone members (cf. de la Porte and Heins, 2016; European Commission, 2022b, 2022c). Moreover, Eurozone members are unable to devalue externally. In addition, countries could implement national fiscal rules to achieve fiscal consolidation. Empirical studies agree that those can lead to fiscal consolidation, although there are strong endogeneity concerns (Badinger and Reuter, 2017; Caselli and Reynaud, 2020; Heinemann et al., 2018; Molnar, 2012). After all, fiscal rules could be used as a signalling tool for governments to show their preferences rather than being useful commitment devices (Debrun and Kumar, 2007). Hence, to make sure that the considered rules have the "capacity to 'tie the hands of policymakers' tempted by deviations from socially optimal choices" (Debrun and Kumar, 2007: 479), it makes sense to only consider strict rules, i.e., such that are monitored independently or for which legal enforcement procedures are applicable. This is in line with empirical evidence arguing that the design of fiscal rules matters (e.g., Caselli and Reynaud, 2020; Wyplosz, 2013) and identifying the lack of enforcement or commitment as a potential cause for consolidation failure (Alesina and Perotti, 1996b). To overcome these problems, the literature has proposed enshrining fiscal rules in the constitution (Asatryan et al., 2018; Grembi et al., 2016). However, effective rules can also result from public negotiations among coalition partners, as in the Netherlands, given that independent monitoring and sanctioning mechanisms are in play (Wyplosz, 2013). Lastly, regarding the type of rule, the literature points to budget balance rules as the most effective instrument (Bergman et al., 2016; Heinemann et al., 2018). Accordingly, we expect legally strong budget balance rules to be a potential causal factor for successful fiscal consolidation.

Finally, we include the political factor "left parties". Left parties are said to pursue macroeconomic policies in line with class-based interests and preferences (Hibbs, 1977; Schmidt, 2022), potentially hindering fiscal consolidation. According to Potrafke (2017), however, the partisan effect has been rather weak since the 1990s. Moreover, he finds ambiguous ideology effects on debt and deficit developments and vague results indicating higher taxation when left parties are in power. Armingeon et al. (2016) argue that the classic picture is reversed in that left governments could even be more eager to pursue fiscal consolidation than centrist or right governments (also: Kraft, 2017; Raess, 2021). Based on a "Nixon-goes-to-China" logic (Cowen and Sutter, 1998; Kitschelt, 2001), this might even mean a more effective retrenchment with left parties in government (Armingeon et al., 2016; but see: Tavares, 2004). Finally, left governments might perceive the necessity to signal fiscal competence by pursuing consolidation (cf. Kraft, 2017; Raess, 2021). If true, this again puts a focus on the design of fiscal consolidation: do left governments pursue rigorous retrenchment, or are they accepting austerity measures as a new normal without, however, losing central ambitions to achieve a fair society (Bremer, 2018)? Such an approach would align with left governments' aim at revenue-based fiscal consolidation through higher taxation instead of cutbacks to deal with fiscal pressures and high debt (Mulas-Granados, 2006; Tavares, 2004).

METHOD

In the previous section, we argued that poverty, debt, and deficit levels could be influenced by many factors, leading us to assume that no single condition likely solves the potential dilemma; instead, this seems more plausible under a combination of conditions (*conjunctural causation*). Moreover, we expect multiple configurations of causal conditions (paths) to lead to the desired outcome (*complex causation*). Being confronted with such a research setting, QCA is best suited as it enables the analysis of equifinality and complex causation (Ragin, 2008). Another advantage is that QCA-analyses are less subject to the omitted variable bias than net-effect analyses (cf. Fainshmidt et al., 2020). We use fuzzy-set QCA (fsQCA) as the included conditions and the outcome are better depicted by partial membership scores than dichotomous coding. In the following, we present the case selection, the operationalisation and calibration of our outcome and conditions.[2]

Case Selection

We investigate all countries of the European Economic Area plus Switzerland between 1994 and 2019, excluding "the rainy day" (2008–2013) of the financial and the sovereign debt crisis. This is justified because we aim to investigate how countries can prepare for crises, not how they should react during crises.[3] Moreover, fiscal consolidation during economic hardship is very unlikely also due to the welfare state's function as an automatic stabiliser which leads to higher spending in times of crisis (Reinprecht et al., 2018). We define 88 cases based on the countries' success or failure in consolidating their budgets in this period (see online appendix). Budget consolidation is assessed by considering general government debt-ratios and non-cyclically adjusted primary balances, whereby positive changes must persist over at least two consecutive years (thereby closely following Wagschal and Wenzelburger, 2008)[4]; accordingly, we refrained from incorporating a lag. More specifically, we consider the following scenarios of successful consolidation:

- Scenario I – In case of primary deficit:
  Average deficit improvement ≥ 0.7 percentage points/year over the consolidation period, whereby the consolidation phase ends if the primary deficit or the debt level increases.
- Scenario II – In case of primary surplus:
  Reduction ≥ 5 per cent of the initial debt-ratio level over the consolidation period, whereby the consolidation phase ends with the first increase in the debt-ratio level or change from primary surplus to deficit.[5]

We identify 47 periods of successful fiscal consolidation using this definition and relying on data from the IMF Fiscal Monitor (IMF, 2022). We also identified another scenario similar to scenario II among the remaining periods. Here, countries reduced their initial debt-ratio level by at least 5% in a consecutive period, but without having a primary surplus. Given the critical role of the primary surplus for a sustainable consolidation of the budget (e.g., Abbas et al., 2013; Alesina and Perotti, 1996c; Wagschal and Wenzelburger, 2008), time periods within this scenario were identified as only "partly" successful. All cases and their classification are displayed in Table A1 in the online appendix.

Operationalisation of Causal Conditions and Outcome

fsQCA requires careful construction of fuzzy-sets for the outcome and its potential causal conditions, indicating the degree of membership of a case to a set. Most important are the three qualitative breakpoints of full membership (1), full non-membership (0) and a crossover point of maximum ambiguity (0.5) (Ragin, 2008). Membership scores >0.5 indicate that a case is more a member than a non-member of a set, with the opposite being true for scores <0.5. Although the precise definition of the 0.5 anchor is crucial for calibrating membership scores (via the direct method of calibration, cf. Ragin, 2008), we followed recommendations to refrain from assigning cases set memberships of 0.5 due to theoretical, analytical and practical reasons (Schneider and Wagemann, 2012: 28 and 101).

Outcome

The outcome captures the essence of the perceived dilemma, achieving fiscal consolidation without increasing poverty. Both aspects are equally considered in the operationalisation and calibration by creating membership scores for each aspect and combining them in a single set. For budget consolidation, cases with successful consolidation were assigned the score "1", and cases without success were given the score "0". Cases with partial success (debt reduction without having a primary surplus) were assigned the score "0.622", equivalent to being "more in than out" (Ragin, 2008). This label is more justified than 0.5 (neither in nor out) since, despite the lack of a primary surplus, we found a substantial debt reduction in most cases classified as "partly" successful.

Relative poverty levels (less than 60% of median-equivalised income) are used to depict the aspect of a fair society, justified by poverty alleviation being a key goal of all welfare states (cf. Goodin et al., 1999). Poverty changes were compared by percentage change (not points), which accounts for different initial poverty levels. Furthermore, we defined three qualitative anchors and applied the direct method of calibration to assign membership scores. Cases with a 20% reduction/increase of the initial poverty level were assigned full membership/non-membership in the set of cases with successful poverty-level developments. The 20% benchmark ensures differentiated membership scores and rewards/punishes strong poverty changes. The 0.5-anchor was set at a one-per-mill increase of initial poverty scores. This ensures that no "real" observation receives the value of 0.5 (cf. Schneider and Wagemann, 2012) and, in addition, that all cases that have at least managed to maintain their poverty level receive a membership score of >0.5. Lastly, we combined both membership scores to create membership scores for our total outcome O as follows:

- Let $P(x)$ and $F(x)$ be the membership score for case x in the poverty development and fiscal consolidation set with $x \in$ {countries used in the analysis}
- Then

$$O(x) = \begin{cases} if\ F(x)=1\ and\ P(x)>0.119: \dfrac{P(x)}{2}+\dfrac{1}{2} \\ if\ F(x)=1\ and\ P(x)\leq 0.119: 0.48 \\ if\ F(x)=0.622\ and\ P(x)>0.378: \max\left\{\dfrac{0.622}{2}+\dfrac{P(x)}{2}, 0.52\right\} \\ if\ F(x)=0.622\ and\ P(x)\leq 0.378: \min\left\{\dfrac{0.622}{2}+\dfrac{P(x)}{2}, 0.48\right\} \\ if\ F(x)=0: \min\left\{\dfrac{P(x)}{2}, 0.48\right\} \end{cases}$$

Defining the total outcome this way ensures that both aspects (poverty and fiscal developments) are weighted equally and that scores of 0.5 are not assigned. Most importantly, it places cases that manage to achieve fiscal consolidation but mostly fail in the poverty set $P(x) \leq 0.119$ "being mostly out", Ragin, 2008) below the 0.5 anchor.

Causal Conditions

We used the seven conditions discussed above to explain the outcome. Although there is no mechanical way to determine the number of conditions, we follow recommendations by using four to seven conditions for ≥ 40 cases (Berg-Schlosser and De Meur, 2009). We refrain from including more than seven conditions because otherwise, the number of truth table rows would strongly exceed the number of observed cases, increasing the issue of limited diversity. All conditions are operationalised as fuzzy-sets.[6] Capital letters indicate the presence and cross out the absence of conditions.

The economic growth (GRWTH) condition is based on the World Bank GDP-per-capita growth indicator (World Bank, 2022b). Fuzzy-set scores were assigned using the complement of a sluggish economic growth set (1-SGRWTH). For the SGRWTH set, membership scores are determined via the direct method, using three qualitative anchors based on the average growth rate: full membership (0%), full non-membership (2%) and the crossover point at 1.5%. The 2%-mark was chosen because it is occasionally referred to as the ideal (long-term) growth rate (cf. Jones, 2016). The 1.5%-mark for the 0.5-anchor is more controversial but has already been used as a dividing line between winners and losers (albeit for economic growth per worker, Durlauf et al., 2005: 571). Moreover, since we exclude the "rainy days", higher average economic growth can be assumed, justifying seeing growth rates $\leq 1.5\%$ as sluggish. This is also confirmed by the data, as a 1.5% GDP-per-capita growth rate is far below the investigated countries' average for the interval of interest [1994–2007, 2014–2019, >2.1%], which stays true even when including the rainy days [1994–2019, >1.6%].

Economic activity (OGAP) is assessed using output gap data based on the AMECO dataset (European Commission, 2022a). While the EC argues for the advantages of its estimation over the IMF or OECD approaches (European Commission, 2015b), our choice is primarily driven by data availability[7] and implicit proximity to EEA countries. Initial fuzzy-set scores were assigned relying on the EC's evaluation of output gap scores, which defines five intervals of economic performance (European Commission, 2015a: 20). Full non-membership (=0) is given to cases with an average output gap of < -4 (*exceptionally bad times*). *Very bad economic times* $(-4 \leq X < -3)$ translate into a score of 0.2. Cases with *bad economic times* ($-3 \leq X < -1.5$) were assigned a membership score of 0.4. The EC defines *normal times* with output gap scores between $-1.5 \leq X < 1.5$, justifying placing cases with such scores above the 0.5-anchor. We used the lower threshold (-1.5) as the crossover point between normal and bad economic times (=0.5). The remaining interval was separated into two parts: scores of $-1.5 < X < 0$ translated into membership scores of 0.6, and cases between $0 \leq X < 1.5$ were assigned scores of 0.8. Full membership was given for cases with *good economic times* ($X \geq 1.5$). Lastly, we relied on the indirect method of calibration (cf. Ragin, 2008), which calculates exact membership scores based on the predefined anchors and original data through a fractional logit model.

The employment condition (EMPL) is based on the World Bank employment-to-population-ratio indicator (World Bank, 2022c). The direct method was used for the calibration. We used Sweden's employment value in 1991 (~65) as a benchmark for defining full membership, as until then, the Swedish model was considered to be a prototype for high employment. Full non-membership is set at 40%, and the crossover point at 55%. This is justified as it makes no sense to speak of high employment if the majority of people are not employed. Hence our operationalisation ensures that cases with an average employment rate of 50% are placed well below the 0.5-anchor.

For trade balance (TRDE), we rely on the external-balance-of-goods-and-services indicator (World Bank, 2022a). A substantial trade surplus of 5% translates into full membership, a trade deficit of −5% translates into full non-membership, and the crossover point of maximum ambiguity is set at 0%. All intermediate values were determined using the direct method of calibration.

Eurozone (EURZN) scores are assigned based on the length of Eurozone membership for each case: not a member of the Eurozone at any point (=0); member of the Eurozone in $0\% < X < 51\%$ of the interval (=0.33); in 51–74% of the interval (=0.67); in over 75% of the time interval (=1).

For the budget balance rule (BRULE) condition, we rely on the technical report of the IMF Fiscal Rules Data Set (Davoodi et al., 2022). Following the literature on effective fiscal rules, rules were only considered when active in at least two-thirds of the interval and if monitored outside the government or when formal enforcement procedures are possible. Fuzzy-set scores were linked to the datasets' legal basis coding: full non-membership (=0) means a case had no rule that conformed to our criteria. A value of 0.4 was given to cases having a BRULE that is legally based on a "political commitment", 0.6 for "political coalition", 0.8 for "statutory", and full membership (=1) was given for constitutionally based rules.

Lastly, we created two left government conditions based on the *leftcab*[8] variable from the Comparative Welfare State Dataset (Brady et al., 2020).

Fuzzy-set scores were assigned using the direct method. The first set describes strong left parties (LEFT) in government (0.5-anchor at 25% of governmental parliamentary seats, full membership at 50%, full non-membership at 0%). The second set describes left majority governments (LEFTM), placing the 0.5-anchor at 50%, full-membership at 100%, and full non-membership at 0%. Given the theoretical controversy regarding left parties for the perceived dilemma, using a second set allows capturing outcome-relevant nuances. This is also in line with calls for more robustness tests in QCA, especially in big N analyses (Emmenegger et al., 2013; Skaaning, 2011). Consequently, two sufficiency analyses were conducted, each with seven conditions. Prior to this, all conditions were tested for necessity (Mello, 2022; Schneider and Wagemann, 2012).

FSQCA ANALYSES

Necessary Conditions

A condition is potentially necessary for the outcome if consistency is ≥ 0.9 and coverage ≥ 0.5 (ibid.; Legewie, 2013). Figure 4.1 displays that good economic performance (OGAP) and economic growth (GRWTH) meet those thresholds. However, when plotting both conditions against the outcome, we dismiss OGAP as a necessary condition as the graph displays true logical contradictory cases (CYP(14–17):0.28/0.60; EST(99–01):0.48/0.75). Hence, the relevance of necessity (cf. Schneider and Wagemann, 2012) was only calculated for economic growth (RoN(GRWTH) = 0.32). Given the important role of economic growth for (fair) fiscal consolidation in the literature, it is treated as a *non-trivial* necessary condition in the subsequent analyses.

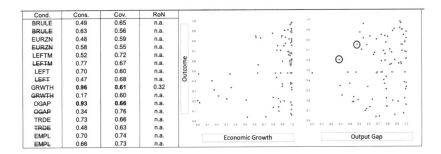

Figure 4.1   Necessity analysis

Sufficient Conditions

Identifying sufficient paths for the outcome requires constructing a truth table based on set membership scores and examining the truth table rows ($2^7 = 128$) for sufficiency. For this, we used a consistency threshold of 0.857, a frequency threshold of 1, considered the occurrence of simultaneous subset relations (PRI > 0.5) and checked for true logical contradictory (TLC) cases.[9] Moreover, only plausible counterfactuals were used in the logical minimisation process to account for limited diversity when generating the intermediate solution. Simplifying assumptions were set in fsQCA guided by directional expectations about the conditions (Legewie, 2013; Ragin, 2008; Schneider and Wagemann, 2012). Lastly, several robustness tests were conducted. Besides running two sufficiency analyses (LEFT-fsQCA and LEFTM-fsQCA), we varied the consistency (0.9) and frequency thresholds (2, 3) as recommended (Maggetti and Levi-Faur, 2013; Schneider and Wagemann, 2012; Skaaning, 2011). We also refer to the results of the parsimonious solution (cf. Baumgartner and Thiem, 2020), for which we follow Ragin (2008: 204) in seeing the ingredients of the parsimonious solution as "*core* causal conditions" ▲ and additional conditions from the intermediate solution as "*complementary* or *contributing* conditions" (▲).

Both sufficiency analyses yield satisfying results (LEFT-fsQCA: 0.74(Cov.)/0.81(Cons.); LEFTM-fsQCA: 0.69/0.86). However, the single recipes vary greatly regarding their coverage of cases, their robustness and whether they display inconsistencies, i.e., the occurrence of cases violating sufficiency ($X > Y$, reported by italic) and TLC cases ($X > 0.5; Y < 0.5$, reported by crossing them out). Overall, the LEFT-solution is more consistent than the LEFTM-solution. For the analyses, we only used recipes that displayed no inconsistencies or passed at least one of three robustness tests.

Table 4.1 displays the results of the robust sufficiency analyses. Economic growth (GRWTH) is present in all sufficient paths, and no path displays poor economic activity (~~OGAP~~). The presence or absence of other conditions varies across the recipes. This is consistent with the analysis of necessary conditions, confirming that full realisation of the economic potential (OGAP) is not necessary, but OGAP can constitute a contributing, yet often not a core causal condition. Consequently, as suspected, solving the perceived dilemma seems to be limited to the "sunny days" since the "rainy days" would imply low economic activity (~~OGAP~~) and growth (~~GRWTH~~). Simultaneously, this does not mean that the perceived dilemma is only solvable under ideal socio-economic conditions, nor that there is only one way to go. Instead, it seems as if the absence of certain socio-economic conditions (~~EMPL~~ or ~~TRDE~~) can be "*compensated*" for by the presence of other conditions. Perhaps the most surprising recipe is GRWTH*OGAP*~~TRDE~~*~~EMPL~~*~~LEFTM~~, which leads to success although lacking both high employment (~~EMPL~~) and trade surplus (~~TRDE~~), implying the important role economic activity and growth can play for fair fiscal consolidation.

However, it is not the socio-economic conditions alone that lead to a successful outcome. There is no sufficient path that does not include specifications regarding the presence or absence of institutional or political conditions. For example, every path with high employment (EMPL) only "works" because, among others, a left-party condition is present (II_{LM}, I_L, V_L), which fits the assumption of higher tax revenues when strong left parties are in government. At the same time, this does not mean that the presence of strong left parties always comes along with high employment (VI_L, VIII_L and III_{LM}). Most interesting in this regard is III_{LM}: GRWTH*OGAP*TRDE*LEFTM*EURZN, which is successful not only due to beneficial economic conditions and being a member of the Eurozone but requires a left majority in government. This path also differs from the other recipes, which include the presence of a strong left government in that most of the successful cases covered by it took place after the financial and sovereign debt crisis (except for BEL(94–07)).

However, this does not mean that partisan politics vanished because we also find several paths requiring the absence of a left majority (I_{LM}, IV_{LM}, V_{LM}) and a strong left (II_L, III_L, VII_L). Starting with the latter, all paths requiring the absence of a strong left (~~LEFT~~) seem to be in line with the *classic stereotype*, whereby the left is unable to consolidate. Paths requiring the absence of a left majority (~~LEFTM~~) could result in biased interpretations if not simultaneously considering the LEFT-fsQCA paths, as eight of the 15 cases covered by I_{LM}, IV_{LM}, V_{LM} require the absence of LEFTM, but the presence of LEFT. There we find complex scenarios in which it is not the left per se that matters, but it is a question of its strength.

Turning to the institutional conditions: being a Eurozone member seems to (not) work independently of a partisan logic or fiscal consolidation strategy. Instead, it is context-dependent, which makes sense given that it entails advantages possibly contributing to reaching the outcome but simultaneously limits countries' monetary policy options. Thus, the European Union's conditional requirements for Eurozone membership have contributed to or perhaps even allowed fair fiscal consolidation in some Member States (for instance, in CEE countries, IV_{LM}, III_L, VII_L). A different picture emerges for budget balance rules. We find a time-related pattern in which the presence or absence of BRULE contributed to the outcome. 11 out of 13 cases covered by paths requiring the presence of BRULE are cases after the financial and sovereign

Table 4.1   Sufficiency analysis

Cond./Rec.	Sufficiency Analysis (Left Majority Condition - LEFTM)							Sufficiency Analysis (Strong Left Condition - LEFT)							
	I$_{LM}$	II$_{LM}$	III$_{LM}$	IV$_{LM}$	V$_{LM}$	VI$_{LM}$	I$_L$	II$_L$	III$_L$	IV$_L$	V$_L$	VI$_L$	VII$_L$	VIII$_L$
Socio-Economic														
GRWTH	◄	◄	◄	(◄)	◄	(◄)	◄	◄	◄	(◄)	◄	◄	◄	(◄)
OGAP	◄	(◄)	(◄)	◄		(◄)	(◄)	◄		◄ ►	(◄)	◄	►
EMPL	►	◄		◄	►	►	◄	►		◄	◄ ►	►		
TRDE	►		◄	◄					(◄)					
Party-Political														
LEFT							◄	►	►		(◄)	(◄)	►	◄
LEFTM	►	◄	◄	►	►									
Institutional														
BRULE		►		►	◄	◄	►			◄	◄	►	◄	◄
EURZN			◄	►		►						◄		►

The perceived dilemma between debt reduction and a fair society

	Sufficiency Analysis (Left Majority Condition - LEFTM)						Sufficiency Analysis (Strong Left Condition - LEFT)						
Covered Cases	ESP(97-07) EST(02-07) FIN(15-17) LVA(01-07) LVA(14-16) MLT(05-07) POL(96-98) POL(99-07) SVK(05-07)	AUT(95-97) CYP(04-07) CZE(96-04) PRT(96-00) ROM(01-07) SWE(96-00)	BEL(94-07) GER(05-07) LTU(15-18) LUX(14-16) LUX(17-19) MLT(14-19) PRT(16-19) SVK(14-19) SVN(15-19)	CZE(05-07) CZE(14-19) NDL(96-01) NOR(14-19) NOR(99-07) POL(16-19)	BLG(14-15) EST(02-07) EST(99-01) FIN(15-17) GBR(15-17) LVA(14-16) LVA(17-19)	BLG(16-18) EST(02-07) HRV(14-19) HUN(14-19) ROM(14-18)	SWE(96-00) AUT(95-97) CYP(04-07) CZE(05-07) CZE(14-19) CZE(96-04) NDL(96-01) NOR(99-07) PRT(96-00) ROM(01-07)	BEL(14-19) BLG(16-18) FIN(15-17) HRV(14-19) HUN(14-19) LUX(96-02) LVA(01-07) MLT(05-07) POL(16-19) SVK(05-07)	AUT(04-07) AUT(98-03) BEL(14-19) CYP(14-17) CYP(18-19) IRE(14-19) IRE(94-07) LUX(96-02) NDL(04-07)	BEL(14-19) BLG(16-18) HRV(14-19) HUN(14-19) PRT(16-19) SVK(14-19) SVN(15-19)	LVA(17-19)	ESP(97-07)	GBR(15-17) FIN(15-17)	EST(99-01) ROM(14-18) EST(02-07)
Incons. (TLC)	3(3)	3(2)	4(2)	2(2)	3(2)	0(0)	4(3)	1(1)	3(2)	0(0)	0(0)	0(0)	0(0)	0(0)
Robustness														
Frequency (2)	No	Yes (id)	Yes (sup)	Yes (sub)	No	No	Yes (id)	Yes (id)	No	Yes (id)	No	No	No	No
Frequency (3)	No	Yes (id)	Yes (sup)	Yes (sub)	No	No	Yes (id)	Yes (id)	No	Yes (sup)	No	No	No	No
Cons. Cut-off (0.9)	Yes (id)	Yes (sup)	Yes (sup)	No	Yes (sup)	Yes (id)	No	Yes (id)	Yes (sup)	Yes (id)	No	Yes (id)	Yes (id)	Yes (id)
Recipe Prop.														
Raw Coverage	0.32	0.30	0.22	0.21	0.15	0.12	0.34	0.32	0.20	0.25	0.11	0.10	0.10	0.07

	Sufficiency Analysis (Left Majority Condition - LEFTM)					Sufficiency Analysis (Strong Left Condition - LEFT)				
Unique Coverage	0.06	0.04	0.02	0.04	0.02	0.01	0.14	0.05	0.05	0.04	0.00	0.02	0.01	0.02
Consistency	0.87	0.90	0.87	0.86	0.86	0.96	0.86	0.89	0.87	0.93	0.93	0.98	0.92	0.99

Note: ▲ – core causal cond. (presence); ▼ – core causal cond. (absence); (▲) – contributing causal cond. (presence) (▼) – contributing causal cond. (absence). Only recipes without inconsistencies or passing at least one of three robustness tests were reported. TLC = True logical contradictory case; id = identical; sup = superset of recipe; sub = subset of a recipe.

debt crisis (exception: EST(99–01)/EST(02–07)), with the opposite being true for cases covered by paths requiring ~~BRULE~~. Moreover, Table 4.1 displays a timely restricted partisan logic before the crisis (1994–2007) in that left government paths only work with ~~BRULE~~ (II_{LM}, I_L, VI_L), again with Estonia being an exception (VIII_L). This pattern does not hold after 2013 ($III_{LM}, V_L, VIII_L$).

Lastly, we run separate necessity and sufficiency analyses for the non-outcome. The results (see online appendix) mirror insights from the outcome analysis in that most sufficient paths included the absence of economic growth (~~GRWTH~~), economic activity (~~OGAP~~) or both. Moreover, they again emphasise the vital link between high employment and left governments. No necessary condition is found.

DISCUSSION AND CONCLUSION

It is *possible to save for a rainy day without taking away people's umbrellas*, i.e., fair fiscal consolidation is not a dilemma in the classical sense. However, the following questions remain: under *what* circumstances, *how* and *by whom* is fair consolidation achieved? Our analysis confirms that achieving the outcome is only possible in the absence of sluggish growth (<1.5% of GDP per capita) and not too large output gaps. This means that countries must make fiscal consolidation efforts during the "sunny days" and that it is impossible to expect governments to achieve fair fiscal consolidation during times of low economic growth. As to the *how*, we find multiple sufficient pathways aiming at different strategies, including such that seem to work via vital economic conditions despite having trade deficits or low employment, via high employment (thus, likely higher tax revenues) or such in line with more liberal accounts focusing on net exports.

However, these strategies only work because institutional and party-political conditions are present or absent. Starting with the former, it is difficult to disentangle clear patterns, but it seems as if the presence or absence of the institutional conditions do not relate to the envisaged strategy but are context-dependent regarding Eurozone membership and time-dependent in the case of budget balance rules. This means fair fiscal consolidation is possible even for Eurozone members, contrary to scholars arguing that Europe would be better off without the Euro (cf. Höpner, 2014; Streeck, 2014). At the same time, the analysis points out that it might be beneficial for certain states not to be a currency union member as we find paths explicitly including the absence of Eurozone membership (covering many CEE countries). For national budget balance rules, time matters. Paths including BRULE cover cases mostly after the financial and debt crisis (2014–2019), as opposed to paths requiring its absence (~~BRULE~~), mainly covering cases before 2008. We assume that this can be attributed to the instalment of a new generation of fiscal rules (in this study, budget balance rules) that are better designed (cf. Ardanaz et al., 2021) and subject to better advising and monitoring, e.g., via fiscal councils (Debrun and Kinda, 2017). Interestingly, sufficient paths including the presence of left governments only work in the absence of budget balance rules, but again are only valid in the time period before the financial crisis.

This brings us to the *who* question. First, the *classic stereotype* whereby left parties in government cannot achieve fiscal consolidation must be rejected as we find multiple paths requiring the presence of left governments to achieve fair debt and deficit reduction. However, this does not mean there is no partisan logic behind fiscal consolidation strategies. For example, we do find sufficient paths in line with liberal arguments that require the absence of left parties in government to achieve the outcome, as well as a recurring link that high employment contributes to the outcome only under the presence of strong left parties in government. This path is in line with arguments whereby the left hopped onto the train of fiscal consolidation (and, according to the data, did this a while ago) without losing central tenets (Bremer, 2018). At the same time, we witness a change of strategy in the aftermath of the financial and sovereign debt crisis. This is best visible in the path GRWTH*OGAP*TRDE*LEFTM*EURZN, which covers most successful left government cases after the crisis, implying that success was achieved not via employment strategies but via a prospering economy, a trade surplus and Eurozone membership.

The question that continues to remain for the future is: what is left for the left? Are progressive governments no longer able to pursue fiscal consolidation via high employment strategies, as the argument of a "trilemma of the social service economy" (Iversen and Wren, 1998) would suggest? Or has the left ideologically surrendered? This question is highly relevant since the free lunch of reducing debt and decreasing poverty through high growth is likely to be a (environmentally damaging) pathway of the past, and "an expansion based on net exports is not available to the world as a whole" (Perotti, 2011: 42). To ensure fair fiscal consolidation does not become a zero-sum game, it is necessary for domestically driven strategies to succeed. The fact that this is not impossible is demonstrated by two cases: Latvia(17–19) in GRWTH*OGAP*EMPL*~~TRDE~~*LEFT*EURZN and the Czech Republic(14–19) in GRWTH*EMPL*OGAP*LEFT*~~BRULE~~. Given the issue's complexity, more research is needed on the effects of specific policy instruments (e.g., McManus et al., 2021; Paulus et al., 2017) and on conditions that have to be in place to make just fiscal consolidations possible.

Supplementary online appendix (e.g., classification of cases, data Matrix fsQCA, truth table fsQCA) can be found here: DOI: 10.6084/m9.figshare.21170812.

NOTES

1. Ideally, we would have included a condition reflecting the progressivity of welfare state design. Due to a lack of comparative data, this was not possible in the analysis, which is why such a condition is not discussed further.
2. In the design and application, we relied on general recommendations for good fsQCA practice (Baumgartner and Thiem, 2020; Legewie, 2013; Mello, 2022; Ragin, 2008; Rihoux and Ragin, 2009; Schneider and Wagemann, 2012) and applications of QCA in comparative welfare-state research in particular (Emmenegger et al., 2013). The analysis was conducted using fsQCA 3.0 (Ragin and Davey, 2016).
3. The years 2008 to 2013 were determined as the times of crisis by referring to the average annual change in the debt-to-GDP ratio and primary deficit for the country selection. Following the indicators, 2014 marks the end of the crisis, which is why we included it as a reference point in the analysis.
4. Non-cyclically adjusted primary balances were used to account for interest payments, although being aware that those disregard the cyclical effects of growth and unemployment. However, this is justified as we are only interested in comprehensive fiscal consolidations that should "not be unduly influenced by cyclical effects" (Alesina and Perotti, 1996c: 118). Moreover, a considerable advantage of this approach lies in its simplicity and transparency (Alesina and Perotti, 1996a; Wagschal and Wenzelburger, 2008). We explicitly refrained from using CAPB, as such are dependent on estimations of potential GDP, which is highly dependent on the statistical technique used (Best et al., 2019). We refrained from using narrative-based approaches (Devries et al., 2011; Romer and Romer, 2010) to capture our period of interest.
5. Setting quantitative thresholds for fiscal consolidation is a subject of discussion (e.g., Molnar, 2012: 131). Accordingly, results may differ with different approaches. However, since our definition closely resembles previously used ones, potential deviations are not expected to be major. Applying our case II definition to a country with a 60% debt-ratio mirrors definitions used in Alesina and Ardagna (2010); Alesina and Perotti (1996a); and European Commission (2007). Using per cent instead of percentage points seemed more appropriate to put cases to a relatively equal hard test. Moreover, a similar definition for case I can be found in Wagschal and Wenzelburger (2008), and a slightly less demanding definition in Tsibouris et al. (2006).
6. As is true for all QCA-analyses, defining universally valid thresholds is not possible, i.e., using other valid definitions could lead to different results. However, slightly adjusting the thresholds did not unduly alter the results. For reasons of transparency and clarity, we only report the technical robustness tests (consistency and frequency thresholds adjustments) in our tables.
7. E.g., the IMF lacks long-term Output Gap data for BLG/HRV/CZE/HUN/ISL/LVA/LIT/POL/ROM/CHE, while AMECO only lacks data on CHE/NOR/ISL, for which we relied on alternative sources: CHE(SECO), NOR(IMF), ISL(Central Bank of Iceland).

8. Leftcab is calculated by the share of seats in parliament held by leftist parties in the most recent government as a percentage of all seats held by the government. We calculated scores for missing years and countries using the datasets' methodology. Values for 2018 and 2019 were added for: AUT/BEL/CHE/DEN/ESP/FIN/FRA/GBR/GER/GRE/IRE/ITA/LUX/NET/NOR/PRT/SWE. Newly added countries: BLG/HRV/CYP/CZE/EST/HUN/ISL/LVA/LIT/MLT/POL/ROM/SVN/SVK.
9. Rows containing TLC cases were only deemed sufficient for the outcome if the majority of other cases fulfilled the criterion of sufficiency (X<Y with X>0.5), whereby a buffer of 0.10 in membership scores was used for the X<Y criterion when X>0.5.

LITERATURE

Abbas SA, Akitoby B, Andritzky J, et al. (2013) *Dealing with High Debt in an Era of Low Growth*. Staff Discussion Notes No. 2013/007, International Monetary Fund.

Agnello L and Sousa RM (2014) How Does Fiscal Consolidation Impact on Income Inequality? *Review of Income and Wealth* 60(4): 702–726.

Alesina A and Ardagna S (2010) Large Changes in Fiscal Policy. *Tax Policy and the Economy* 24(1): 35–68.

Alesina A and Ardagna S (2013) The Design of Fiscal Adjustments. *Tax Policy and the Economy* 27(1): 19–68.

Alesina A and Perotti R (1996a) *Fiscal Adjustments in OECD Countries: Composition and Macroeconomics Effects*. National Bureau of Economic Research Paper No. 5730.

Alesina A and Perotti R (1996b) Fiscal Discipline and the Budget Process. *American Economic Review* 86(2): 401–407.

Alesina A and Perotti R (1996c) Reducing Budget Deficits. *Swedish Economic Policy Review* 3: 113–134.

Alesina A, Perotti R and Tavares J (1998) The Political Economy of Fiscal Adjustments. *Brookings Papers on Economic Activity* 29(1): 197–266.

Algieri B (2013) An Empirical Analysis of the Nexus Between External Balance and Government Budget Balance. *Economic Systems* 37(2): 233–253.

Ardanaz M, Cavallo E, Izquierdo A, et al. (2021) Growth-Friendly Fiscal Rules? Safeguarding Public Investment from Budget Cuts through Fiscal Rule Design. *Journal of International Money and Finance* 111: 102319.

Armingeon K, Guthmann K and Weisstanner D (2016) Choosing the Path of Austerity. *West European Politics* 39(4): 628–647.

Asatryan Z, Castellón C and Stratmann T (2018) Balanced Budget Rules and Fiscal Outcomes. *Journal of Public Economics* 167: 105–119.

Badinger H and Reuter WH (2017) The Case for Fiscal Rules. *Economic Modelling* 60: 334–343.

Ball L, Furceri D, Leigh D, et al. (2013) *The Distributional Effects of Fiscal Consolidation*. IMF Working Paper No. 13/151.

Barro RJ (1974) Are Government Bonds Net Wealth? *Journal of Political Economy* 82(6): 1095–1117.

Baumgartner M and Thiem A (2020) Often Trusted but Never (Properly) Tested. *Sociological Methods and Research* 49(2): 279–311.

Bell T (2018) The End of Austerity? https://www.resolutionfoundation.org/comment/the-end-of-austerity-not-so-much/ (accessed 26 August 2022).

Bergman UM, Hutchison MM and Jensen SEH (2016) Promoting Sustainable Public Finances in the European Union. *European Journal of Political Economy* 44: 1–19.

Berg-Schlosser D and De Meur G (2009) Comparative Research Desgin Case and Variable Selection. In: Rihoux B and Ragin C (eds) *Configurational Comparative Methods*. Los Angeles: Sage, pp. 19–32.

Best T, Bush O, Eyraud L, et al. (2019) Reducing Debt Short of Default. In: Abbas SA, Pienkowski MB, and Rogoff K (eds) *Sovereign Debt*. Oxford: Oxford University Press, pp. 225–274.

Blanchard O and Leigh D (2013) Fiscal Consolidation. *VoxEU.org*. https://voxeu.org/article/fiscal-consolidation-what-speed (accessed 3 June 2022).

Blyth M (2013) *Austerity: The History of a Dangerous Idea*. Oxford: Oxford University Press.

Brady D, Huber E and Stephens JD (2020) *Comparative Welfare State Dataset, 2020*. https://www.lisdatacenter.org/wp-content/uploads/CWS-data-2020.xlsx (accessed 3 June 2022).

Bremer B (2018) The Missing Left? *Party Politics* 24(1): 23–38.

Caselli F and Reynaud J (2020) Do Fiscal Rules Cause Better Fiscal Balances? *European Journal of Political Economy* 63: 101873.

Ciminelli G, Ernst E, Merola R, et al. (2019) The Composition Effects of Tax-Based Consolidation on Income Inequality. *European Journal of Political Economy* 57: 107–124.

Cowen T and Sutter D (1998) Why Only Nixon Could Go to China. *Public Choice* 97(4): 605–615.

Darrat AF (1988) Have Large Budget Deficits Caused Rising Trade Deficits? *Southern Economic Journal* 54(4): 879–887. DOI: 10.2307/1059523.

Davoodi HR, Elger P, Fotiou A, et al. (2022) *Fiscal Rules at a Glance: An Update 1985–2021*. IMF.

de la Porte C and Heins E (2016) A New Era of European Integration? In: de la Porte C and Heins E (eds) *The Sovereign Debt Crisis, the EU and Welfare State Reform*. London: Palgrave Macmillan, pp. 15–41.

Debrun X and Kinda T (2017) Strengthening Post-Crisis Fiscal Credibility. *Fiscal Studies* 38(4): 667–700.

Debrun X and Kumar M (2007) *Fiscal Rules, Fiscal Councils and All That*. SSRN. http://www.ssrn.com/abstract=2004371 (accessed 1 June 2022).

Devries P, Guajardo J and Pescatori A (2011) *A New Action-based Dataset of Fiscal Consolidation*. IMF Working Paper No. 11/128.

Dollar D, Kleineberg T and Kraay A (2013) *Growth Still Is Good for the Poor*. Washington, DC: World Bank.

Durlauf SN, Johnson PA and Temple JRW (2005) Growth Econometrics. In: Phillipe A and Durlauf SN (eds) *Handbook of Economic Growth*. Amsterdam: Elsevier, pp. 555–677.

Emmenegger P, Kvist J and Skaaning S-E (2013) Making the Most of Configurational Comparative Analysis. *Political Research Quarterly* 66(1): 185–190.

European Commission (2007) *European Economy: Public Finances in EMU*. https://ec.europa.eu/economy_finance/publications/pages/publication338_en.pdf (accessed 11 April 2023).

European Commission (2015a) *Making the Best Use of the Flexibility within the Existing Rules of Stability and Growth Pact*. https://ec.europa.eu/economy_finance/economic

_governance/sgp/pdf/2015-01-13_communication_sgp_flexibility_guidelines_en.pdf.
European Commission (2015b) *Quarterly Report on the Euro Area*, Vol. 14(3). https://op.europa.eu/de/publication-detail/-/publication/cf7d5eb4-9e8f-11e5-8781-01aa75ed71a1/language-en (accessed 7 April 2022).
European Commission (2022a) *AMECO Database*. https://ec.europa.eu/info/business-economy-euro/indicators-statistics/economic-databases/macro-economic-database-ameco/ameco-database_en (accessed 6 April 2022).
European Commission (2022b) *The Corrective Arm*. https://ec.europa.eu/info/business-economy-euro/economic-and-fiscal-policy-coordination/eu-economic-governance-monitoring-prevention-correction/stability-and-growth-pact/corrective-arm-excessive-deficit-procedure/legal-basis-and-related-stages_en (accessed 1 June 2022).
European Commission (2022c) *The Preventive Arm*. https://ec.europa.eu/info/business-economy-euro/economic-and-fiscal-policy-coordination/eu-economic-governance-monitoring-prevention-correction/stability-and-growth-pact/preventive-arm/legal-basis-and-related-stages_en (accessed 1 June 2022).
Fainshmidt S, Witt MA, Aguilera RV et al. (2020) The contributions of qualitative comparative analysis (QCA) to international business research. *Journal of International Business Studies* 51(4): 455–466.
Feldstein M and Horioka C (1980) Domestic Saving and International Capital Flows. *The Economic Journal* 90(358): 314–329.
Furcerci D, Tovar Jalles J and Loungani P (2015) Fiscal Consolidation and Inequality in Advanced Economices. In: Clements BJ, Mooij RA de, Gupta S, et al. (eds) *Inequality and Fiscal Policy*. IMF, pp. 141–158.
Goodin RE, Headey B, Muffels R, et al. (1999) *The Real Worlds of Welfare Capitalism*. Cambridge: Cambridge University Press.
Gootjes B, de Haan J and Jong-A-Pin R (2021) Do Fiscal Rules Constrain Political Budget Cycles? *Public Choice* 188(1): 1–30.
Grembi V, Nannicini T and Troiano U (2016) Do Fiscal Rules Matter? *American Economic Journal: Applied Economics* 8(3): 1–30.
Guichard S, Kennedy M, Wurzel E, et al. (2007) *What Promotes Fiscal Consolidation*. OECD Working Papers No. 553.
Hagemann RP (2012) *Fiscal Consolidation: Part 6. What Are the Best Policy Instruments for Fiscal Consolidation?* OECD Working Papers No. 937.
Heinemann F, Moessinger M-D and Yeter M (2018) Do Fiscal Rules Constrain Fiscal Policy? *European Journal of Political Economy* 51: 69–92.
Hibbs DA (1977) Political Parties and Macroeconomic Policy. *American Political Science Review* 71(4): 1467–1487.
Höpner M (2014) Europe Would be Better Off Without the Euro. *Labor History* 55(5): 661–666.
IMF (2022) *Fiscal Monitor*. https://data.imf.org/?sk=4be0c9cb-272a-4667-8892-34b582b21ba6&sId=1390030341854 (accessed 4 April 2022).
Inman P (2019) Has the Age of Austerity Really Come to an End? *The Guardian*. https://www.theguardian.com/business/2019/sep/05/has-the-age-of-austerity-really-come-to-an-end-sajid-javid (accessed 26 August 2022).
Irving Z (2021) The Legacy of Austerity. *Social Policy and Society* 20(1): 97–110.
Iversen T and Wren A (1998) Equality, Employment, and Budgetary Restraint. *World Politics* 50(4): 507–546.

Jones CI (2016) The Facts of Economic Growth. In: Taylor JB and Uhlig H (eds) *Handbook of Macroeconomics*. Amsterdam: Elsevier, pp. 3–69.

Kitschelt H (2001) Partisan Competition and Welfare State Retrenchment. In: Pierson P (ed.) *The New Politics of the Welfare State*. Oxford: Oxford University Press, pp. 265–302.

Kraft J (2017) Social Democratic Austerity. *Journal of European Public Policy* 24(10): 1430–1449. DOI: 10.1080/13501763.2016.1231708.

Legewie N (2013) An Introduction to Applied Data Analysis with Qualitative Comparative Analysis. *Forum: Qualitative Social Research* 14(3): art. 15.

Maggetti M and Levi-Faur D (2013) Dealing with Errors in QCA. *Political Research Quarterly* 66: 198–204.

McManus R, Ozkan FG and Trzeciakiewicz D (2021) Fiscal Consolidations and Distributional Effects. *Oxford Economic Papers* 73(1): 317–349.

Mello PA (2022) *Qualitative Comparative Analysis*. Georgetown: Georgetown University Press.

Molnar M (2012) Fiscal Consolidation. *OECD Journal: Economic Studies* 2012(1): 123–149.

Mulas-Granados C (2006) *Economics, Politics and Budgets*. Basingstoke: Palgrave Macmillan.

Okun AM (2015) *Equality and Efficiency: The Big Tradeoff*. Washington, DC: Brookings Institution Press.

Paulus A, Figari F and Sutherland H (2017) The Design of Fiscal Consolidation Measures in the European Union. *Oxford Economic Papers* 69(3): 632–654.

Perotti R (2011) *The "Austerity Myth"*. National Bureau of Economic Research Paper No. 17571.

Pierson P (2001) *The New Politics Of The Welfare State*. Oxford: Oxford University Press.

Potrafke N (2017) Partisan Politics. *Journal of Comparative Economics* 45(4): 712–750.

Raess D (2021) Globalization and Austerity. *Political Studies*: 00323217211015811.

Ragin CC (2008) *Redesigning Social Inquiry*. Chicago: University of Chicago Press.

Ragin CC and Davey S (2016) *Fuzzy-Set/Qualitative Comparative Analysis 3.0*. Irvine, CA. https://www.socsci.uci.edu/~cragin/fsQCA/software.shtml.

Rault C and Afonso A (2009) Bootstrap Panel Granger-Causality Between Government Budget and External Deficits for the EU. *Economic Bulletin* 29(2): 1027–1034.

Reinhart CM, Reinhart VR and Rogoff KS (2012) Public Debt Overhangs. *Journal of Economic Perspectives* 26(3): 69–86.

Reinprecht C, Seeleib-Kaiser M and Sowula J (2018) Mythen der vergleichenden Sozialpolitikforschung? *Sozialer Fortschritt* 67(8–9): 783–805.

Rihoux B and Ragin C (2009) *Configurational Comparative Methods*. Los Angeles: Sage.

Romer CD and Romer DH (2010) The Macroeconomic Effects of Tax Changes: Estimates Based on a New Measure of Fiscal Shocks. *American Economic Review* 100(3): 763–801.

Schmidt MG (2022) Parties. In: Bland D, Morgan KJ, Obinger H, et al. (eds) *The Oxford Handbook of the Welfare State*. Oxford: Oxford University Press, pp. 298–312.

Schneider CQ and Wagemann C (2012) *Set-Theoretic Methods for the Social Sciences*. Cambridge: Cambridge University Press.

Siničáková M, Sulikova V and Gavurova B (2017) Twin Deficits Threat in the European Union. *Ekonomie a Management* 20(1): 144–156.

Skaaning S-E (2011) Assessing the Robustness of Crisp-set and Fuzzy-set QCA Results. *Sociological Methods & Research* 40(2): 391–408.
Streeck W (2014) *Buying Time: The Delayed Crisis of Democratic Capitalism*. Brooklyn, NY: Verso.
Summers L (1988) Tax Policy and International Competitiveness. In: Frenkel JA (ed.) *International Aspects of Fiscal Policies*. Cambridge: University of Chicago Press, pp. 349–386.
Tavares J (2004) Does Right or Left Matter? *Journal of Public Economics* 88(12): 2447–2468.
Tsibouris G, Horton M, Flanagan M, et al. (2006) *Experience With Large Fiscal Adjustments*. No. 246, IMF Occasional Publication, 14 July.
von Hagen J and Strauch RR (2001) Fiscal Consolidations. *Public Choice* 109(3): 327–346.
Wagschal U and Jäkel T (2010) Öffentliche Finanzen im Stresstest. *dms* 3(2): 295–320.
Wagschal U and Wenzelburger G (2008) Roads to Success. *Journal of Public Policy* 28(3): 309–339.
World Bank (2022a) *External Balance on Goods and Services (% of GDP)*. https://data.worldbank.org/indicator/NE.RSB.GNFS.ZS.
World Bank (2022b) *GDP Per Capita Growth (Annual %)*. https://data.worldbank.org/indicator/NY.GDP.PCAP.KD.ZG.
World Bank (2022c) Population to employment ratio (15+). https://data.worldbank.org/indicator/SL.EMP.TOTL.SP.ZS.
Wyplosz C (2013) Fiscal Rules: Theoretical Issues and Historical Experiences. In: Alesina A and Giavazzi F (eds) *Fiscal Policy after the Financial Crisis*. Chicago: University of Chicago Press, pp. 495–525.
Xie Z and Chen S-W (2014) Untangling the Causal Relationship Between Government Budget and Current Account Deficits in OECD Countries. *International Review of Economics and Finance* 31: 95–104.

5. The evolution of welfare attitudes in Europe over the past four decades[1]
Gianna Maria Eick

INTRODUCTION

The recent crises have highlighted how crucial generous social policy measures are (Taylor-Gooby et al. 2017; Greve 2021). Thus, a new Social Question in Europe serves as the starting point for this chapter. It reproduces the dual challenges of economic disruption and social and institutional reconstruction across and within European countries.

This chapter focuses on the public opinion towards welfare states from a bird's-eye perspective over the past four decades to determine the legitimacy of current welfare arrangements. That is because, amongst others, analysing welfare attitudes over long periods can help to disentangle the views of the general population with those of the more powerful elites that frequently claim to speak for the general population (Schakel et al. 2020).

Notably, the field produced some conclusions about welfare attitudes in Europe. As points of departure for this chapter, the three most prominent rationales for explaining public support for the welfare state are used. First, according to self-interest reasoning, those who are most likely to profit from welfare state resources will also be those who support the welfare state and particular welfare policies (Dallinger 2010). This suggests that people's employment status and exposure to socioeconomic risks are indicators of their preference for government redistribution (Rehm 2009).

Second, ideology reasoning entails that political socialisation shapes welfare attitudes (Neundorf and Soroka 2018). Since ideological positions are not entirely endogenous, previous studies demonstrate that more inclusive attitudes are often related to more generous welfare attitudes. For example, political partisanship (Gingrich and Häusermann 2015), economic individualism (Blekesaune 2007), or deservingness (van Oorschot 2000).

Third, institutional reasoning serves as an indicator of public support for government redistribution (Rothstein 1998). Studies usually argue that institutional risks and crises are related to more generous welfare attitudes. For example, income inequality (Finseraas 2009) or economic decline (Dallinger 2010). Institutional reasonings suggest that the welfare regime theory explains public opinion towards welfare policies in light of institutional setups (such as the welfare state's structure), political dynamics (such as the influence of right-wing parties), and cultural history (such as religious diversity) (Esping-Andersen 1990). Another body of literature focuses on the interaction between institutions and public opinion regarding their accomplishments, notably the effects of policy feedback (Busemeyer et al. 2019).

While important conclusions already emanated from the field that differed in substance and emphasis, more comprehensive analyses still lag. This chapter uses the wealth of existing knowledge on welfare attitudes to shed light on the larger developments over the past four decades. The few studies that examine welfare attitudes across time demonstrate increasing preferences for government redistribution (Burgoon et al. 2012; Jæger 2013). However, these studies mainly deal with general government redistribution and more detailed studies that examine welfare policies and socioeconomic divides across time are still lacking. This chapter contributes to this debate by taking a bird's-eye perspective on the evolution of welfare attitudes in Europe across time, socioeconomic groups, and welfare policies. Hereby, this chapter will identify a profile of the demands for change and reforms.

A comparative viewpoint is especially useful for addressing issues related to the formation and modification of attitudes. This is because it helps us better understand the factors that influence attitudes. Unfortunately, a scarcity of data has hampered the research field for many decades. With the formation and expansion of large survey programmes that include both time-series and comparative data, the field has since advanced immensely. Now it is possible to analyse public attitudes towards European welfare states during the past four decades. For this chapter, the following three representative survey programmes will be included:

- European Social Survey (ESS) 2002–2018
- International Social Survey Programme (ISSP) 1985–2015
- European Value Survey (EVS) 1981–2017.

Starting with the year 1981 and ending with 2018, these surveys include Europe's confrontation with several crises, such as the financial crisis, the refugee crisis and Brexit. The data sets end before the COVID and Ukraine crises, but similar or even more pronounced trends can be expected in the future. Overall year-means, country-year-means, region-year-means and group-year-means are calculated. To ensure the quality of the results, design weights were applied and "don't know" answers were treated as missing values. The results from the EVS analysis are not shown in this chapter, but they indicate that the findings are overall robust.

WELFARE ATTITUDES ACROSS COUNTRIES

The analysis starts with the most prominent survey item that is covered by the current data: attitudes on general government redistribution in Europe. This section examines ESS data that was gathered every two years between 2002 and 2018. Respondents evaluate the following statement:

The government should take measures to reduce differences in income levels.

Figure 5.1 demonstrates that the public in Europe overall supports the government's efforts to decrease income disparities. Over the past 20 years, support for income redistribution has generally increased. The variation averages 0.15 on a 1–5 scale during the past 20 years. This is not a dramatic increase, but public attitudes tend to be relatively steady over time, and European welfare states have a long history of receiving solid levels of support (Sainsbury 2001). An intriguing finding from Figure 5.1 is that support for income redistribution increased more during the 2007–2008 financial crisis. Although the increase appears to be relatively small (from 3.8 to 3.9 on the scale), it is the largest in the observed period.

The results are consistent with research showing that people's perceptions of economic hardship increased during the financial crisis of 2007–2008 (Taylor-Gooby et al. 2017). This is because the public demand for government redistribution (across different policy areas) increased in bad times when the economic conditions are poor or when unemployment levels are high and vice versa (Blekesaune 2007; Dallinger 2010). The lack of control many individuals experienced throughout the crises may be the cause of the increased support for income redistribution. Possibly, the need for government assistance is seen as less of an individual responsibility in crisis times. It's important to note that similar trends can be observed using the same item in other survey programmes, such as the ISSP (1985–2015) and EVS (1981–2017).

Additionally, Figure 5.1 breaks down average welfare attitude trends across five regions of Europe: North, East, South, West, and Anglo. These findings back up the notion that contextual factors influence public attitudes towards redistribution (Dallinger 2010). Overall, the public supports reducing income differences less where redistribution is already higher/more salient, and vice versa. However, the low demand for redistribution in the Anglo countries is in line with the welfare regime theory, which postulates that the demand for redistribution is lowest in such a low-spending Liberal regime (Finseraas 2009).

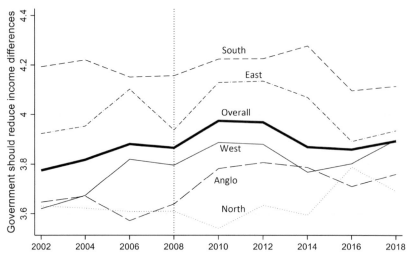

Notes: "North" = Denmark, Finland, Iceland, Norway and Sweden; "East" = Bulgaria, Croatia, Czech Republic, Estonia, Hungary, Latvia, Lithuania, Poland, Ukraine, Romania, Russia, Slovakia and Slovenia; "South" = Cyprus, Italy, Malta, Spain, Portugal and Greece; "West" = Austria, Belgium, France, Germany, Luxembourg, the Netherlands and Switzerland; and "Anglo" = Ireland and the United Kingdom.
Data: European Social Survey, 1 = disagree strongly to 5 = agree strongly, 418,713 individuals, 33 countries, dotted line indicates the financial crisis in 2008.

Figure 5.1 *"Government should reduce differences in income levels" (mean) in European regions, 2002–2018*

Additional analyses demonstrate a strong relationship (R-squared=0.232) between the support for government redistribution and income inequality, measured as the Gini index of equivalised disposable income (OECD Database 2020). Even such simple snapshots suggest that public demand for redistribution is lower at lower levels of income inequality, and higher at higher levels of income inequality (see also Jæger 2013).

Further, the relationship between the attitude "Government should reduce differences in income levels" in 2002 and the change in this attitude between 2002 and 2019 is analysed. This method helps in spotting β-convergence, which occurs when country cases show low values on an indicator initially (in this chapter, mean attitude), but show above-average increases in this indicator over time (Barro and Sala-i-Martin 1992). Indeed, the findings show a strong negative and statistically significant association between previous levels of attitudes towards income differences and later changes (R-squared=0.122), indicating that support for redistribution has increased, especially in countries where it had been particularly low initially.

Next, the prospective convergence of attitudes towards income reduction is investigated, i.e. the yearly mean absolute deviation of a country's attitudes from the cross-country average. This is related to the concept of σ(sigma)-convergence, i.e. the relative convergence of observation units to a common mean (Cornelisse and Goudswaard 2002). And indeed, the results reinforce a clear trend of convergence in attitudes across Europe. This might indicate a certain degree of harmonisation of welfare attitudes across European countries. Such a process, particularly in times of crisis, has the potential to strengthen welfare legitimacy across Europe.

WELFARE ATTITUDES ACROSS SOCIOECONOMIC GROUPS

Next, this chapter examines general attitudes towards income redistribution in Europe across socioeconomic groups using the ESS data. Specifically, the individual data for different groups in this section were aggregated in each ESS wave, also called quasi-panel data (Jæger 2013). The group-level variables include a dummy item for each socioeconomic group to enable a meaningful convergence analysis over time. Using this approach, one can increase the variation in social risk exposure while taking the regular sample sizes of each ESS country and wave into account (around 1000 to 2000 respondents). The results represent all groups in each country and period.

First, Figure 5.2 depicts socioeconomic divisions between those with higher and lower income and between those with and without tertiary education. According to the findings for both groups, those who have less income and those without tertiary education support income redistribution more than their counterparts, which is consistent with the literature (Rehm 2009). These groups converge rather than diverge over time, particularly those with different education levels. These patterns demonstrate how the literature frequently produces premature correlations between labour market vulnerability and income/education. When investigating this relationship, it is important to keep in mind that more insecure employment sectors, including the service industry, have grown over the past several decades in countries that are becoming more post-industrial. As a result, higher income and education groups that were previously in more secure employment positions are now more vulnerable in the labour market (Häusermann et al. 2015), which may encourage these groups to support the welfare state more strongly. The findings point to a rising likelihood of pro-welfare coalitions involving those with higher and lower levels of income and education. This could be a result of two interrelated social risks that these groups have faced in the workforce that are related to their preferences for more generous welfare states. These are intriguing patterns that go across economic and educational divides and may help us better understand polarisation, solidarities, and the politics of the welfare state.

Second, Figure 5.2 demonstrates that women favour redistribution more than men, despite the fact that these cleavages have remained constant over

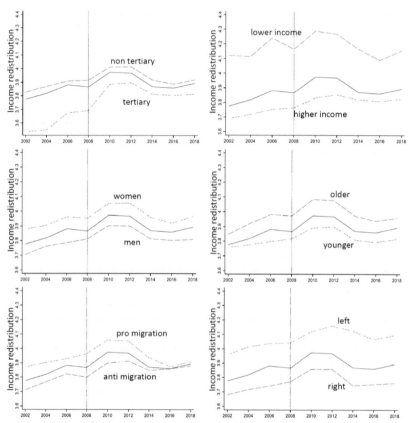

Notes: Continuous line shows the overall mean. Measuring education (tertiary versus non-tertiary educated), income (highest three income deciles versus lowest six income deciles), age (over 50 versus under 50), gender (men versus women), allow many/few migrants of different race/ethnic group from the majority (allow versus do not allow) and left–right identification (highest five versus lowest six). Country sample, see Figure 5.1.
Data: European Social Survey, 1 = agree strongly to 5 = disagree strongly, 418,713 individuals, 33 countries, dotted line indicates the financial crisis in 2008.

Figure 5.2   *Convergence and divergence of "Government should reduce differences in income levels" (mean) across socioeconomic groups (2002–2018)*

the years. Given the large increase in female labour force participation, this finding is intriguing. It could imply that women still rely more on welfare state programmes than men or that they generally have a more solidaristic approach to redistribution. The results show a greater disparity between younger and older groups; While younger groups' support for redistribution is declining, older groups are favouring it more and more. This may be because older populations rely on pension plans. In fact, current retirees are more secure and well paid than any past retirees and likely also compared to future retirees. On the contrary, the ageing populations in most European countries result in a greater tax burden for the younger generations.

Third, Figure 5.2 analyses the evolution of two ideological groups, namely groups that support and oppose migration as well as groups that lean to the left and right ideologically. The results support the long-held claim in the literature that welfare attitudes have ideological underpinnings, and they also highlight the significance of these divisions throughout Europe. It is commonly argued that pro-migration groups also belong to higher socioeconomic status groups (Burgoon et al. 2012), which are less supportive of the welfare state though the results from Figure 5.2 show that the opposite is true. Regardless, here the cleavages are closing, which is an interesting observation. The results for left-versus right-oriented groups align with the current literature that assumes that left-oriented individuals support the welfare state more (Kriesi et al. 2008). The left–right gap is increasing, which is not surprising, considering that European societies have become increasingly polarised (Greve 2021). However, these results are puzzling, considering that lower socioeconomic status groups tend to vote for right-wing parties (Gingrich and Häusermann 2015). One can only speculate at this point that the evolution of welfare attitudes across ideological groups can be explained by welfare state recalibration and the restructuration of partisan politics.

WELFARE ATTITUDES ACROSS POLICIES

Last but not least, this chapter shifts from general developments in public views towards income redistribution to attitudes across different welfare policies. Even though there is fewer time-series data on policy-specific welfare attitudes, this topic is crucial because the "government responsibility for reducing income differences" differs from other welfare state objectives, such as insurance, compensation or social investment. Therefore, it can be argued that redistribution support is a problematic measure that requires clarification as to which welfare policies should be redistributed and to whom.

The final analysis focuses on policy-specific welfare attitudes measurements. In particular, the ISSP includes repeated measures between 1985 and 2015: "Listed below are various areas of government spending. Please show whether you would like to see more or less government spending in each area. Remember that if you say 'much more', it might require a tax increase to pay for it. (1) Health, (2) The police and law enforcement, (3) Education, (4) The military and defence, (5) Old-age pensions, (6) Unemployment benefits, (7) Culture and the arts."

The average attitude patterns across Europe are shown in Figure 5.3. The regional differences are similar to the findings from the previous section. The results show overall convergence among welfare policies once more, although with a few caveats: the trends reinforce the well-known conclusion that some policies, such as education, receive more support than others, such as unemployment assistance (Busemeyer et al. 2018). Furthermore, compared to other government bodies (i.e. culture, military, police and environment) that are not a part of the welfare state, the public is more in favour of increased government expenditure on old-age, health and education policies. The levels of support have been reasonably stable and robust even or because of the stresses of the global financial crisis.

The ISSP also includes items on the beneficiaries of such policies. Here the patterns are similar; the most deserving groups are sick people and students.

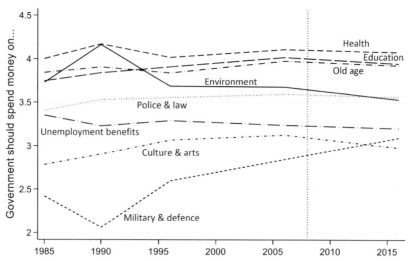

Notes: Countries include Belgium, Croatia, Czech Republic, Denmark, Finland, France, Georgia, Germany, Hungary, Iceland, Ireland, Italy, Latvia, Lithuania, Norway, Poland, Russia, Slovakia, Slovenia, Spain, Sweden, Switzerland and United Kingdom.
Data: International Social Survey Programme, 1 = Spend much less to 5 = Spend much more, 82,870 individuals, 23 countries, dotted line indicates the financial crisis in 2008.

Figure 5.3   *Different government areas where spending should be increased/decreased (mean) in Europe, 1985–2015*

This further demonstrates that strengthening specific policies is quite popular across Europe. And while there is still room for more research into whether there may be convergence across many different social policy fields, it is telling that there are some familiar patterns in the levels of support across different welfare beneficiaries.

Related to this, researchers find clear differences in support for welfare policies, depending on whether they are provided universally or selectively (Rothstein 1998). Universal encompassing programmes such as pensions and healthcare receive strong support, while more targeted or selective policies such as unemployment benefits and social assistance are usually supported less (Svallfors 2012). Furthermore, the literature argues that social investment policies (such as education or childcare) gain popularity over traditional compensation policies (such as unemployment benefits or social assistance). This is because expanding social investments may have the potential to diminish social inequalities as well as to promote growth in service-based knowledge economies (Busemeyer et al. 2018).

The question remains why the levels of support for unemployment benefits are relatively low and decreasing over time. Possibly, the deservingness theory can help here (van Oorschot 2000). The unemployed are usually perceived as one of the least deserving social groups of welfare support by the public. This is because unemployment is often considered to be the individual's fault and not a systematic failure. Consequently, granting support to unemployed people is based on their observable efforts to re-enter the labour market. Furthermore, unlike other welfare beneficiary groups, such as pensioners, the unemployed face stronger conditionality for welfare support, because even though some unemployed have already contributed a lot to the system, they are seen as less deserving because people make judgements about their "reciprocity", which is typically higher for other groups, such as pensioners. To put it differently, the public might think that they have not earned the benefits they are paid.

The declining support towards unemployment benefits seems worrying, also because similar patterns can be found using another item from the ISSP on support for the government's role in ensuring the standard of living of unemployed people and how it changes over time. However, the unemployed may receive higher levels of public support when the questions are related to social investment, namely active labour market policies (ALMPs). In line with this, it is argued that there is a shift in the preferred balance between social rights and social obligations when it comes to employment policies (Roosma and Jeene 2017). This means stricter conditions imposed on the unemployed, such as actively looking for work, can increase support for these policies. Consequently, such activation policies have been marketed as trampoline policies rather than as safety nets. Interestingly, the ISSP data on ALMPs from 1985 to 2015 demonstrates that ALMPs are indeed overall more popular than unemployment benefits. Overall, the cross-time results on employment policies are quite telling since other research suggests that in the short term (and during a crisis), there is particular demand for social compensation, not investment. However, looking at the big picture, the results do not show evidence of this.

CONCLUSION AND POTENTIAL FOR FUTURE RESEARCH

Public attitudes on welfare matter for the future of individuals, for national welfare states and for the European social integration. Welfare support is crucial to ensuring economic and social stability, particularly in times of crisis when incomes are dropping, inequality and poverty are rising, and working conditions are becoming more precarious (Taylor-Gooby et al. 2017). Although there is still widespread support for the welfare state in Europe, welfare attitudes are becoming more conditional towards specific groups, like migrants (Eick and Larsen 2022).

This chapter empirically investigates the evolution of public welfare attitudes over the past four decades from a bird's-eye perspective. To do that, the chapter reviewed existing quantitative surveys on welfare attitudes. First, the chapter finds that the public shows overall high and relatively stable levels of support for more government redistribution. During the post-crisis years after 2007/2008 (the global financial crisis) some (upward and downward) convergence trends across countries and time in attitudes were reinforced. The COVID-19 crisis may serve as a foundation for establishing stronger policy stances on the long-standing divisions over the future of European welfare states. Crises, in general, may offer a chance to develop welfare states even more, especially when coupled with generous government responses (unlike austerity measures that likely reinforce negative attitudes towards those in need).

Second, social investment policies such as education enjoy increasing levels of support, while the opposite trends can be observed for compensation policies, such as unemployment benefits. This may be because unemployment is increasingly perceived as a personal decision and the support for unemployment benefits thus relies on this group to demonstrate the willingness to re-enter the labour market (van Oorschot 2000). So, even if welfare solidarity is still generally strong, it is also subject to certain conditions, such as a rising understanding that those who are vulnerable are expected to do more to help themselves out of a difficult situation. The chapter also discovers considerable support for measures that stimulate the labour market and are less punishing, such as investments in training and lifelong learning. Future policy measures should be well justified to the public by policymakers if they are to improve redistribution across various policies.

Third, important socioeconomic cleavages are declining over time too, and there seems to be potential for strengthening welfare alliances across Europe. The upward convergence between the higher and lower educated groups is most intriguing because the higher educated are traditionally regarded as labour market insiders with distinctly different preferences. Faced with increasing inequality and labour market precariousness, high-skilled insiders might start to feel more like outsiders in demanding protection from the welfare state (Häusermann et al. 2015), which could explain their increasing welfare solidarity. However, the challenge for policymakers will be to address both the needs of the groups that traditionally received welfare provisions and of the groups that need welfare provisions because of the development of new social risks and who are particularly vocal and heterogeneous.

Importantly, the trajectory of European economic and social policy has demonstrated that social policy convergence does not happen automatically but requires decisive political action. The results hint at public preferences for increasing welfare spending in general and recalibrating and/or reforming the European welfare state from compensation to social investment models. In fact, against the fear of overall welfare state retrenchment, many countries have already expanded social investment policies as they serve – in comparison to compensation policies – long-term social equality strategies (Eick et al. 2021). Still, reorienting the welfare state towards social investment constitutes a complex and multidimensional challenge of policy recalibration and raises daunting political problems. The temporal mismatch between social investment reforms and their returns requires a degree of political patience on the side of current voters and politicians, which is not always disposable in contemporary democracies (Ferrera 2017).

Finally, this study offered a view into important research gaps in a field with plenty of potential for future research that might benefit the process of future welfare policymaking. First, there is a need for more cross-time studies to analyse the reasons for the convergence/divergence of attitudes on the macro and cross-national level. While the more recent rounds of the large survey programmes include many countries that are sufficiently institutionally specific, such data is missing for earlier periods (the 1980s, 1990s), and not all countries are included in all waves. In particular, longitudinal panel data across countries is largely missing in the field. A comparative panel would establish the time order of events, making it possible for the analyst to establish causal effects.

Second, the field could benefit from more (cross-time) studies on policy trade-offs and qualitative studies. This is because attitudes are often diffuse, multifaceted, multidimensional or downright contradictory (Roosma et al. 2013). However, more such projects are only just emerging in this field, such as "Investigating in Education" (INVEDUC), "Welfare State Futures: Our Children's Europe" (WelfSOC), "welfarepriorities", or "The Future of European Social Citizenship" (EUSOCIALCIT).

Still, the patterns presented in this chapter suggest that the available data provided by international survey programmes is a valuable data source for exploring the evolution of welfare attitudes in Europe. To sum up, this chapter finds an overall emerging welfare solidarity across and within European countries and demonstrates that such preferences increase in times of rising social risks and crises.

NOTE

1. This chapter is available Open Access on ElgarOnline.com. This Open Access publication was supported by the publication fund of the University of Konstanz.

REFERENCES

Barro, Robert J. and Sala-i-Martin, Xavier. 1992. "Convergence." *Journal of Political Economy* 100(2): 223–251.
Blekesaune, Morten. 2007. "Economic Conditions and Public Attitudes to Welfare Policies." *European Sociological Review* 23(3): 393–403.
Burgoon, Brian, Koster, Ferry and Van Egmond, Marcel. 2012. "Support for Redistribution and the Paradox of Immigration." *Journal of European Social Policy* 22(3): 288–304.
Busemeyer, Marius R., Abrassart, Aurélien and Nezi, Roula. 2019. "Beyond Positive and Negative: New Perspectives on Feedback Effects in Public Opinion on the Welfare State." *British Journal of Political Science* 51: 137–162.
Busemeyer, Marius R., Garritzmann, Julian, Neimanns, Erik and Nezi, Roula. 2018. "Investing in Education in Europe: Evidence from a New Survey of Public Opinion." *Journal of European Social Policy* 28(1): 34–54.
Cornelisse, Peter A. and Goudswaard, Kees P. 2002. "On the Convergence of Social Protection Systems in the European Union." *International Social Security Review* 55(3): 3–17.
Dallinger, Ursula. 2010. "Public Support for Redistribution: What Explains Cross-National Differences?" *Journal of European Social Policy* 20(4): 333–349.
Eick, Gianna M., Burgoon, Brian and Busemeyer, Marius R. 2021. "Measuring Social Citizenship in Social Policy Outputs, Resources and Outcomes across EU Member States from 1985 to the Present." *EUSocialCit*, Working Paper.
Eick, Gianna M. and Larsen, Christian A. 2022. "Welfare Chauvinism across Benefits and Services." *Journal of European Social Policy* 32(1): 19–32.
Esping-Andersen, Gosta. *The Three Worlds of Welfare Capitalism*. Princeton, NJ: Princeton University Press, 1990.
Ferrera, Maurizio. 2017. "Impatient Politics and Social Investment: The EU as 'Policy Facilitator'." *Journal of European Public Policy* 24(8): 1233–1251.
Finseraas, Henning. 2009. "Income Inequality and Demand for Redistribution: A Multilevel Analysis of European Public Opinion." *Scandinavian Political Studies* 32(1): 94–119.

Gingrich, Jane and Häusermann, Silja. 2015. "The Decline of the Working-class Vote, the Reconfiguration of the Welfare Support Coalition and Consequences for the Welfare State." *Journal of European Social Policy* 25(1): 50–75.

Greve, Bent. *Handbook on Austerity, Populism and the Welfare State*. Cheltenham, UK and Northampton, MA, USA: Edward Elgar Publishing, 2021.

Häusermann, Silja, Kurer, Thomas and Schwander, Hanna. 2015. "High-Skilled Outsiders? Labor Market Vulnerability, Education and Welfare State Preferences." *Socio-Economic Review* 13(2): 235–258.

Jæger, Mads. 2013. "The Effect of Macroeconomic and Social Conditions on the Demand for Redistribution: A Pseudo Panel Approach." *Journal of European Social Policy* 23(2): 149–163.

Kriesi, Hanspeter, Grande, Edgar, Lachat, Romain, Dolezal, Martin, Bornschier, Simon and Frey, Timotheos. *West European Politics in the Age of Globalization*. Cambridge: Cambridge University Press, 2008.

Neundorf, Anja and Soroka, Stuart. 2018. "The Origins of Redistributive Policy Preferences: Political Socialisation With and Without a Welfare State." *West European Politics* 41(2): 400–427.

OECD Database. 2020. "Income Distribution and Poverty Database." Retrieved 27 July 2021. https://stats.oecd.org/Index.aspx?DataSetCode=IDD.

Rehm, Philipp. 2009. "Risks and Redistribution: An Individual-level Analysis." *Comparative Political Studies* 42(7): 855–881.

Roosma, Femke and Jeene, Marjolein. 2017. "The Deservingness Logic Applied to Public Opinions Concerning Work Obligations for Benefit Claimants." In Wim van Oorschot, Femke Roosma, Bart Meuleman and Tim Reeskens (Eds.) *The Social Legitimacy of Targeted Welfare* (pp. 189–206). Cheltenham, UK and Northampton, MA, USA: Edward Elgar Publishing.

Roosma, Femke, Gelissen, John and van Oorschot, Wim. 2013. "The Multidimensionality of Welfare State Attitudes: A European Cross-National Study." *Social Indicators Research* 113(1): 235–255.

Rothstein, Bo. *Just Institutions Matter: The Moral and Political Logic of the Universal Welfare State*. Cambridge: Cambridge University Press, 1998.

Sainsbury, Diane. 2001. "Welfare State Challenges and Responses: Institutional and Ideological Resilience or Restructuring?" *Acta Sociologica* 44(3): 257–265.

Schakel, Wouter, Burgoon, Brian and Hakhverdian, Armen. 2020. "Real but Unequal Representation in Welfare State Reform." *Politics & Society* 48(1): 131–163.

Svallfors, Stefan. 2012. "Welfare States and Welfare Attitudes". In Stefan Svallfors (Ed.) *Contested Welfare States: Welfare Attitudes in Europe and Beyond* (pp. 1–24). Stanford: Stanford University Press.

Taylor-Gooby, Peter, Leruth, Benjamin and Chung, Heejung (Eds.). *After Austerity: Welfare State Transformation in Europe after the Great Recession*. Oxford: Oxford University Press, 2017.

van Oorschot, Wim. 2000. "Who Should Get What, and Why? On Deservingness Criteria and the Conditionality of Solidarity Among the Public." *Policy & Politics* 28(1): 33–48.

6. Climate change and its effect on welfare states
Ian Greener

INTRODUCTION

Climate change represents an existential threat to humanity, with the effects of rising temperatures having the potential to cause sea levels to rise, change existing climate patterns in ways that are extremely difficult to predict, and causing the displacement of millions (at best) of people. This chapter argues that we must consider climate change in relation both to our prevailing model of economic growth and its relation to the welfare state, in order to understand what action we must now take, as well as what the effects on the future welfare state might be. To consider this, it makes use of a revised version of Jessop's 'governance of welfare' model, considering how capitalism has developed since its original formulation in the early 2000s, and incorporating climate change to a far greater extent. It suggests that we must radically revisit the model of capitalism prevailing in the 2020s if we are to have a chance of both preventing climate disaster as well as protecting the poorest from the worst effects of our current model of economic growth.

First the chapter considers the relationship between climate change and the governance of welfare, updating Jessop's model to give a framework to analyse the current situation. It then examines the prospect of the current model for confronting climate change, before suggesting that a far more radical approach needs to be taken in order to confront the challenge ahead.

CLIMATE CHANGE AND THE GOVERNANCE OF WELFARE

The chapter's first claim is that, in order to consider the relationship between climate change and welfare states, we have to consider the inter-relationships between the two, as well as between both climate change and welfare, and the prevailing model of economic accumulation. Unless we can understand how these three are linked, we cannot understand the problems the world is having in either confronting climate change, or the difficulties that welfare states are experiencing in terms of either their legitimacy or their performance. To explore this topic, it first presents Jessop's 'governance of welfare' model, before updating it to consider how capitalism has changed in the last 20 years, and to place a greater emphasis on the role of climate change within it.

JESSOP'S 'GOVERNANCE OF WELFARE' FRAMEWORK

Jessop developed a framework outlining the key dimensions of the governance of welfare across a string of highly cited and influential publications spanning a decade (Jessop, 1992, 1994, 1999, 2002). Jessop's work is also often incorporated into Social Policy textbooks as a framework for considering how welfare systems have changed (Lister, 2010). As his work developed, it considered state governance in terms of four inter-related elements: the mode of economic growth; the role of the welfare state; the scale of governance; and the mode of governance. Jessop suggested that, from the 1970s onwards especially, the dominant mode of economic growth has shifted from Keynesian (demand-management, concerned with full employment) to Schumpeterian (supply-side management, concerned with inflation), with the state placing a far greater emphasis on creating the conditions for effective competition in a global economy and less concerned with intervening through fiscal policy to try and achieve full employment, as it had been in the decades following the Second World War. This outline is broadly in line with accounts of the 'paradigm' shift in economic policy occurring in the 1970s (Hall, 1990, 1993) as well as with the idea that states were now more concerned with positioning their economies to deal with increased global competition than had been necessary in the 1940s, 1950s and 1960s (Cerny, 1997). As such, this first dimension – of the prevailing model of economic growth or accumulation – has a great deal in common with accounts of the same period. However, Jessop's contribution is in linking it to his other three dimensions of governance.

Jessop's second dimension of governance is perhaps his least developed. Jessop suggests a shift from 'welfare', in which welfare rights and benefits were conferred as a citizenship right (fitting in broad terms the path suggested by Marshall (1950)), to 'workfare', which Jessop defines in terms of social policy becoming subordinate to economic policy. This marks a shift towards a more instrumental approach to welfare in which the primary purpose of social policy moves away from supporting the most vulnerable, to ensuring economic growth can continue. As such, the primary purpose of education becomes to train people for work (rather than to participate as citizens as well as work), and individuals might expect far more scrutiny should they not wish to participate in the labour market and draw benefits (although the extent of the lack of conditionality in the 'welfare' model is often under-estimated as a reading of the Beveridge Report (1942) makes clear). As such, economic growth and social policy become more closely entwined, but with the former more obviously driving the latter.

Jessop's next dimension of governance is its scale, which again links to the previous two dimensions. Jessop suggests there has been a shift in the dominant scale from 'national' to 'postnational', with a shift upwards (in terms of globalisation and global competition) as well as downwards (with a greater emphasis in regional- and city-level governance). This has resulted in the national state losing power both upwards and downwards in scale. This shift is linked to the fourth of Jessop's dimensions, that of the mode of governance, where he suggests a change from 'state' to 'regime', which reflects the need for the state to work with supra-national organisations (such as the European Union, NATO and G7) as well as regional- and city-level bodies in order to be effective. This puts in place a need for network-style governance, with power spread across the different bodies, rather than being located more obviously in the state.

A key part of Jessop's work is the idea of the 'fix' – that capitalism inevitably contains contradictions which dominant modes of governance attempt to paint over or conceal, but which will inevitably emerge and result in crises of one kind or another. This is grounded in the basic insight of Offe (1984) that on the one hand capitalism cannot live with the welfare state – for the latter is too expensive and diverts resources away from growth. However, capitalism also cannot live without the welfare state, as it requires a state-based organisation to educate its workers, and provide them with money to consume should they not be able to work. Within Jessop's Schumpeterian Workfare Postnational Regime, various possibilities of tensions and fractures exist – should the state try and put in place a highly educated workforce to compete at the global level ('flexicurity') then it risks over-spending on welfare and giving workers rights that will reduce profits because of the additional training and staffing costs involved. If it tries to compete at a lower cost ('flexploitation') it risks being forever undercut by other countries which can be even cheaper, leading to rising unemployment and governments losing power through lack of public support. These two responses are polarised, but most states have attempted mixtures of the two, with Scandinavian countries often comparatively emphasising towards the former, and the UK and USA the latter. Jessop presents the fullest account of his model in his 2002 book *The Future of the Capitalist State* (Jessop, 2002), of which the above aspires to be a short summary of an extraordinarily rich and far-reaching book.

It would be hard to argue that Jessop's 2002 book places climate change or the environment as its main focus. However, he does make some prescient comments that can be built upon in updating his framework. First, Jessop points to a basic problem in thinking about the economy – that natural resources should be available to be economically exploited simply by lying within the geographic confines of a particular country. Second, he points to the short time horizons prevalent in economic growth models that do not take the exploitation of nature into account. Both are crucial points in considering how climate change might be incorporated more fully into an updating of his framework.

The first dimension we need to reconsider is that of the dominant mode of economic governance. Jessop, as outlined above, suggested a transition from the demand-side macroeconomic management of Keynesianism, which was geared towards trying to achieve full employment as its main focus, to what he called Schumpeterianism, which was borne out of the crisis of Keynesianism in the 1970s, when fiscal policy appeared to break down in the face of oil price shocks, economic stagnation and rising inflation. Schumpeterianism put an emphasis on supply-side economics, being especially concerned with trying to reshape national economies to make them more competitive on the global scale. This meant the state had no business in attempting to achieve full employment, but instead should aim to create a economic environment in which such competitiveness could be achieved, especially by trying to ensure a low-inflation economy.

Jessop's account of economic governance change has strong parallels with others developed in the 1980s and 1990s but, from the perspective of the 2020s, it perhaps misunderstood the complex changes taking place. First, although Jessop provides a key role for the financial services industry, including its rapid growth and its global reach in his accounts, with hindsight he under-estimated the scale and character of the changes the massive 'financialisation' (Allen and Snyder, 2009) of the 1990s and 2000s led to. What we can now see is that the explosive growth of the financial services industry was largely due to the creation of new speculative financial instruments (such as derivatives), with finance becoming increasingly less oriented towards the 'real' economy, and more focused on the rather higher gains that could be achieved through more speculative enterprise instead. The deregulation of the financial industry in the 1990s, apparently forgetting the key lessons of the economic crash of the 1930s (Casey, 2011), created a massive speculative bubble that eventually led to the financial crisis of 2007/8. However, the implications of the growth of the financial services industry go far beyond even that.

The huge growth of speculative financial services, which often serve no purpose in the non-financial economy, and certainly no social purpose (Financial Services Authority, 2009), helped conceal the lack of the growth in the economy outside of finance, and led to governments (perhaps most clearly in the UK (Richards, 2010)), not regulating their unsustainable growth because of the taxation benefits it was bringing. This made the financial crisis, when it came, even more damaging as governments were left without a viable model with which to fund the growth in welfare services that they had helped fund.

However, the growth in speculative financial services also created the conditions for resistance to international attempts to address climate change. Regulatory capture means that it becomes harder to put in place rules that might disrupt the status quo, even after the events of 2007/8 (Financial Services Authority, 2009). One element of this is ideological, and the other ideational. The ideological element is the campaigning of financial institutions against regulatory attempts to curb their speculation, which formed part of an anti-government agenda in which markets were seen to have far greater wisdom than regulators – whether financial or environmental (Peterz and Schroedel, 2009). Market-based solutions were regarded as being inherently superior to government-based ones, with the debate around climate change being framed in terms of financial instruments such as carbon trades from which further profits could be generated (Klein, 2014) rather than being seen as representing a wider social and economic challenge. This attempt to depoliticise and marketise climate change ultimately failed, but systematically under-estimated the scale and significance of the challenge before us.

The ideational challenge of speculative financial services is that the profits they appeared to generate concealed the need for governments to rethink the ways their economies were failing to develop in other spheres, while at the same time generating an infrastructure of regulatory contempt and short-term pursuit of profit which are antithetical, as Jessop reminds of us, of the needs of the environment. Natural resources are generally non-replaceable, and the short timescales of speculative capitalism mean that the incentive to exploit them in the short term can be overwhelming, even where that exploitation leads to both it being unavailable for future generations, and to damage due to extraction and to any pollution that occurs as a result of its use – as in the case of gas and oil. The short-term time horizons in finance were summarised in the work Tett (2009) did in relation to the financial crisis and summarised in the acronym IWBH, YWBH (I won't be here, you won't be here) used by financial traders fully aware that their actions generated no real value, were exploiting loopholes or misunderstandings in the present to generate paper-profits only, but also that they were unlikely to have to bear the consequences. We often seem to have a similar approach to the environment – exploiting natural resources for our short-term needs that will not be available to those that have to follow us, while we also cause huge environmental damage through their extraction and use. The shortening of time horizons in finance makes it more legitimate to consume natural resources now with far less regard for the future.

Jessop's 'Schumpeterianism' does not quite capture the shift needed to understand the change in economic governance that has become more apparent over the last 20 years. Much of the competition between products and services that we see as consumers is actually traceable back to a small number of multinational corporations which dominate those markets (Galbraith, 1993; Greener, 2018). It is certainly true that new entrants into markets may face significant competitive pressures from existing corporations should they achieve any degree of success, with that often leading to an anti-competitive strategy from existing multinationals, or more simply them being bought out in areas such as the technology industry where there is still at least a little room for new entrants. What we are seeing is the domination of large-scale corporations, but in an environment where economic growth for most major economies has been sluggish at best. This means that the balance of profitability between financial and non-financial areas of the economy has swung heavily in favour of the former (Piketty, 2017) even though many of the gains seen in finance are speculative and subject to massive corrections that might retrospectively wipe out the majority of the gains seen there (Engelend et al., 2011).

What this points to is a mode of economic governance organised around massive multinational corporations that are increasingly engaged in short-term extractive practices (often linked to financial instruments) rather than long-term investment in the non-financial economy (Krugman, 2009a). This mindset is antithetical to the needs of the environment, but also to the long-term needs of most of those living and working within it. In honour of the economist who identified the trend in the economy towards corporatisation, the use of advertising to create new needs, and the deleterious effects of financial speculation, this mode of economic governance might be better labelled as 'Galbraithian' after J.K. Galbraith (Galbraith, 1958, 1993, 1996), not because he believed that this mode of economic growth was good or sustainable, but because of his trenchant critique of it.

Galbraith also foresaw the effects on welfare of this mode of capitalism. Amongst other phrases he coined, 'private opulence and public squalor' is one of the most resonant. The full quote from chapter 18 of his 1958 book *The Affluent Society* is: 'In a community where public services have failed to keep abreast of private consumption things are very different. Here, in an atmosphere of private opulence and public squalor, the private goods have full sway.' Galbraith realised that mass advertising by massive corporations led to the construction of want, designed to ensure the expansion of the consumer society. However, as people grow more affluent, they come to prioritise such private consumption as a way of life, resenting their taxation contribution to public services (as it prevents further private consumption), and leading to governments that promise lower taxes becoming more popular. This leads to the dynamic outlined by Taylor-Gooby (2013), in which the demand for lower taxation leads to public services becoming starved of resources, which in turn leads to poorer quality public services, and demands to reduce the funding for such services even further because they are not meeting the demands of the public. This is mostly obvious since 2007/8 in public budgets no longer expanding in the same way as they had in the previous decade, yet being put under pressure to provide an increased range of services to fulfil the commitments policymakers have committed to.

The affluent society, in which in material terms we are almost unimaginably richer than our grandparents were, but often mired in debt and chasing ever more consumer goods, is due to our need to measure our material wellbeing in terms of our position in society relative to others (Frank, 2007), rather than whether it is actually helping to make us happy. This is fuelled by mass advertising, but alongside that an economic model based on short-term gain, encouraging us to take on more debt, and with the houses in which we live turning into commodities to be bought and sold rather than lived in, driving up the costs of rent or home ownership to unsustainable levels, fuelling the need to take on even greater debt.

All of these pressures feed directly into the relationship between work and welfare which manifest differently in different countries, but with some common tendencies. The Galbrathian model of economic growth prioritises massive corporations demanding ever more lenient terms from governments in order to continue employing people in their countries, requiring labour market practices to become more flexible, and increased corporate welfare that can reduce taxation receipts, and so the resources available to governments, even further. The labour market becomes segregated into those who have (relatively) secure employment, those who find themselves in a variety of precarious employment relationships (Hutton, 1996; Standing, 2014) but are able to survive (often with their low wages being supplemented by the state), and those whose precarity leaves them in poverty and in receipt of benefits which impose increasingly harsh conditions upon their recipients. Such a political and social environment leaves little room for investing in the need to nurture the lifelong development of the skills and capabilities that are needed so that people can make their fullest contribution to society, or have meaningful work to support their wellbeing.

Reduced taxation and pressures for political parties to compete in terms of their ability to meet the needs of multinational corporations leads to the state having few resources to invest in long-term infrastructure. This is most visible in the literally crumbling bridges and roads in the USA, but also includes the long-term projects which would move the economy towards being more sustainable.

Jessop's location of the dominant scale of economic and welfare governance being at the postnational level is insightful into the predicament we face but, in the light of the financial crisis of 2007/8, requires a little modification. The national state has lost power, compared to the situation of the 1950s and 1960s, in now being part of a global economy in a more interconnected way, in which vast volumes of financial flows can enter and leave in seconds. However, when the financial system failed in 2007, it was down to national economies to organise the bailouts needed to prevent that system from collapsing entirely. National governments still have a great deal of power, but have voluntarily ceded large parts of their ability to regulate their own economies to global financial systems which appear to offer far less in return than they should do (Prospect Magazine, 2009). The problem here is a collective action one – in order to prevent the massive speculative flows that do little to serve any wider social good, national economies must legislate in a co-ordinated way, but individual states that choose to avoid such legislation can become enriched by financial corporations then favouring them as a base for their financial transactions. This 'race to the bottom' of financial legislation perpetuates a system that benefits few that are not directly employed within it, and causes actual harm in terms of the short-term economic model it propagates and supports through the damage it does to public goods in the process.

THE GOVERNANCE OF WELFARE IN THE 2020s

The above sections suggest a different lens to consider the governance of welfare than in relation to Jessop's original 'Schumpeterian Workfare Postnational Regime', instead suggesting we might better consider a configuration which is Galbrathian, organised around Affluence rather than Workfare, and while the dominant scale of the political economy of both welfare and the environment is Postnational, it is clearly national governments that are still tasked with attempting to broker agreements to limit the worst excesses of the current mode of economic growth. This final element of Jessop's framework is the Regime, which was counterposed to the 'State' in suggesting that state-based actors increasingly have to work through a range of actors located at different scales and different locations in order to make policy work. This is certainly true. However, it also appears that the dominant mode of governance has become increasingly extractive, both in terms of its approach to economics, in which the living standards of the poorest are remaining static at best, but also in terms of the environment, where the dominance of polluting multinational corporations and their close relationships with governments means that neither the climate nor the plight of the poorest is prioritised. International attempts to prevent further climate change struggle to achieve the kinds of agreements needed (with the disagreements present at COP 26 being a clear example), and actual achievement against these weak agreements often falls short. Making agreements is difficult not only because richer countries do not wish to change, but also because less developed countries regard already-industrialised countries as blocking their path to prosperity while doing little to share green technology or compensate them for not industrialising. This is a massive collective action problem that does not make for a promising future.

Instead of Jessop's notion of 'Regime' in his new governance formulation, then we might characterise the closed world of international policymaking, which appears able to overlook the challenges those most vulnerable in our societies face, while not confronting climate change at the scale needed, to be Oligarchic in nature. Rather than government of the people, by the people, for the people, we appear to be experiencing government of the many, by the few, for the few, with corporate elites dominating our lives to levels not seen since the 1920s (Piketty, 2017), and with apparently little regard to the future they are creating for anyone outside of their own private worlds (Winters, 2011; Mount, 2013). Such elites may have never experienced poverty, and believe that they will be insulated against climate change by their wealth, but for both the working and increasingly middle classes (Frank, 2007), this will not be the case. The governance of both welfare and climate change appear to be dominated by those who do not accept that widespread poverty is something they need to be more concerned about, or that the disastrous effects of not changing course in terms of our economies to avoid climate change is a sufficiently urgent problem.

This formulation of the Galbrathian Affluent Postnational Oligarchy leads to an obvious question – why do the many allow themselves to be led by those who do not share their interests? The overwhelming evidence in countries such as the UK and USA is that the rewards of economic growth have not been shared since the 1970s (Krugman, 2009b). It will be the poorest, who will be unable to absorb the costs of adapting to climate change (where such adaptation is possible), that will be worse off as the planet warms. The answers to this are complex. The consumer-led society emphasised by Galbrathian economic governance is dominated by the generation of false consumer needs, and it is going to be extraordinarily difficult to divert people away from the disastrous effects this is having on both wellbeing and on the environment – we are now so immersed in consumerism that it may have become central to many of our identities (Barber, 2007).

Discourses around welfare have become so successful – especially in the USA and UK – in painting large groups of people as being undeserving of support (Garthwaite, 2011) that the social solidarity that was far more prevalent in the 1940s, at the founding of our current welfare states, will be difficult to recapture. We do see, however, rises in support for more generous welfare systems in times of recession, and given the world economic situation in 2022, this at least creates the potential for a more compassionate approach appearing. This approach may even extend internationally as the war in Ukraine has demonstrated, but still appears highly selective in terms of who developed countries are prepared to extend a hand of support to, and who they are not.

This last point will be especially crucial as the effects of climate change begin to appear even more clearly in countries which richer nations may have less obvious links to.

The weakness of international institutions in addressing the serious challenges before us has also become clearer in the 2020s. Despite the crucial need for legally binding agreements between countries to address climate change, they have not appeared. Attempts to create carbon trading markets are one road forward, but are ideologically located within the same framework as the existing economic paradigm, so do not appear to bring much hope of securing change on the scale that is required (Klein, 2014). Equally, without such trading agreements being binding with clear sanctions for any breaches – which has so far been the case – then there is little hope of them working. Part of this inability to establish binding agreements is our economic dependence on countries which do not want to sign such agreements, and who are able to veto them because of our growing dependence on them for further economic growth or natural resources. Part of this is the lack of willingness of richer nations to address past injustices and devote a larger part of their wealth to supporting the greener development of other nations. However, unless we are prepared to consider the fates of all those on our planet as interconnected, and to accept every country has a role to play in that, it is hard to see how we will be able to divert ourselves from the worst effects of climate change.

What is doubly frustrating is that there are clear proposals for what international agreements would look like that could move us onto a different mode of economic governance. They are not based on complex principles – they would tax things we accept are damaging our world, and aim to subsidise and support things that support human flourishing (Stiglitz, 2012). We can tax polluters at rates that require them to clear up the full cost of their activities, tax socially useless international financial transactions, and use those funds to support sustainable economic development and research greener technologies to meet our energy needs better in the future. The barrier to these agreements is the lack of vision of our politicians and the influence international corporations hold over them, and so this too needs to be addressed.

Reich (2009) suggests that richer countries should remove corporation tax and, at the same time, clear away any right of multinational corporations to lobby governments – no taxation, no representation. We also need fuller disclosures of conflicts of interest between those in power and corporations with those who are not prepared to put aside their own material gain being excluded from office in an attempt to get them to govern for all of their people. It even seems, astonishingly, that those in power are sometimes actively attempting to avoid taxation in their own countries. All of these things must stop.

CONCLUSION

This chapter has argued that, to understand welfare and the climate crisis, we need to locate both within the wider political economy. By updating Jessop's governance of welfare framework to take into account the events of the last 20 years, we can propose an alternative formulation that captures the direction and key elements of the current situation, in which a Galbrathian Affluent Postnational Oligarchy is in danger of becoming dominant.

This formation is Galbrathian in the sense that it is dominated by large multinational corporations with business models that are based on the generation of consumer demand through large-scale advertising. These corporations may compete with one another, but the vast majority of products we see on the shelves we visit come from relatively few different such corporations, giving an illusion of competition which may be very real for smaller companies seeking to compete, but which is profoundly limited at base for those seeking to purchase products. These corporations have massive influence as employers, but also have significant sway over governments, especially given the revolving door between government and corporation work. Such corporations are able to claim a significant amount of 'corporate welfare' from governments in order to locate their operations in their country (Farnsworth, 2013), and expect to have a strong voice in lobbying for laws that support their business, as we have seen in the examples relating to financial services above.

This new ideal-type governance is Affluent in that it depends upon the generation of false needs through mass advertising for economic growth, and accepts that the vast majority of people are, compared to their own grandparents, vastly better off financially. However, with affluence comes a range of new problems. Housing costs have risen beyond what anyone could have imagined 50 years ago, and the pressures to meet such costs and continue to expand consumption appears to be having profound consequences on our mental health (Barber, 2007). Even if people try to escape from judging their lives in terms of what others have, rising inequality levels appear to be causally linked to poorer health and wellbeing outcomes for us all (Wilkinson and Pickett, 2010). Increased Affluence has not given us more free time and greater wellbeing – instead it appears to have made us work even harder and reduced our happiness. This claim about Affluence does not mean poverty no longer exists – most poverty is relative. Compared to those in the 1930s the vast majority of people have extraordinary choice over their lives. However, that is not how we judge our wellbeing – such judgements are inherently relative, and while the richest continue to accumulate, most are being left behind. It is also the case that increased consumption cannot go on forever without even further environmental consequences (Klein, 2014). If we are to being to address the mental health and environment consequences of endless consumption, then we need to find a different road based instead around prioritising wellbeing rather than consumerism.

As such, the key role of the welfare state, in countering Affluence, is in re-emphasising wellbeing rather than consumerism, and seeking a more equal distribution of resources within our societies. This, if combined with a serious attempt to imagine an economy in which endless economic growth is not the main priority, provides a potential future which is much more sustainable both in terms of our planet, but also in terms of our mental health. Welfare is not a separate system from our economy, but the two are embedded in one another.

Our world is postnational in that both welfare and the environment depend on us being able to create international agreements to tackle the challenges we face. Introducing a tax on socially useless financial transactions, and taxing corporations that pollute, would allow far greater support for the most vulnerable and allow significant investment in green technologies. That we do not embrace this agenda, and that so many are prepared to argue against it, shows the entrenchment of focus on the short term, and their personal investment in the damaging economic model which underpins it.

Finally, the chapter has suggested that the prevailing mode of governance is not that of the 'regime', as Jessop suggested, but is becoming increasingly oligarchic, in that it is overseen by a small global elite ruling to maintain their own interests. That elite appears disinterested in making the significant changes needed to both address climate change and the consequences of the Galbrathian form of capitalism that predominates as they are part of it themselves.

REFERENCES

Allen, R. and Snyder, D. (2009) 'New Thinking On the Global Financial Crisis', *Critical Perspectives on International Business*, 5(1/2), pp. 36–55.

Barber, B. (2007) *Consumed: How Markets Corrupt Children, Infantilize Adults and Swallow Citizens Whole*. London: W.W. Norton and Co.

Beveridge, W. (1942) *Social Insurance and Allied Services*. London: HMSO.

Casey, T. (2011) *The Legacy of the Crash: How the Financial Crisis Changed America and Britain*. Basingstoke: Palgrave Macmillan.

Cerny, P. (1997) 'Paradoxes of the Competition State: The Dynamics of Political Globalization', *Government and Opposition*, 32(2), pp. 251–274.

Engelend, E. et al. (2011) *After the Great Complacence: Financial Crisis and the Politics of Reform*. Oxford: Oxford University Press.

Farnsworth, K. (2013) 'Bringing Corporate Welfare Back In', *Journal of Social Policy*, 42(1), pp. 1–22.

Financial Services Authority (2009) *The Turner Review: A Regulatory Response to the Global Banking Crisis*. London: Financial Services Authority.

Frank, R. (2007) *Falling Behind: How Rising Inequality Harms the Middle Class*. Oakland, CA: University of California Press.
Galbraith, J.K. (1958) *The Affluent Society*. London: Penguin.
Galbraith, J.K. (1993) *The Culture of Contentment*. London: Penguin.
Galbraith, J.K. (1996) *The Good Society: The Humane Agenda*. London: Sinclair-Stevenson.
Garthwaite, K. (2011) '"The Language of Shirkers and Scroungers?" Talking about Illness, Disability and Coalition Welfare Reform', *Disability and Society*, 26(3), pp. 369–372.
Greener, I. (2018) *Social Policy after the Financial Crisis: A Progressive Response*. Cheltenham, UK and Northampton, MA, USA: Edward Elgar Publishing (New Horizons in Social Policy).
Hall, P. (1990) *The Power of Economic Ideas*. Princeton, NJ: Princeton University Press.
Hall, P. (1993) 'Policy Paradigms, Social Learning and the State', *Comparative Politics*, 25, pp. 275–296.
Hutton, W. (1996) *The State We're In*. London: Vintage.
Jessop, B. (1992) 'Fordism and Post-Fordism: A Critical Reformulation', in M. Storper and A. Scott (eds) *Pathways to Industrialisation and Regional Development*. Abingdon: Routledge, pp. 42–62.
Jessop, B. (1994) 'The Transition to Post-Fordism and the Schumpeterian Workfare State', in R. Burrows and B. Loader (eds) *Towards a Post-Fordist Welfare State?* Abingdon: Routledge, pp. 13–37.
Jessop, B. (1999) 'The Changing Governance of Welfare: Recent Trends in its Primary Functions, Scale and Modes of Coordination', *Social Policy and Administration*, 33(4), pp. 348–359.
Jessop, B. (2002) *The Future of the Capitalist State*. Cambridge: Polity Press.
Klein, N. (2014) *This Changes Everything: Capitalism vs the Climate*. London: Penguin.
Krugman, P. (2009a) *The Conscience of a Liberal*. London: Penguin.
Krugman, P. (2009b) 'The Return of Depression Economics: Part 3: The Night they Reread Minsky', *Lionel Robbins Memorial Lecture, London School of Economics* [Preprint].
Lister, R. (2010) *Understanding Theories and Concepts in Social Policy*. Bristol: Policy Press.
Marshall, T.H. (1950) *Citizenship and Social Class*. Cambridge: Cambridge University Press.
Mount, F. (2013) *The New Few: Or a Very British Oligarchy*. London: Simon and Schuster.
Offe, C. (1984) *Contraditions of the Welfare State*. London: Hutchinson.
Peterz, P. and Schroedel, J. (2009) 'Financial Regulation in the United States: Lessons from History', *Public Administration Review*, July/August, pp. 603–612.
Piketty, T. (2017) *Capital in the Twenty-first Century*. Translated by A. Goldhammer. Cambridge, MA and London: The Belknap Press of Harvard University Press.
Prospect Magazine (2009) 'How to Tame Global Finance', *Prospect* [Preprint].
Reich, R. (2009) *Supercapitalism: The Battle for Democracy in an Age of Big Business*. London: Icon Books.
Richards, S. (2010) *Whatever It Takes: The Real Story of Gordon Brown and New Labour*. London: Fourth Estate.
Standing, G. (2014) *The Precariat: The New Dangerous Class*. London: Bloomsbury.

Stiglitz, J. (2012) *The Price of Inequality*. London: Penguin.
Taylor-Gooby, P. (2013) *The Double Crisis of the Welfare State and What We Can Do About It*. Basingstoke: Palgrave MacMillan.
Tett, G. (2009) *Fool's Gold: How Unrestrained Greed Corrupted a Dream, Shattered Global Markets and Unleashed a Catastrophe*. London: Little, Brown.
Wilkinson, R. and Pickett, K. (2010) *The Spirit Level: Why Equality Is Better for Everyone*. London: Penguin.
Winters, J. (2011) *Oligarchy*. Cambridge: Cambridge University Press.

7. Keynesian economics steering is back – end of liberal economic policy?
Mogens Ove Madsen

7.1 INTRODUCTION

The global pandemic has triggered unprecedented economic events in modern times. It required strict restrictions on economic activity, which effectively closed large parts of the global economy. Governments have responded with enormous fiscal support and central banks have stepped up their unconventional monetary policy. The nature of policy responses has varied across countries, reflecting differences in political preferences, differences in the severity of the impact of the pandemic, and institutional differences in pre-COVID welfare systems.

The main question raised in this chapter is whether in economic theory and economic policy there is a lasting paradigm shift in public finances due to COVID-19? Or is the pandemic just a Keynesian "moment" disappearing with COVID-19? Furthermore, will Keynesian sensitivities be aroused only when it is the "real economy" that is in distress, or will financial and sectoral crises also be met with countercyclical measures?

Until the pandemic, even large-scale crises such as the one in 2008 did not seem to pose a real danger to the primacy of neoliberal principles. In fact, it can be argued that such crises have been used as a justification for carrying out far-reaching state interventions against the common good to stabilize the neoliberal system. The interesting thing is whether the measures taken by states to combat COVID-19 have shaken the neoliberal edifice so much that there is a real possibility of returning to the Keynesian paradigm as a basis for understanding the economy and for economic policy actions.

Skidelsky (2009) has in his book on Keynes a chapter comparing the performance of the world economy between the "golden age" period of 1951 to 1973, when Keynesian politics was dominant, with the Washington Consensus period of 1981 to 2008, when free market policies were adopted by leading governments. This phase division will be used subsequently with a focus on the period 1981 to 2008, followed by a special focus on what happened after 2008 and whether the "golden age" period of 1951 to 1973 can be re-established in some form.

7.2 THE HEYDAY OF NEOLIBERALISM

In the early 1970s, when the Keynesian Bretton Woods system collapsed and economic crises intensified in the United States and Europe, it challenged Keynesian economic policy. At the same time, neoliberal ideas began to enter the mainstream. Milton Friedman – the first man of monetarism – has a quite unequivocal comment on this relationship, claiming that when the time came for a change, there was an alternative ready to be picked up.

Friedman delivers political concepts, principles, and policies to neoliberalism, but Friedrich August von Hayek and James Buchanan also play a central role. Everyone wrote about both political philosophy and political economy. The themes of their work provide a good portrait of the political doctrine of neoliberalism.

These three economists place their emphasis on criticizing the Keynesian arguments for government intervention. Hayek (1941 [2007]) focuses on public spending and the actions of monetary authority. Hayek argues that the Keynesians' dependence on simple economic aggregates obscures how capital and investment are structured across the economy.

As is well known, Friedman (1959) developed the doctrine of monetarism, which claims that inflation is a monetary phenomenon, and that inflation and economic conditions can be governed by monetary policy. Thus, fiscal policy instruments are effectively put out of force.

In addition, Friedman does not have much left over for monetary policy makers. They know too little to use monetary policy to manage the economy. Instead, central banks must be bound by a rule that would lead to gentle inflation. The only focus should be on increasing the monetary base in line with economic growth to prevent a collapse in the money supply and thereby avoid some forms of recession.

Thus, Friedman and Buchanan are both concerned about Keynesian claims that recessions are due to declining aggregate demand. Therefore, they cannot recommend debt-financed fiscal stimulus.

However, Buchanan's critique of Keynes also differs from Friedman's, although their critique is mutually reinforcing. Buchanan (1987, 1999) delivers a critique that governments are staffed with politicians and officials who are most concerned with benefiting themselves and particular interest groups. Thus, Buchanan's angle on debt-financed economic stimulus is that it is directed more at politicians' preferred groups than at the places where stimulus money is most needed – which is referred to as the danger of government failure (Buchanan and Tullock 1962).

Policies that follow the neoliberal mindset basically involve a reduction or elimination of trade barriers and capital controls: "Neoliberalism sought to dismantle or suppress extra market forms of economic coordination ... Concretely, its policies involved the elimination of institutionalized post-Depression and post-World War II policy conventions, such as redistributive taxation and deficit spending, controls on international exchange, economic regulation, public goods and service provisions, and active fiscal and monetary policies" (Centeno and Cohen 2012, p. 318).

But generally, neoliberal theorists sharply reject the most common justification for the welfare state, namely, to pursue an egalitarian view of social justice. Hayek (1978) is very clear and rejects the very idea of social justice. He believes that the idea of social justice is confused by the fact that justice cannot be applied to specific market results because they are not the result of direct, conscious choices. The state can thus not be used to obtain a precise distribution of income.

Daniel Stedman Jones (2012) describes neoliberalism as "a kind of neoliberal international": a transatlantic network of academics, businessmen, journalists, and activists. The rich backers of the movement funded a series of think tanks that would refine and advance the ideology. Among them were the American Enterprise Institute, the Heritage Foundation, the Cato Institute, the Institute of Economic Affairs, the Center for Policy Studies, and the Adam Smith Institute. They also funded academic positions and departments, particularly at the universities of Chicago and Virginia, and with the help of particularly sympathetic journalists and political advisers, elements of neoliberalism, particularly its monetary policy regulations, were adopted by Jimmy Carter's administration (1977–1981) in the United States and Jim Callaghan's government in Britain (1976–1979).

After Margaret Thatcher (1979–1990) and Ronald Reagan (1981–1989) took power in the United Kingdom and the United States, more of the policy followed: massive tax cuts for the rich, the crushing of trade unions, deregulation, privatization, outsourcing, and competition in public services. Through the International Monetary Fund (IMF), the World Bank, the Maastricht Treaty, and the World Trade Organization, neoliberal policies were imposed on large parts of the world (Hermann 2007; Monbiot 2017).

The Rome Treaties from 1957 were signed during the golden age of the Keynesian welfare state. According to Mark Pollack (1998) there was a stark cleavage between the liberal advocates of free trade on the one hand, and the primarily French advocates of a less liberal, more regulated Europe on the other. From Rome to Maastricht, the fundamental thrust of the treaties has been neoliberal, in the sense that each of the Community's constitutive treaties facilitated the creation of a unified European market.

The Single European Act (1986) and The Maastricht Treaty (1992) therefore represent the extension of the European neoliberal agenda from the internal market to a neoliberal economic and monetary policy based on Friedman's views on the central bank's political independence and in practice inspired by the German Bundesbank's way of working.

However, the Treaty of Amsterdam (1998) introduces an employment chapter into the overall treaty. Likewise, the Treaty of Amsterdam gave the Council of Ministers the right to take initiatives to combat not only poverty, but also social exclusion, i.e., exclusion from the labor market. This can be taken as an expression of an intention of regulated capitalism. The idea of a new Employment Chapter was created as a precondition for the adoption of a German requirement for a stability pact, that presented two completely arbitrary figures: a 3 percent budget deficit with regards to Gross National Product (GNP) and 60 percent for overall debt.

The Lisbon Agenda of 2000 again underlined the neoliberal agenda, with the European Union (EU) becoming the most competitive region in the world. Deregulation and increased competition – not least in the labor market – played a key role in achieving this. Thus, the Lisbon Summit also promoted social citizenship as a noticeable target for European cooperation. In line with its target to strengthen the social investment dimension of social citizenship, the Lisbon Process explicitly coupled the economic and social policy agendas of the integration process (Eick, Burgoon and Busemeyer 2021, p. 11).

This had the consequence that two divergent but interconnected economic models gradually developed in the center and on the periphery of the EU in the 2000s. One was the export growth-based, neo-mercantilist model, which characterized the center of the EU, and the other model was based on debt and dependent financing and import dependence on the periphery of the EU.

In these years of neoliberalism, the state domain has been reduced. Instead, neoliberal theory claims that people can exercise choices in the economic market, for example, through consumption spending. But some have more to spend than others – the market-votes are not evenly distributed. The result is powerlessness among the poorest and this denial of power also turns into denial of the right to vote. Conversely, the triumph of neoliberalism also seems to reflect a kind of political failure of the left.

7.3 THE FINANCIAL CRISIS

In the United States, financial deregulation was initiated in the early 1980s. This meant that it was now possible to allow a higher leverage, which led to a large increase in liquidity, which fueled a housing bubble. Wealth effects from housing and innovative financial instruments were instrumental in supporting excessive household consumption. Consumption increases and the fiscal deficits needed to finance the wars in Iraq and Afghanistan simultaneously created large US trade deficits and global imbalances.

Furthermore, the Federal Reserve pursued an expansive monetary policy from the late 2000s during the Great Recession and in this way also supported consumer demand through credit rather than wage increases. The overall result was the development of a comprehensive subprime bubble.

When the bubble economy burst, the financial system froze, and interbank loans stalled along with bank lending to companies. The impact on the real economy was extensive. Governments in the United States and Europe set in motion quickly – not to immediately prevent unemployment, but to save the big banks that had been culpable for the crisis.

However, the banks resisted the political pressure from Washington to establish a collective defense with their own resources. The banks told the government that they were only responsible for their own balances and not responsible for dealing with any systemic threat.

Following the financial crisis, there were calls to bring the separation of retail banking and investment banking back to the Glass–Steagall Act. This was abolished under the Clinton administration and had prompted banks to engage in risky trades in search of high profits.

Despite their severe crisis of legitimacy, the financial elite was able to resist reforms and more Keynesian-oriented reforms were stopped. The final version of the legislation became a diluted version of the Volcker Rule, which in its original wording would have prohibited banks from engaging in real estate trading or using depositors' money to trade in the banks' own accounts, but the Volcker Rule had some unintended effects (Skold 2011; Bui and Putnins 2018).

It has subsequently been highlighted that the banking reform in the United States was a case where the regulated captured the regulators. It was up to the government to come up with taxpayer-funded resources to save the banks and save the system, not the banks themselves. The banking sector also did not fear being nationalized.

During the banking crisis of 2008, prominent economic journalists and economists began arguing for Keynesian stimulus. It rubbed off on the policy makers who announced major stimulus packages in the hope of averting the possibility of a global depression. The IMF, OECD, and G20 countries were concerned about this. In January 2009, newly elected President Barack Obama unveiled a plan for comprehensive domestic spending to combat the recession, further reflecting Keynesian thinking. The plan was signed by him in February 2009. At the beginning of 2009, there was thus broad acceptance among the world's economic decision makers about the need for fiscal stimulus. But by the end of 2009, consensus among economists began to collapse and by 2010 a widespread depression had been averted, although unemployment in many countries was still high.

A marked shift in the direction of Keynesian thinking took place among prominent economists. Some, such as Paul Krugman, James Galbraith, and Brad DeLong, were already Keynesians, but in 2008 they began to receive significantly more attention from their proponents of Keynesian politics, Richard Posner and Martin Feldstein, who had previously been associated with anti-Keynesian thinking, but in 2009 they publicly converted to Keynesian economics, which had a major impact on other economists. Posner's 2009 article on the failures of capitalism was a critique of laissez-faire capitalism and its ideologues. A showdown that was also based on criticism of neoliberal thinking.

A trigger for the growing Keynesian commitment was a critique of the unsustainability of the rational expectation hypothesis that provided the theoretical basis for the effective market hypothesis. These two theories collapsed with the onset of the global financial crisis in 2007–2008, when financial market participants collectively lost faith in market valuations, panicking and engaging in "irrational" herd behavior. Precisely this put not only the financial market but entire economies in great danger, which led to the discrediting of neoliberalism in general.

The scale of the recession prompted New Keynesians to reassess the potential for major stimulus, and their debates with New Classical economists, who were often completely opposed to the stimulus, became significant. However, some post-Keynesian economists accused this new Keynesian system of being so integrated with the neo-classical influences of the pro-free market that the brand "Keynesian" in this case could be considered a misleading term.

However, a counter-reaction to the Keynesian proposals came into play. In 2009, more than 300 professional economists, led by three Nobel laureates in economics, James M. Buchanan, Edward C. Prescott, and Vernon L. Smith, signed a declaration against more public spending, arguing that lower tax rates and a reduction in government burden are the best ways to use fiscal policy to boost growth.

In March 2010, while accepting that the resurgence had stalled, Paul Krugman expressed optimism about the long-term prospects of achieving a lasting shift towards Keynesianism in both mainstream economics and policymaking. In May, Krugman (2012) published a book on ending the depression, in which he reiterated his calls for greater use of fiscal stimulus, although his proposals, according to the *Financial Times*, were both "modest" and "cautious," reflecting opposition to such measures since the end of the resurgence.

Keynesianism can be said to have made a powerful comeback during the financial crisis, but it did not repress neoliberal orthodoxy.

In turn, concerns about public debt rose and became the rationale for holding back on Keynesian fiscal policy. Unconventional monetary policy continued to be used in attempts to increase economic activity. In Europe in particular, there was an increase in rhetoric calling for immediate fiscal tightening, following events such as the Greek debt crisis and the change of government in Britain after the May 2010 election. European political leaders embarked on significant savings. In July 2010, leading European economic policy maker Jean-Claude Trichet, President of the European Central Bank (ECB), stated that it was time for all industrialized nations to stop stimulating and start tightening up.

In immediate response to the financial crisis, some key European politicians and technocrats proclaimed that fiscal tightening was necessary to cut public debt and make the economy grow again (Blyth 2013). This laid the groundwork for an extended period of austerity policy in some European countries.

A striking example is the initiative to resolve the Greek debt crisis from 2009 to 2012. A troika consisting of the EU, the ECB, and the IMF negotiated with the Greek government. The latter undertook to implement several savings packages. These packages resulted in major cuts, which included a reduction in the public sector, a higher retirement age, and reduced wages and social benefits.

Any economic policy initiative carries the risk of ending up as a lesson of failure, and this may affect future failures at the macro level. The outcome of this situation with its potential for learning and failure has been worked through in an analysis of European integration and the failure of the Eurozone (Jones, Kelemen and Meunier 2015). Here, the view is that incomplete learning in the 1990s and early 2000s resulted in a weak governance architecture in the Eurozone, which brought this into deep crisis. However, this was sought to be counteracted by partial reforms. Paradoxically, this persistent cycle of incomplete reforms followed by crisis has resulted in further integration pressures – which has allowed the EU project to "fail going forward" (Jones, Kelemen and Meunier 2015; Dunlop 2017), which means a growing mismatch between the EU's normative striving towards a "Union of values" and the political and institutional limits imposed.

There is no doubt that the management of the crisis in 2010–2012 at the EU level was deeply rooted in the national policies of the surplus countries – not least Germany (Puetter 2016), but it would later turn out that the COVID crisis had a different starting point.

7.4　FROM AUSTERITY TO COVID-19

From 2008 to 2009, there was a fiscal expansion to mitigate the effects of the global financial crisis. But already in 2010–2012, a fiscal contraction began, even though the economic situation in many countries was fragile, with poverty, unemployment, and hunger. Public spending was reduced already from 2010 and from 2013 to 2015 the fiscal contraction intensified. According to IMF forecasts, the extent and depth of austerity measures had picked up significantly in this latest phase of the crisis (Ortiz et al. 2015).

However, it must be emphasized that after the financial crisis of 2008, there has been a revival in Keynesian thinking among political decision makers such as Obama in favor of robust government intervention. The *Financial Times* described this as an "astonishing reversal of the orthodoxy of recent decades" (Giles, Atkins and Guha 2008). Keynesianism again became a more central inspiration for politicians to give a global response to the 2007–2010 financial crisis.

On the other hand, the austerity approach was supported by Harvard economists Reinhart and Rogoff (2010), who attracted much political attention by arguing that if states went over a 90 percent debt-to-GDP ratio it would be a turning point that could harm the US economy for decades. Subsequently, economists at the University of Massachusetts at Amherst found computational errors and questionable analytical design in this research and concluded that a debt-to-GDP ratio above 90 percent is not dramatically different than when the debt-to-GDP ratio is lower.

It would turn out, however, that conditions in fact backfired on Keynesianism. A major recession took effect from 2008 to 2012. There was a crisis in the real estate market and real estate bubbles in several countries. The active fiscal policies of the peripheral EU states were being challenged and by the end of 2009 the peripheral Eurozone Member States were virtually unable to repay or refinance their sovereign debt or rescue their besieged banks without the help of third-party financial institutions. These included the ECB, the IMF, and ultimately the European Financial Stability Facility (EFSF).

In 2010, Republicans in the United States won control of the House of Representatives. From 2011 onwards, congressional Republicans used key deadlines – from the expiration of the debt ceiling to government funding – to extract larger and larger spending cuts from the Obama administration. Bivens (2016), the Economics Policy Institute's research director, concluded that the Republicans should be blamed for a subsequent weak economic recovery.

Although it came late, the European Commission abandoned the austerity policy in March 2020 and activated a general flight clause in the Stability and Growth Pact that allows Member States to exceed normal deficit and debt limits due to the sudden economic shock caused by the COVID-19 pandemic. These rules will remain suspended until 2023.

Since the beginning of this century and accelerated by the pandemic crisis, infrastructure funds have become key promoters of the ecological and digital transition, initiating investments in carbon-free assets, renewable energy, recycling and circular economy, smart cities, new forms of productivity, and new ways to work and collaborate.

One more reason why the COVID-19 pandemic has already had such a severe economic impact is that countries have organized their societies under neoliberalism in ways that make them extremely vulnerable. Such embedded vulnerability means that many societies face a more drastic shock than if they create greater resilience in their public administrative institutions.

At the same time, it can be argued that COVID-19 was a springboard towards new fiscal paradigms, just as it was a groundbreaking accelerator for latent policy shifts that were already underway. These included policies which had received positive feedback at the micro level over time, but which had not been directly adopted at the macro scale. Prominent among these are tax stimulus categories including social protection programs, such as basic income regulations, income protection programs, and employment protection programs. Such programs gained accelerated political legitimacy because of their suitability as response measures in the economic crisis. In fact, the story of COVID-19 as a path-clearing accelerator is based not only on evolving trends, such as social protections, but also on how latent and smoldering social problems bubbled up with acute intensity.

The pandemic served as a focus event that opened a unique political window for government intervention of an unprecedented magnitude in most countries. For government balances, the pandemic marked a new equilibrium, so that in countries such as the United States and Australia, the stimulus in the early stages accounted for almost 12 percent of all national economic output. Yet the range of interventions varied meaningfully between countries, both in absolute and relative terms. For some developing countries, a relatively small stimulus outflow was managed in a targeted way to maximize pro-poor policies, and the pandemic therefore served as a groundbreaking accelerator for policies aimed at constructing the rudiments of a social protection system. For other countries, such as Brazil, even a relatively large fiscal package in absolute and relative terms could not be translated into an effective policy.

The Biden administration has proposed something far beyond the pandemic-related stimulus in the form of the administration's Build Back Better (BBB) plan. The BBB plan has three major long-term components: the American Rescue Plan Act; the American Jobs Plan; and the American Families Plan, which together amount to $7 trillion in proposed funding over a decades-long horizon. The focus of the BBB plan is on genuine Keynesian objects of interest: infrastructure, employment, technology, (renewable) energy, affordable housing, wages, industry, and transport. It also dives into important elements of social protection such as childcare, women's employment, years of free public education, educational improvements, and tax breaks for lower-income families.

A follow-up to this is an important spillover effect on Europe from US policies that will come from financial risks, as the financial markets are highly internationalized. The breaking of these bubbles could damage the Eurozone's financial system and trigger renewed tensions on government interest rates in fragile countries. The expected, but uncertain, positive macroeconomic spillover effects of US policies should not obscure the need for the Euro area to accompany the recovery with an appropriate policy mix and to continue to prevent the emergence of a new wave of financial turmoil.

The design and scope of emergency policy responses to COVID-19 will vary widely from country to country in ways that reflect at least partially existing national political heritage. The policy responses to COVID-19 seek to reduce uncertainty, stabilize incomes, and prevent an economic free fall, at least in part shaped by existing policy legacies, including those linked to specific policy areas and welfare regimes (e.g., the balance between targeted and universal benefits), as well as with concrete instruments used (e.g., wage subsidies vs. temporary unemployment) or territorial arrangements (e.g., centralization–decentralization link).

The COVID crisis has led to a far-reaching monetary and fiscal stimulus reflecting a Keynesian theoretical understanding. At the EU level, as early as March 2020, the ECB launched a €750 billion Pandemic Emergency Purchase Program (PEPP) aimed at national and regional authorities – both surplus and deficit economies.

Three months later, in June 2020, the ECB almost doubled PEPP (to €1.35 trillion) and made bond purchases, which should remove the uncertainty as to whether ECB purchases will continue throughout the cycles of the health crisis. In total, the volume of PEPP rose so much that it doubled as the Fed's relative to its GDP ratio.

Adam Tooze (2018) claimed that the Fed did better than the more conservative ECB in the previous financial crisis, but the same cannot be said about the COVID crisis. The difference is that the Fed had already started using quantitative easing to combat the great recession in 2008. In three different rounds, the central bank bought assets worth more than $4 trillion between 2009 and 2014.

Until 2015, however, the ECB openly refused to admit quantitative easing, but in January 2015 the European Central Bank announced an "extended asset buyback program" in which €60 billion a month of Euro area bonds from central banks, governments, agencies, and European institutions would be purchased. In 2016, the Bank announced that it would continue this policy with increased monthly bond purchases and from November 2019, the ECB resumed purchases of government bonds in the Euro area as an attempt to encourage governments to borrow more and spend on domestic investment projects.

It should be emphasized here that there were also negotiations on "corona bonds," but these broke down. In return, it succeeded in establishing a coordinated EU-wide fiscal policy package, which had been difficult to imagine before the outbreak of the COVID crisis in 2020. The package was called the Next Generation EU (NGEU) – and had a value of €750 billion and where climate change and digitalization are high priorities.

Some of the elements of this newly formulated Keynesian initiative are set to expire automatically with the end of the health crisis. It is unprecedented in the history of the Euro that the clauses in the Stability and Growth Pact have been temporarily repealed, but they will return after the end of the COVID crisis. This is emphasized by the Finance Ministers of the Eurogroup and by the European Fiscal Board.

7.5   WHAT ARE THE PROSPECTS?

As soon as it became clear that it would be necessary to take extraordinary measures to control the COVID-19 virus, there were demands for assessments of the economic effects. Estimates of the potential impact on energy consumption and greenhouse gas emissions (GHG) soon followed. Proposals for stimulus packages came not long after, with a general feeling that policy makers were more "ready" for the green stimulus than in 2008–2009. However, it can be argued that the economic effects of the pandemic at the sectoral level are more important than the results at the macro level, both for economic and environmental reasons. Unlike in 2008–2009, the economic crisis we are currently facing is initially rooted in reduced levels of consumer spending rather than reduced levels of investment.

The situation is radically different from the 2008–2012 crisis in Europe. Here, the norm or response to the crisis was austerity, but it applies to both the heads of state of the European countries and the European Union that the prospect of an even greater recession gave rise to thinking in new directions around economic policy. The implementation of a new fiscal activism in the form of the NGEU at the EU level may be sluggish and associated with some uncertainty.

However, with the onset of the 2008 crisis, the fragility of the neoliberal approach became more apparent. Instead of tackling the fundamental problem of the division of labor and capital and creating sustainable structures for development on the European periphery, the austerity approach opted for a radicalization of the neoliberal approach to integration.

As during the financial crisis in 2008, the social security systems proved to be very strong automatic stabilizers. The socio-political reactions to COVID-19 have been significant in size and scope, with policy packages in many countries representing new departures. Conversely, COVID-19 emergency policies were inherently different from the savings- and work-related policies pursued in several countries in the decade before the onset of the COVID-19 crisis. Nevertheless, several countries continued the dual transformation of social protection that has taken place in recent decades, which on the one hand abolished income-related benefits for the long-term unemployed and atypically employed and extended social security to the so-called "new social risks" on the other side. The more generous treatment of COVID-19-related social risks compared to ordinary unemployment may in some countries have even exacerbated the differences between well-protected core workers and outsiders in the labor market.

The point is thus that economic and social recovery policies will be extremely demanding for the national welfare states. GDP has fallen while social spending reaches unprecedented levels. The COVID-19-related costs come on top of the cost of aging and the efforts needed for climate change, while the increase in unemployment that will follow the abolition of rescue measures will take place during digitalization, which in itself will have a negative impact on employment opportunities for the low-skilled.

There is little doubt that the pandemic will bring the welfare state to a critical point in its history while reminding us why we need welfare states. The answer to the initial questions is how welfare states, albeit with large differences, have impressively coped with the consequences of this unprecedented crisis.

The neoliberal EU integration model has not solved the problems associated with the imbalance in the distribution in Europe between the two inhomogeneous, interconnected economic models in the center and on the periphery of Europe.

A political and economic perspective on the history of the United States and the EU clearly shows that European integration has not been a linear process – nor do the policy initiatives in the United States. On the two continents there have been collapses and crises with quite extensive consequences. However, there is a difference between the crises and thus also the economics advice. The financial crisis of 2007–2008 had a different course with a brief introduction of Keynesian expansive policy, which, however, was quickly replaced by a public debt problem, where a neoliberal austerity policy became the solution in the long run. On the other hand, the COVID-19 crisis has had a far more extensive impact, whether it has made it obvious to pursue a detailed Keynesian policy and do away with several neoliberal features in the individual states and rules that have been monetarist-inspired.

There is great uncertainty associated with economic forecasts. If the economic turmoil increases after the COVID crisis is reduced, the arrow points more to Keynesian countermeasures than neoliberal initiatives. However, the scope will vary based on the individual countries' past performance.

REFERENCES

Bivens, Josh (2016). *Why is Recovery Taking So Long – and Who's to Blame?* Economics Policy Institute, Washington, DC.

Blyth, M. (2013). *Austerity*. Oxford: Oxford University Press.

Buchanan, James (1987). Budgetary bias in post-Keynesian politics: The erosion and potential replacement of fiscal norms. In James Buchanan, Charles Rowley and Robert Tollison (eds.), *Deficits*. New York: Blackwell, pp. 180–198.

Buchanan, James (1999). *The Logical Foundations of Constitutional Liberty*. Indianapolis, IN: Liberty Fund.

Buchanan, James and Gordon Tullock (1962). *The Calculus of Consent*. Ann Arbor, MI: University of Michigan Press.

Bui, Christina and Talis Putnins (2018). The intended and unintended effects of the Volcker Rule. https://pdfs.semanticscholar.org/fd14/d7676343c5a9ba118cfa0902b7e38d4ffe8a.pdf.

Centeno, M. A. and J. N. Cohen (2012). The arc of neoliberalism. *Annual Review of Sociology*, 38, 317–340.

Dunlop, Claire A. (2017). Policy learning and policy failure: Definitions, dimensions and intersections. *Policy and Politics*, 45(1), 3–18.

Eick, Gianna M., Brian Burgoon and Marius R. Busemeyer (2021). *Measuring Social Citizenship in Social Policy Outputs, Resources and Outcomes across EU Member States from 1985 to the Present*. EuSocialCit Working Paper. file:///C:/Users/mom/Downloads/D6.1%20Measuring%20social%20citizenship.pdf

Friedman, Milton (1959). *A Program for Monetary Stability*. New York: Fordham University Press.

Giles, Chris, Ralph Atkins and Krishna Guha (2008). The undeniable shift to Keynes. *Financial Times*, December 29.

Hayek, F. (1941 [2007]). *The Pure Theory of Capital*. Chicago: University of Chicago Press.

Hayek, F. (1978). *Law, Legislation and Liberty: Volume 2: The Mirage of Social Justice*. Chicago: University of Chicago Press.

Hermann, Christoph (2007). *Neoliberalism in the European Union*. Thematic Paper, Project: Dynamics of National Employment Models (DYNAMO), Working Life Research Centre, Vienna.

Jones, Daniel Stedman (2012). *Masters of the Universe: Hayek, Friedman, and the Birth of Neoliberal Politics*. Princeton, NJ: Princeton University Press.

Jones, E., R. D. Kelemen and S. Meunier (2015). Failing forward? The Euro crisis and the incomplete nature of European integration. *Comparative Political Studies*, 49(7), 1010–1034. doi:10.1177/0010414015617966

Krugman, Paul (2012). *End this Depression Now*. New York: W. W. Norton & Co.

Monbiot, George (2017). *How Did We Get Into This Mess? Politics, Equality, Nature* (Reprint edn). Brooklyn, NY: Verso.

Ortiz, Isabel, Matthew Cummins, Jeronim Capaldo and Kalaivani Karunanethy (2015). *The Decade of Adjustment: A Review of Austerity Trends 2010–2020 in 187 Countries*. International Labour Office, Geneva (Extension of Social Security Series No. 53).

Pollack, Mark A. (1998). *Beyond Left and Right? Neoliberalism and Regulated Capitalism in the Treaty of Amsterdam*. Working Paper Series in European Studies, Vol. 2, No. 2.

Posner, Richard A. (2009). A failure of capitalism: The crisis of '08 and the descent into depression. *Journal of Affordable Housing & Community Development Law*, 19(1).

Puetter, Uwe (2016). The centrality of consensus and deliberation in contemporary EU politics and the new intergovernmentalism. *Journal of European Integration*, 38(5), 601–615.

Reinhart, Carmen A. and Kenneth S. Rogoff (2010). Growth in a time of debt. *American Economic Review: Papers and Proceedings*, 100(2), 573–578.

Skidelsky, Robert (2009). *Keynes: The Return of the Master*. London: Penguin.

Skold, Alida S. (2011). *Intended and Unintended Consequences of the Proposed Volcker Rule*. Munich Personal RePEc Archive. mpra.ub.uni-muenchen.de

Tooze, Adam (2018). *Crashed: How a Decade of Financial Crises Changed the World*. London: Penguin.

8. The welfare state and handling health challenges
Caroline Rudisill

8.1 INTRODUCTION

Welfare states face several challenges related to the health of the populations they serve. There are policy levers to improve some challenges while others are much more intractable. Ageing populations, increasing inequality and the changing nature of work have health and financial implications requiring policy focus. Specific to health, obesity, mental health, substance abuse, lack of physical activity and infectious disease (e.g. antibiotic resistance) all pose financial and quality of life costs to populations.

While the challenges set forth by population health changes are very real and require both consideration and action, several approaches can help. The chapter aims to outline those tools and review what we know about their effectiveness. It will start with briefly defining what is meant by the term 'welfare state' in the context of health and health care, particularly for an American audience. Then we will outline the health challenges faced by welfare states that motivate efforts to wisely respond to these needs. This section will build the case as to why welfare states and health policy must consider unique approaches to population health concerns. Topics such as the role of prevention and the prudent use of funds will be covered in this section. Then we will discuss how present health challenges can be supported in three ways: health systems focusing on value; harnessing the role of technology in care delivery; and using low-cost/costless interventions such as nudges.

8.2 CONTEXT FOR THE WELFARE STATE AND HEALTH

The term 'welfare state', in this chapter, is deemed to mean expenditures by government for the purposes of the economic and social wellbeing of its population.[1] We depend on the classic social-welfare maximization problem where the goal is to maximize society's welfare. Social-welfare maximization occurs in a resource-constrained model with three parameters – tastes (preferences for alternative goods), technology (as limited by production functions for goods both in terms of capital and labor) and resources (stock of capital and labor available to the economy's production function to produce goods that people both desire and that can be produced given technological and resource limitations) (Barr 1998). The state then gets involved through four means (as named in Barr 1998): regulation (e.g. the Affordable Care Act in the US requiring coverage of pre-existing conditions by insurers); financing (e.g. changing cigarette prices via taxes or paying for all COVID-19 shots); production of goods or services (e.g. running schools, Veterans Health Administration in the US); or income transfers (e.g. Child Tax Credit in the US).

The government's involvement in public health and health care is thus a response to contexts where the market cannot settle on a socially acceptable solution for society's preferences. For example, there is large agreement that regulation is needed to ensure that medicines and other named products are safe for the population's health (e.g. European Medicines Agency and the Food and Drug Administration in the US). There is less agreement across nations about who pays for health care and what the structure of health care delivery and financing should look like.

Regardless of how these decisions get settled, a major component of any country's public expenditure is on health and health care. This is also true in the US, which spends a greater percentage of its social expenditure on health (8.4% in 2019) than any other OECD country except France (8.5% in 2019) (OECD 2019). In 2019, overall expenditures on health were highest in the US as a percentage of GDP (16.8%) with the closest European countries being Germany (11.7%), Switzerland (11.3%) and France (11.1%) (OECD 2021).

In the US in 2020, 91.4% of Americans had health insurance and of those, 34.8% had insurance via public programs (Keisler-Starkey and Bunch 2021). Of the public programs, Medicare (primarily those 65+ years) has the most beneficiaries (18.4% of all health insurance coverage) and then Medicaid (e.g. low-income families – children, pregnant women, some seniors and people with disabilities) (17.8%) (Keisler-Starkey and Bunch 2021). Employment-based insurance (occupational-based welfare) is a key feature of the US system (54.4% of the insured).

Alternatively, private health spending in European countries is often lower as a percentage of total health spending (OECD 2021) but on average, 32% of the European Union population has private health insurance (Papanicolas et al. 2019). Private health insurance takes a variety of forms in Europe. It can be substitutive (e.g. Germany), complementary (e.g. France) or the dominant form of cover (e.g. the Netherlands). Private health insurance can also be financed by public expenditure in many countries including the US where insurance access is subsidized depending on income and state. Thus, support to receive private health insurance is provided indirectly via the tax system. Employment-based insurance can be complementary or supplementary (e.g. the United Kingdom (UK)) and is voluntary across Europe. Employers, however, can play a key role in financing the public system alongside of employee contributions (e.g. in Germany, the employee and employer split the 14.6% of gross income contribution (Blümel et al. 2020)).

There are many reasons for differences in the size, breadth and modalities of European and US public expenditures on health care. Cross-country comparisons of the welfare state in health are beyond the scope of this chapter. The ways in which money flows in each system do have implications for the levers that can be employed to encourage health outcomes under resource constraints. Nonetheless, the considerations for bringing tools to bear within the context of financial pressures due to population health needs are relevant to European and North American health systems even though policy details vary due to system design.

8.3 HEALTH ISSUES AND THE WELFARE STATE

Health systems are under expenditure pressure not only due to acute demands from COVID-19 but also underlying population health factors. America's Health Rankings® examines the key challenges for health and health care in the US each year (*America's Health Rankings: Annual Report 2021* 2021). Disparities across race, ethnicity, income and in some cases, gender for disease burden and care access pose ongoing issues in the US. Mental health, drug use and e-cigarette use also persist as issues. Clinical care provider availability (providers/100,000 population) in mental health and primary care is increasing but disparities in access exist between geographies (*America's Health Rankings: Annual Report 2021* 2021).

These topics layer on top of underpinning trends in chronic disease incidence and related costs such as ageing populations, obesity and mental health. The UK has some similar issues to the US. The burden of disease related to mental health has been increasing over the past 25 years with disproportionate illness amongst lower-income populations (McKee et al. 2021). Alcohol and drug use-related disease and death have also increased more recently (McKee et al. 2021). More broadly, other threats persist such as antimicrobial resistance and continued disparities in life expectancy gains for individuals across Europe according to education, income and job type (Mackenbach, Karanikolos, and McKee 2013).

There are also underlying dynamics in recent years driving new phenomena. The COVID-19 pandemic has changed the ways people work (e.g. individuals retiring earlier, working at home). The increased percentage of retirees in the total US population may be a temporary phenomenon but we do not know yet.

Work can, however, hedge against the risk of social isolation. Thus, larger swathes of the population who are retirees may be at risk of isolation and its negative health impacts (e.g. cardiovascular disease and cognitive decline; Shankar et al. 2013; National Academies of Sciences, Engineering, and Medicine 2020). Evidence from Europe and Israel examining early retirees during COVID-19 found increased COVID-19-related preventive behaviors (e.g. not leaving home, leaving home less often to meet friends, shop, go for a walk) and less mobility to negatively impact the mental health of *single* early retirees in particular but *not* overall (Bertoni et al. 2021).

Prevention is a key aspect of many population health challenges affecting health systems today. Market failures present in public health are clear. They include the role externalities play in vaccination decisions and preference structures of individuals not following time intransient features and overweighting utility associated with behavior today (e.g. drinking, drug use, food choices) that produces future disutility. The public sector intervenes through making many vaccines free and/or required for schooling and implementing taxes on cigarettes, alcohol and in some settings sugary beverages (e.g. France, Norway, Mexico, some local US settings) to reduce consumption (Fichera et al. 2021; Cawley et al. 2019; Chaloupka, Powell, and Warner 2019; Powell et al. 2013). Taxes can be a very effective tool but the political appetite for higher rates has limits and thus other tools augment such policies.

8.4 ADDITIONAL LEVERS FOR HANDLING HEALTH CHALLENGES

The health challenges named only stand to increase the financial burden related to health on welfare states. Health systems have standard tools of regulation, financing, production of goods and services and income transfers (Barr 1998) but there are some nuances available within these broad buckets of instruments. Health expenditure can sharpen its focus on value, use technology to help ameliorate existing challenges and, finally, uptake low-cost interventions such as nudges (e.g. changes in choice architecture to encourage health-benefiting choices like exercise) where we have evidence that they can help.

8.4.1 Focus on Value for Health Systems

'Value' in health systems can have a number of definitions (Landon, Padikkala, and Horwitz 2021). It focuses on providing the right treatment at the right time and discouraging the use of clinically ineffective treatments. Money is thus spent on clinically appropriate services on the clinically appropriate population as opposed to services that are not useful and thus a financial waste and perhaps even harmful to patients. Specific policies have been aimed at these issues. For example, the UK Quality Outcomes Framework (QOF) encourages high-value care through incentives to primary care for performing specific evidence-based activities (Marshall and Roland 2017). The Choosing Wisely campaign, started in the US in 2012 (Wolfson, Santa, and Slass 2014) and now in over 20 countries (Born, Kool, and Levinson 2019), discourages low-value care by offering lists of such care by specialty as developed by specialist bodies.

Sometimes the term 'value for money' is used. This connects expenditure explicitly to the idea of value. 'Value for money' brings in notions of cost-effectiveness. Cost-effectiveness analysis (CEA) or other forms of economic evaluation such as cost–benefit or cost–utility analysis distinguish between alternative choices. Methods of economic evaluation are a toolset that can be used in the quest for value in health care. Other means are at policy makers' disposals, however, such as payment arrangements and demonstration models that test novel delivery and financing ideas.

8.4.1.1 Payer arrangements focused on value

Germany, the UK and the US have all undertaken value-based care models. The key behind these experiences is a focus on integration and payment that encourages coordination across care settings.

The UK recognizes gaps in coordinating care, achieving desired outcomes and meeting changing population health needs. The Five Year Forward View released in 2014 focused on care integration and outcomes-led health service delivery (Bains, Warriner, and Behrendt 2018). These efforts continued in 2019 with the NHS long-term plan, a 10-year plan to continue service improvement efforts in an environment of diminished funding growth, increasing health care needs and declining health system performance. Changes in payment models have accompanied integration efforts that include networks sharing in gains and losses and the encouragement of primary care networks (Collins 2019).

In the US, the Centers for Medicare and Medicaid Services (CMS) have introduced a number of models aimed at improving value for money in the Medicare and Medicaid programs. Value-based insurance design (VBID) is a broad term describing arrangements between providers and purchasers of care that incentivize both quality and reduced cost (Fendrick, Chernew, and Levi 2009). VBID is not specifically about value-based user charges (i.e. higher co-payment for a branded drug than a generic drug) (Thomson, Schang, and Chernew 2013). It moves beyond individual patient transactions into how the health system is organized and funded to provide quality care (i.e. timely and appropriate health service delivery to patients according to clinical evidence).

Accountable care organizations (ACOs) are integral to the Affordable Care Act (2010) and were built out of demonstration projects[2] by the CMS (McClellan et al. 2010). They vary in design (e.g. hospital vs physician-led) but share the goal of delivering quality improvements alongside of cost reductions and that providers and network members collaborate in caring for patients together (McClellan et al. 2010). They have a set pool of patients for which all providers are accountable and depending on the financial arrangements, they would share in savings or be penalized for costs associated with patient care.

ACOs in contracts with Medicare have met overall savings (i.e. care spend is lower than the CMS benchmark) (Trombley et al. 2019; McWilliams et al. 2016; McWilliams, Landon, and Chernew 2015; CMS 2020) even when considering risk selection (McWilliams et al. 2020) although the nonrandom exit of high-cost clinicians from ACOs appears to impact findings about savings (Markovitz et al. 2019). There is, however, heterogenous individual-level experience with savings amongst ACOs, which has been found to be depend on factors such as ACO characteristics (e.g. region and higher morbidity of populations; Gusland, Herbold, and Larson 2017). Medicaid ACOs have seen early success in improving care delivery and in some cases containing cost growth (Rutledge et al. 2019). However, costly interventions run by ACOs such as care management and coordination have not necessarily met either outcomes or costs goals as expected (Ouayogodé et al. 2019). There is still much work to do to understand what interventions provide value for money and for what populations of patients with needs.

Germany has been making efforts towards more integrated care since 2000 when the German Statutory Health Insurance Reform Act permitted insurers to offer greater integration with physician networks and health care management companies. In 2004, money could flow from insurers to physicians for integrated care (Milstein and Blankart 2016). The resulting models look a lot like what we see in the US now in the form of shared savings models and ACOs (Marill 2020). Evidence on cost and quality impacts is not routinely reported apart from specific research studies (Milstein and Blankart 2016), however, much existing evidence is positive. One such study on a program (Gesundes Kinzigtal in Baden-Württemberg) that targeted chronic disease, demonstrated cost savings on a per patient per year basis along with decreased mortality, improved cooperation amongst providers and fewer people changing insurers but increased hospital admissions with a decreased length of stay on those admissions (Busse and Stahl 2014).

Across these systems, we see a general acknowledgment of the value in coordinating care to improve population health. These efforts are also taking place in countries not discussed here such as the Netherlands (Tsiachristas et al. 2011). Evidence thus far suggests that greater care integration has positive effects on patient satisfaction, perceived care quality and access to care but the impact on costs is mixed according to an international systematic review (Baxter et al. 2018). Tests and experiments about the right interventions and for which populations, including risk segmentation, will help hone judicious expenditure in the search for value.

8.4.1.2 New models of care aimed at population health

One of the clear positive by-products of financing models that encourage integration and coordination of care is the ability for health care providers to focus on issues of local population importance. One that is relevant across all health systems is the role conditions in the place where someone was born, lives, learns and works impact their health. The social determinants of health (SDoH) are receiving more attention and investment than ever in the US by health care systems and payers (Horwitz et al. 2020; Murray, Rodriguez, and Lewis 2020). Part of this is due to the testing of new population health-focused models that allow for expenditures outside of traditional health care means. Identification of patients for services cannot be based only on SDoH factors but they can play a part under Medicare Advantage plans (CMS 2022). Medicare Advantage programs have started offering supplemental benefits for non-Medicare-covered items that are 'primarily health related' such as meal delivery, transport and at-home carpet cleaning (CMS 2019).

8.4.2   Harnessing the Role of Technology

While technology changes and the COVID-19 crisis have put and continue to put pressure on welfare states, they have also encouraged the use of tools to shape responses to present health challenges. Technology has the potential to offer significant gains in equity by making health care services available to patients who might otherwise be unable to access them due to geography- (rural), transport- or time-related constraints (e.g. hourly employees attending an appointment represents income lost). Telehealth provides a tremendous opportunity to extend care into larger population groups, including those less likely to access traditional health care or those for whom specialists are out of reach. Technology has also enabled more 'hospital at home' care and remote monitoring of chronic conditions. Alongside of some of these interventions are apps and programs for encouraging behavioral change that pair with clinical readings (e.g. HbA1c readings and then diet nudges).

The COVID-19 crisis provided a real-life test pilot of expanding telehealth availability. Importantly, such services can be billed for in the US under specific contexts (e.g. chronic care remote patient monitoring) and now acute conditions (e.g. COVID-19) (Congress 2020). While there are still many unknowns about remote patient monitoring including which patients would most benefit in every context, it offers a transformative care opportunity (Mecklai et al.

2021). Increasingly, evidence generation specifies the cost-effectiveness for services based on disease classification. For example, usual care along with tele-monitoring was found to be cost-effective for chronic heart failure patients with New York Heart Association (NYHA) class II to IV but not for the entire population of class I to IV in a modeling study for a US sample (Jiang, Yao, and You 2020).

The UK is relying heavily on technology to improve primary care access for specific populations such as the frail and to target interventions to those most in need (Alderwick and Dixon 2019). With challenges in health care staffing across the US and Europe, particularly related to nursing and rural health care in general, technology can help in some cases. For example, a qualitative study of telehealth consultations for nursing home residents in rural areas of Germany demonstrated its acceptability and ability to support the lack of specialists in these regions (May et al. 2021).

Virtual visits relative to in-person primary care visits have been found to be preferred by those who might face distance and parking cost barriers with in-person visits in northern California (Reed et al. 2020). Reliable internet access is also necessary though and this cannot be assumed. Lack of internet is related to rurality; therefore, virtual visits are not necessarily even an option for all. Across a number of specialties such as pediatrics (Shah and Badawy 2021), obstetrics and gynecology (DeNicola et al. 2020), and otolaryngology (Gupta, Gkiousias, and Bhutta 2021), virtual visits exhibit promise when used in the appropriate populations. Focusing how to use them in overcoming transportation barriers is a key next step. Using technology to support and engage patients offers great promise but without explicit consideration of barriers, constraints such as poor internet access and lack of technology in the very populations who could benefit most may undermine goals to improve access and equitable delivery of services.

8.4.3 Low-cost/Costless Interventions such as Nudges

One of the common threads amongst key health challenges facing populations today is the role of health behaviors and prevention. Behavioral economics, or how insights from economics and psychology can help us better understand, predict and encourage decision-making under uncertainty provides some help here. A key tool from this literature is the 'nudge'. Nudges present a suite of options that preserve choice but steer people in the optimal direction for their own interest (Thaler and Sunstein 2021). Nudges are attractive in public policy because of their liberty-maintaining and costless nature (Thaler and Sunstein 2021). Framing an informational flyer or setting a different default in a benefit registration system poses no incremental cost. Behavioral economics has been part of public policy discourse in over 20 countries including the US, the UK,

Germany, the Netherlands and international organizations (World Bank and the United Nations) (Halpern and Sanders 2016).

A meta-analysis of different types of nudges found that of all the intervention types (decision information, structure and assistance), those that focus on the structure of choices are most effective. Of all the behavioral domains tested (health, food, environment, finance, pro-social and other), food was the domain where nudging had most effect. Therefore, food choice is a behavioral domain where a nudge that supports decision structure (e.g. changing choice default) is more likely to be successful than other types of nudges (Mertens et al. 2022).

Nudges have been found to be effective for some of the population health challenges facing policy makers. These include antibiotic prescribing, exercise and initiatives in substance abuse for opioid users. For antibiotic prescribing, a global concern because of antibiotic resistance, many countries (e.g. Australia, the UK, the US) have used nudges and peer feedback to encourage clinically appropriate prescribing. Nudges have increased the opening of reports about prescribing feedback in Ontario, Canada (Daneman et al. 2022). Precommitment letters where providers agree to publicly post letters committing to appropriate antibiotic prescribing resulted in lower rates of inappropriate antibiotic prescribing in five clinics in Los Angeles, California (Meeker et al. 2014). Generally, nudges that include precommitment letters, peer feedback, particularly when it comes from key health system leaders (Hallsworth et al. 2016) and justification alerts (where clinicians must include a reason for prescribing) have been found to reduce inappropriate antibiotic prescribing (Richards and Linder 2021). Moreover, changes can be dramatic, especially when considered at scale and with the low costs associated (Richards and Linder 2021).

Nudges look different for exercise as they focus on the formation and maintenance of new habits. The timing profile of exercise benefits is challenging for policy since the costs (and opportunity costs) of exercise happen today and benefits occur in the future (Leonard and Shuval 2017). Present time bias (focusing on today rather than tomorrow) and status quo bias (not wanting to change behaviors because it is easier to just keep doing what we have been doing) need consideration in using nudges and other tools of behavioral economics to promote exercise (Shuval et al. 2017). Individual-level targeting may not be as beneficial as framing physical activity for society generally and changing the environment and culture to affect norms (Zimmerman 2009). This argument is much like what has been seen with smoking bans changing social norms about smoking. Commitment devices (i.e. voluntary agreement to undertake a behavior with consequences for not sticking to the goal; Rogers, Milkman, and Volpp 2014) have also been found to help people reach exercise goals (Bhattacharya, Garber, and Goldhaber-Fiebert 2015).

Finally, substance misuse, particularly for opioids, may also benefit from nudges. On the patient side nudges, alongside of a risk management education program, more than education alone have been found to encourage the disposal of extra opioids prescribed from an acute health event (Voepel-Lewis et al. 2020). For prescribers, letters to highlight prescribing levels and size have helped decrease initial opioid prescription size (Ahomäki et al. 2020).

8.5 CONCLUDING REMARKS

In the current setting of health care challenges from population and disease trends and financial pressures on government expenditure, the public sector has to consider strategies to improve allocative efficiency and society's health and wellbeing. Payer arrangements can alter how money moves around health systems in efforts to seek value and new models of care and financing can directly tackle population health challenges. Population health dynamics such as ageing, related multimorbidity and behavioral health needs require re-visiting traditional approaches to delivery and financing. Technology appears to offer promising answers to fundamental issues of geographic and SDoH-related disparities facing health systems. And finally, nudges are low or no cost but maintain individual choice and offer answers for food and other choice settings where prior commitment can benefit outcomes.

While demands on health policy makers' budgets are strenuous and likely growing due to population health challenges, promising strategies set forth here can be examined for appropriate local application and assist in ameliorating these needs. The list of tools discussed here is not exhaustive and only delves minimally into their potential applications and supporting body of knowledge. Additional policy experience and experimentation will generate greater evidence about what works, in which contexts and for whom. With dissemination of these successes and failures, we can further refine applicability and the promise of these tools to help society when handling our current and future health challenges.

NOTES

1. There are rich discussions about the welfare state encompassing more than just public expenditure. Society's welfare is dependent on many parameters including public and private sector wages and volunteer work, however, we focus on the role of the public sector in this chapter (Barr 1998).
2. Demonstration projects are where CMS tests a policy idea amongst a set of stakeholders who evaluate results to feedback for policy development.

REFERENCES

Ahomäki, I., V. Pitkänen, A. Soppi, and L. Saastamoinen. 2020. Impact of a physician-targeted letter on opioid prescribing. *Journal of Health Economics* 72: 102344. https://doi.org/10.1016/j.jhealeco.2020.102344.

Alderwick, Hugh, and Jennifer Dixon. 2019. The NHS long-term plan. *BMJ* 364: l84. https://doi.org/10.1136/bmj.l84. https://www.bmj.com/content/bmj/364/bmj.l84.full.pdf.

America's Health Rankings: Annual Report 2021. 2021. United Health Foundation. https://assets.americashealthrankings.org/app/uploads/americashealthrankings-2021annualreport.pdf.

Bains, Manpreet, David Warriner, and Katja Behrendt. 2018. Primary and secondary care integration in delivery of value-based health-care systems. *British Journal of Hospital Medicine* 79 (6): 312–315. https://doi.org/10.12968/hmed.2018.79.6.312. https://doi.org/10.12968/hmed.2018.79.6.312.

Barr, Nicholas. 1998. *The Economics of the Welfare State* (3rd edn). Oxford: Oxford University Press.

Baxter, S., M. Johnson, D. Chambers, A. Sutton, E. Goyder, and A. Booth. 2018. The effects of integrated care: a systematic review of UK and international evidence. *BMC Health Services Research* 18 (1): 350. https://doi.org/10.1186/s12913-018-3161-3.

Bertoni, Marco, Martina Celidoni, Chiara Dal Bianco, and Guglielmo Weber. 2021. How did European retirees respond to the COVID-19 pandemic? *Economics Letters* 203: 109853. https://doi.org/https://doi.org/10.1016/j.econlet.2021.109853. https://www.sciencedirect.com/science/article/pii/S0165176521001300.

Bhattacharya, Jay, Alan M. Garber, and Jeremy D. Goldhaber-Fiebert. 2015. *Nudges in Exercise Commitment Contracts: A Randomized Trial.* National Bureau of Economic Research.

Blümel, M., A. Spranger, K. Achstetter, A. Maresso, and R. Busse. 2020. Germany: Health System Review. *Health Systems in Transition* 22 (6): 1–272.

Born, Karen, Tijn Kool, and Wendy Levinson. 2019. Reducing overuse in healthcare: advancing Choosing Wisely. *BMJ* 367: l6317. https://doi.org/10.1136/bmj.l6317. https://www.bmj.com/content/bmj/367/bmj.l6317.full.pdf.

Busse, Reinhard, and Juliane Stahl. 2014. Integrated care experiences and outcomes in Germany, the Netherlands, and England. *Health Affairs* 33 (9): 1549–1558. https://doi.org/10.1377/hlthaff.2014.0419. https://doi.org/10.1377/hlthaff.2014.0419.

Cawley, J., A. M. Thow, K. Wen, and D. Frisvold. 2019. The economics of taxes on sugar-sweetened beverages: a review of the effects on prices, sales, cross-border shopping, and consumption. *Annual Review of Nutrition* 39: 317–338. https://doi.org/10.1146/annurev-nutr-082018-124603.

Chaloupka, Frank J., Lisa M. Powell, and Kenneth E. Warner. 2019. The use of excise taxes to reduce tobacco, alcohol, and sugary beverage consumption. *Annual Review of Public Health* 40 (1): 187–201. https://doi.org/10.1146/annurev-publhealth-040218-043816. https://doi.org/10.1146/annurev-publhealth-040218-043816.

CMS. 2019. *Announcement of Calendar Year (CY) 2020 Medicare Advantage Capitation Rates and Medicare Advantage and Part D Payment Policies and Final Call Letter.* Centers for Medicare & Medicaid Services.

CMS. 2020. *Shared Savings Program Fast Facts – As of January 1, 2020.*

CMS. 2022. *Value-Based Insurance Design (VBID) Model's Health Equity Incubation Program*. Center for Medicare & Medicaid Innovation: Centers for Medicare & Medicaid Services.

Collins, B. 2019. *Payments and Contracting for Integrated Care: The False Promise of the Self-Improving Health System.* The King's Fund. https://www.kingsfund.org.uk/publications/payments-contracting-integrated-care.

Congress, US. 2020. *HR 6074: Coronavirus Preparedness and Response Supplemental Appropriations Act, 2020*.

Daneman, N., S. Lee, H. Bai, C. M. Bell, S. E. Bronskill, M. A. Campitelli, G. Dobell, L. Fu, G. Garber, N. Ivers, M. Kumar, J. M. C. Lam, B. Langford, C. Laur, A. M. Morris, C. L. Mulhall, R. Pinto, F. E. Saxena, K. L. Schwartz, and K. A. Brown. 2022. Behavioral nudges to improve audit and feedback report opening among antibiotic prescribers: a randomized controlled trial. *Open Forum Infectious Diseases* 9 (5): ofac111. https://doi.org/10.1093/ofid/ofac111.

DeNicola, N., D. Grossman, K. Marko, S. Sonalkar, Y. S. Butler Tobah, N. Ganju, C. T. Witkop, J. T. Henderson, J. L. Butler, and C. Lowery. 2020. Telehealth interventions to improve obstetric and gynecologic health outcomes: a systematic review. *Journal of Obstetrics and Gynaecology* 135 (2): 371–382. https://doi.org/10.1097/aog.0000000000003646.

Fendrick, A. M., M. E. Chernew, and G. W. Levi. 2009. Value-based insurance design: embracing value over cost alone. *American Journal of Managed Care* 15 (10 Suppl): S277–S283.

Fichera, E., T. Mora, B. G. Lopez-Valcarcel, and D. Roche. 2021. How do consumers respond to 'sin taxes'? New evidence from a tax on sugary drinks. *Social Science and Medicine* 274: 113799. https://doi.org/10.1016/j.socscimed.2021.113799.

Gupta, T., V. Gkiousias, and M. F. Bhutta. 2021. A systematic review of outcomes of remote consultation in ENT. *Clinical Otolaryngology* 46 (4): 699–719. https://doi.org/10.1111/coa.13768.

Gusland, C., J. S. Herbold, and A. Larson. 2017. What predictive analytics can tell us about key drivers of MSSP results. Accessed September 28, 2020. https://ae.milliman.com/nl-NL/insight/what-predictive-analytics-can-tell-us-about-key-drivers-of-mssp-results.

Hallsworth, Michael, Tim Chadborn, Anna Sallis, Michael Sanders, Daniel Berry, Felix Greaves, Lara Clements, and Sally C. Davies. 2016. Provision of social norm feedback to high prescribers of antibiotics in general practice: a pragmatic national randomised controlled trial. *The Lancet* 387 (10029): 1743–1752. https://doi.org/https://doi.org/10.1016/S0140-6736(16)00215-4. https://www.sciencedirect.com/science/article/pii/S0140673616002154.

Halpern, David, and Michael Sanders. 2016. Nudging by government: progress, impact, and lessons learned. *Behavioral Science & Policy* 2 (2): 52–65.

Horwitz, Leora I., Carol Chang, Harmony N. Arcilla, and James R. Knickman. 2020. Quantifying health systems' investment in social determinants of health, by sector, 2017–19. *Health Affairs* 39 (2): 192–198. https://doi.org/10.1377/hlthaff.2019.01246. https://doi.org/10.1377/hlthaff.2019.01246.

Jiang, X., J. Yao, and J. H. You. 2020. Telemonitoring versus usual care for elderly patients with heart failure discharged from the hospital in the United States: cost-effectiveness analysis. *JMIR mHealth and uHealth* 8 (7): e17846. https://doi.org/10.2196/17846.

Keisler-Starkey, K., and L. N. Bunch. 2021. *Health Insurance Coverage in the United States: 2020.* U.S. Government Publishing Office, Washington, DC. https://www.census.gov/content/dam/Census/library/publications/2021/demo/p60-274.pdf.

Landon, S. N., J. Padikkala, and L. I. Horwitz. 2021. Defining value in health care: a scoping review of the literature. *International Journal for Quality in Health Care* 33 (4): mzab140. https://doi.org/10.1093/intqhc/mzab140.

Leonard, Tammy, and Kerem Shuval. 2017. Behavioral economics: tools for promotion of physical activity. In Y. Hanoch, A. J. Barnes, and T. Rice (eds.), *Behavioral Economics and Healthy Behaviors: Key Concepts and Current Research.* Abingdon: Routledge, pp. 70–89.

Mackenbach, Johan P., Marina Karanikolos, and Martin McKee. 2013. The unequal health of Europeans: successes and failures of policies. *The Lancet* 381 (9872): 1125–1134. https://doi.org/https://doi.org/10.1016/S0140-6736(12)62082-0. https://www.sciencedirect.com/science/article/pii/S0140673612620820.

Marill, M. C. 2020. From rural Germany, integrated care grows into a global model. *Health Affairs* 39 (8): 1282–1288. https://doi.org/10.1377/hlthaff.2020.01063. https://www.healthaffairs.org/doi/abs/10.1377/hlthaff.2020.01063.

Markovitz, A. A., J. M. Hollingsworth, J. Z. Ayanian, E. C. Norton, P. L. Yan, and A. M. Ryan. 2019. Performance in the Medicare Shared Savings Program after accounting for nonrandom exit: an instrumental variable analysis. *Annals of Internal Medicine* 171 (1): 27–36. https://doi.org/10.7326/M18-2539. https://www.ncbi.nlm.nih.gov/pubmed/31207609.

Marshall, Martin, and Martin Roland. 2017. The future of the Quality and Outcomes Framework in England. *BMJ* 359: j4681. https://doi.org/10.1136/bmj.j4681. https://www.bmj.com/content/bmj/359/bmj.j4681.full.pdf.

May, Susann, Kai Jonas, Georgia V. Fehler, Thomas Zahn, Martin Heinze, and Felix Muehlensiepen. 2021. Challenges in current nursing home care in rural Germany and how they can be reduced by telehealth: an exploratory qualitative pre-post study. *BMC Health Services Research* 21 (1): 925. https://doi.org/10.1186/s12913-021-06950-y. https://doi.org/10.1186/s12913-021-06950-y.

McClellan, Mark, Aaron N. McKethan, Julie L. Lewis, Joachim Roski, and Elliott S. Fisher. 2010. A national strategy to put accountable care into practice. *Health Affairs* 29 (5): 982–990. https://doi.org/10.1377/hlthaff.2010.0194. https://doi.org/10.1377/hlthaff.2010.0194.

McKee, Martin, Karen Dunnell, Michael Anderson, Carol Brayne, Anita Charlesworth, Charlotte Johnston-Webber, Martin Knapp, Alistair McGuire, John N. Newton, David Taylor, and Richard G. Watt. 2021. The changing health needs of the UK population. *The Lancet* 397 (10288): 1979–1991. https://doi.org/https://doi.org/10.1016/S0140-6736(21)00229-4. https://www.sciencedirect.com/science/article/pii/S0140673621002294.

McWilliams, J. M., B. E. Landon, and M. E. Chernew. 2015. Performance in year 1 of pioneer Accountable Care Organizations. *New England Journal of Medicine* 373 (8): 777. https://doi.org/10.1056/NEJMc1507320. https://www.ncbi.nlm.nih.gov/pubmed/26287859.

McWilliams, J. M., L. A. Hatfield, M. E. Chernew, B. E. Landon, and A. L. Schwartz. 2016. Early performance of Accountable Care Organizations in Medicare. *New England Journal of Medicine* 374 (24): 2357–2366. https://doi.org/10.1056/NEJMsa1600142. https://www.ncbi.nlm.nih.gov/pubmed/27075832.

McWilliams, J.M., L. A. Hatfield, B. E. Landon, and M. E. Chernew. 2020. Savings or selection? Initial spending reductions in the Medicare Shared Savings Program and considerations for reform. *Milbank Quarterly* 98 (3): 847–907. https://doi.org/10.1111/1468-0009.12468.

Mecklai, Keizra, Nicholas Smith, Ariel D. Stern, and Daniel B. Kramer. 2021. Remote patient monitoring: overdue or overused? *New England Journal of Medicine* 384 (15): 1384–1386. https://doi.org/10.1056/NEJMp2033275. https://www.nejm.org/doi/full/10.1056/NEJMp2033275.

Meeker, Daniella, Tara K. Knight, Mark W. Friedberg, Jeffrey A. Linder, Noah J. Goldstein, Craig R. Fox, Alan Rothfeld, Guillermo Diaz, and Jason N. Doctor. 2014. Nudging guideline-concordant antibiotic prescribing: a randomized clinical trial. *JAMA Internal Medicine* 174 (3): 425–431. https://doi.org/10.1001/jamainternmed.2013.14191. https://doi.org/10.1001/jamainternmed.2013.14191.

Mertens, S., M. Herberz, U. J. J. Hahnel, and T. Brosch. 2022. The effectiveness of nudging: a meta-analysis of choice architecture interventions across behavioral domains. *Proceedings of the National Academy of Sciences of the United States of America* 119 (1): e2107346118. https://doi.org/10.1073/pnas.2107346118.

Milstein, R., and C. R. Blankart. 2016. The Health Care Strengthening Act: the next level of integrated care in Germany. *Health Policy* 120 (5): 445–451. https://doi.org/10.1016/j.healthpol.2016.04.006.

Murray, Genevra F., Hector P. Rodriguez, and Valerie A. Lewis. 2020. Upstream with a small paddle: how ACOs are working against the current to meet patients' social needs. *Health Affairs* 39 (2): 199–206. https://doi.org/10.1377/hlthaff.2019.01266. https://doi.org/10.1377/hlthaff.2019.01266.

National Academies of Sciences, Engineering, and Medicine. 2020. *Social Isolation and Loneliness in Older Adults: Opportunities for the Health Care System*. Washington, DC: The National Academies Press.

OECD. 2019. *Social Expenditure Database (SOCX)*.

OECD. 2021. Health expenditure. In *Health at a Glance 2021: OECD Indicators*.

Ouayogodé, M. H., A. J. Mainor, E. Meara, J. P. W. Bynum, and C. H. Colla. 2019. Association between care management and outcomes among patients with complex needs in Medicare Accountable Care Organizations. *JAMA Network Open* 2 (7): e196939. https://doi.org/10.1001/jamanetworkopen.2019.6939.

Papanicolas, Irene, Elias Mossialos, Anders Gundersen, Liana Woskie, and Ashish K. Jha. 2019. Performance of UK National Health Service compared with other high income countries: observational study. *BMJ* 367: l6326. https://doi.org/10.1136/bmj.l6326. https://www.bmj.com/content/bmj/367/bmj.l6326.full.pdf.

Powell, L. M., J. F. Chriqui, T. Khan, R. Wada, and F. J. Chaloupka. 2013. Assessing the potential effectiveness of food and beverage taxes and subsidies for improving public health: a systematic review of prices, demand and body weight outcomes. *Obesity Reviews* 14 (2): 110–128. https://doi.org/10.1111/obr.12002.

Reed, M. E., J. Huang, I. Graetz, C. Lee, E. Muelly, C. Kennedy, and E. Kim. 2020. Patient characteristics associated with choosing a telemedicine visit vs office visit with the same primary care clinicians. *JAMA Network Open* 3 (6): e205873. https://doi.org/10.1001/jamanetworkopen.2020.5873.

Richards, Alexandra R., and Jeffrey A. Linder. 2021. Behavioral economics and ambulatory antibiotic stewardship: a narrative review. *Clinical Therapeutics* 43 (10): 1654–1667. https://doi.org/https://doi.org/10.1016/j.clinthera.2021.08.004. https://www.sciencedirect.com/science/article/pii/S0149291821003015.

Rogers, T., K. L. Milkman, and K. G. Volpp. 2014. Commitment devices: using initiatives to change behavior. *JAMA* 311 (20): 2065–2066. https://doi.org/10.1001/jama.2014.3485.

Rutledge, R. I., M. A. Romaire, C. L. Hersey, W. J. Parish, S. M. Kissam, and J. T. Lloyd. 2019. Medicaid Accountable Care Organizations in four states: implementation and early impacts. *Milbank Quarterly* 97 (2): 583–619. https://doi.org/10.1111/1468-0009.12386.

Shah, A. C., and S. M. Badawy. 2021. Telemedicine in pediatrics: systematic review of randomized controlled trials. *JMIR Pediatrics and Parenting* 4 (1): e22696. https://doi.org/10.2196/22696.

Shankar, A., M. Hamer, A. McMunn, and A. Steptoe. 2013. Social isolation and loneliness: relationships with cognitive function during 4 years of follow-up in the English Longitudinal Study of Ageing. *Psychosomatic Medicine* 75 (2): 161–170. https://doi.org/10.1097/PSY.0b013e31827f09cd.

Shuval, Kerem, Tammy Leonard, Jeffrey Drope, David L. Katz, Alpa V. Patel, Melissa Maitin-Shepard, On Amir, and Amir Grinstein. 2017. Physical activity counseling in primary care: insights from public health and behavioral economics. *CA: A Cancer Journal for Clinicians* 67 (3): 233–244.

Thaler, R., and C. Sunstein. 2021. *Nudge: The Final Edition*. New York: Penguin Books.

Thomson, Sarah, Laura Schang, and Michael E. Chernew. 2013. Value-based cost sharing in the United States and elsewhere can increase patients' use of high-value goods and services. *Health Affairs* 32 (4): 704–712. https://doi.org/10.1377/hlthaff.2012.0964. https://doi.org/10.1377/hlthaff.2012.0964.

Trombley, M. J., B. Fout, S. Brodsky, J. M. McWilliams, D. J. Nyweide, and B. Morefield. 2019. Early effects of an Accountable Care Organization model for underserved areas. *New England Journal of Medicine* 381 (6): 543–551. https://doi.org/10.1056/NEJMsa1816660. https://www.ncbi.nlm.nih.gov/pubmed/31291511.

Tsiachristas, Apostolos, Bethany Hipple-Walters, Karin M. M. Lemmens, Anna P. Nieboer, and Maureen P. M. H. Rutten-van Mölken. 2011. Towards integrated care for chronic conditions: Dutch policy developments to overcome the (financial) barriers. *Health Policy* 101 (2): 122–132.

Voepel-Lewis, T., F. A. Farley, J. Grant, A. R. Tait, C. J. Boyd, S. E. McCabe, M. Weber, C. M. Harbagh, and B. J. Zikmund-Fisher. 2020. Behavioral intervention and disposal of leftover opioids: a randomized trial. *Pediatrics* 145 (1): e20191431. https://doi.org/10.1542/peds.2019-1431.

Wolfson, D., J. Santa, and L. Slass. 2014. Engaging physicians and consumers in conversations about treatment overuse and waste: a short history of the Choosing Wisely campaign. *Academic Medicine* 89 (7): 990–995. https://doi.org/10.1097/acm.0000000000000270.

Zimmerman, Frederick J. 2009. Using behavioral economics to promote physical activity. *Preventive Medicine* 49 (4): 289–291. https://doi.org/https://doi.org/10.1016/j.ypmed.2009.07.008. https://www.sciencedirect.com/science/article/pii/S0091743509003417.

9. Welfare states, growth regimes, and the emergence of the knowledge economy: social policy in turbulent times

Julian L. Garritzmann and Bruno Palier

9.1 INTRODUCTION

Karl Polanyi (1944) famously recognized the emergence of market economies, connected with industrialization and the rise of nation states, as the "Great Transformation" of the 19th and early 20th century, shattering societies and politico-economic systems. The "Great Transformation" of our time is the shift from industrial to post-industrial knowledge economies, centered around human skills and capabilities. Just like its 19th-century predecessor, this Great Transformation has far-reaching economic, social, and political consequences. In the words of this book, the emergence of the knowledge economy triggers "turbulent times."

The knowledge economy can be defined as a socio-economic system placing "a greater reliance on intellectual capabilities than on physical inputs or natural resources, combined with efforts to integrate improvements in every stage of the production process" (Powell & Snellman 2004: 201). More concretely, this materializes in several big co-trends: massive educational expansion – particularly in upper-secondary and higher education (Garritzmann et al. 2022c), systematic labor market changes (implying both sectoral and occupational shifts) (Oesch 2013), new types of production and capitalist organization and relatedly new skill needs by employers particularly for high-skilled labor (Durazzi 2019) but also a substantial low-skill service sector, an increased focus on technology resulting in skill-biased and task-biased technological change (Autor et al. 2003), and – as a consequence of these co-trends – new types of social risks (Bonoli 2007). While the emergence of the knowledge economy is most visible in the rich capitalist democracies of Western Europe, the Baltics, North America, and North-East Asia, it is essentially a global phenomenon and spreading to countries on all continents, even if to different degrees and at different points in time.

These transformations towards knowledge economies challenge welfare states around the globe. The main reason why this is so is that most welfare states were founded and shaped in the 19th century during the era of industrialization and tailored to the risks and socio-economic needs of the industrial economy, especially of male industrial workers. Consequently, the mature welfare states in (Western) Europe (Esping-Andersen 1990; Huber & Stephens 2001) as well as in the Americas (Segura-Ubiergo 2007) and in the productivist Asian welfare states (Holliday 2000; Kim 2016) have been until the present day shaped and influenced by these legacies. Against this background, social policy scholars and policy-makers have started to realize from the late 1990s and increasingly throughout the 2000s and 2010s that the established traditional welfare states focused merely on compensatory benefits for (largely male) industrial workers might be increasingly unfit to meet the demands and challenges of the post-industrial knowledge economy and that welfare readjustments are necessary (Esping-Andersen et al. 2002; Bonoli 2007; Morel et al. 2012; Hemerijck 2012).

In this chapter, we trace these challenges and welfare responses in "turbulent times" (Greve, Chapter 1, this book).[1] First, using empirical data covering 100+ economies around the globe over the last century we identify two "mega-trends" connected to the emergence of the knowledge economy: educational expansion, on the one hand, and skill-biased labor market change, on the other. Second, we explain how these co-evolutive mega-trends challenge welfare states; more specifically, we argue that these global trends challenge different welfare regimes differently, pointing at differences in countries' growth and welfare regimes. That is, we argue that while the emergence of the knowledge economy challenges all welfare states, the concrete challenges differ quite substantially depending on the type of preexisting welfare legacies and growth regimes. Third, we sketch four potential welfare reform scenarios to these challenges, including social investments, basic income, social protectionism, or market liberalism.

9.2 TWO MEGA-TRENDS: EDUCATIONAL EXPANSION AND LABOR MARKET CHANGES

The "knowledge economy" has become a buzzword in scholarly and public debates alike. But to what degree can countries around the globe really be characterized as knowledge economies? In order to address this question, we start with some empirical evidence, tracing two key features of the knowledge economy across countries and over time. On the one hand, we look at the *supply* of skills in the economy by exploring how enrollment in education has changed over time. Here, we identify a massive educational expansion over the last 150 years taking place in many countries worldwide. On the other hand, we investigate the *demand* for skills in the economy by taking an empirical look at labor markets, studying patterns of sectoral and occupational change with a particular focus on skills. In a nutshell, we will show that both demand and supply of skills have increased substantially – but that there is considerable variation across countries in the degree of changes and accordingly the degree to which these countries can be classified as knowledge economies.

9.2.1 Education Expansion Around the Globe

We start with the *supply* side, focusing on educational expansion. The three plots in Figure 9.1 show the enrollment rates in primary, secondary, and tertiary education, respectively, i.e., the number of students in the respective education level divided by the size of the population that could be enrolled at that age at that level in a given country. The data stems from Lee and Lee (2016), an updated version of the Barro–Lee dataset on educational enrollment,[2] and covers 110 countries on all continents from 1870 until 2010. We group the countries in eight country clusters – for the rationale for and details of the composition of the clusters, see Garritzmann et al. (2022c). The group-averages in Figure 9.1 are weighted by the respective countries' population sizes in order to achieve a more representative picture.

Figure 9.1 reveals a number of interesting observations. First of all, and most importantly, we see a strong expansion trend that is visible in all education levels and all country groups. Across the globe, more and more children are participating in education and stay in education for ever longer periods of time. Obviously, this is a key indication that countries around the globe are moving towards knowledge-based economies.

A closer look reveals, second, that this educational expansion has subsequently spread from primary education to secondary and finally tertiary education. Primary education had been expanded already in the 19th century in many countries (Ansell & Lindvall 2021), reaching quasi-universal enrollment rates in most richer economies already by 1930 and in others later during the post-war decades. Enrollment rates in secondary education have expanded much later – this is rather a post-World War II phenomenon, as enrollment rates in secondary education were below 20 percent in almost all countries until 1950. From the 1950s to 1970s, however, secondary education was strongly expanded, reaching quasi-universal enrollment rates in most countries in the 1990s with the exception of sub-Saharan Africa. The third – and so far final – step in this process is the expansion of tertiary education, which has started to unfold since the 1970s. It deserves highlighting, though, that this process is currently still ongoing – in most countries tertiary education rates are still below 60 percent, often even below 40 percent. The most common degree is still secondary education, and we only currently witness the "tertiari-

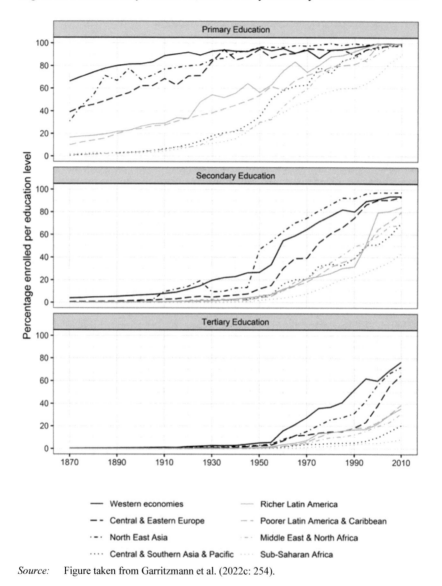

Source: Figure taken from Garritzmann et al. (2022c: 254).

Figure 9.1   Enrollment rates in primary, secondary, and tertiary education (regional averages are weighted by country-population size)

zation" of education. In this sense, the knowledge economy is coming, but still not fully materialized.

Third, we can investigate country differences. What we notice is that although educational expansion is happening across the globe, the degree and timing of this expansion is quite uneven across world regions. Figure 9.1 shows that the "Western" economies, as well as Central and Eastern Europe and North-East Asia have been pioneers in the expansion of education, outpacing the rest of the world by around 60 years in the expansion of primary education, and around 30 years in secondary and tertiary education. From a global perspective, the educational expansion happens the slowest in Africa, particularly sub-Saharan Africa. That is, while the knowledge economy is spreading everywhere, it has done so to different degrees and at different points in time.

In sum, we witness a global, but uneven, spread of the knowledge economy in terms of the *supply* of skills.

9.2.2 Labor Market Change

To cut a long story short, a similar conclusion can be drawn for *demand* for skills: we also see a global but uneven change in labor markets, as these increasingly become reliant on high skills. To start with, this can be seen when looking at data for *sectoral* change (not displayed here for reasons of space). Usually, we distinguish three broader economic sectors: the primary (agriculture and resources), secondary (industry, manufacturing, construction), and tertiary (service) sectors. Industrialization has shifted employment from the primary to the secondary sector and required different and higher skill levels. Subsequently, the ongoing de-industrialization has shifted economic activity from the secondary to the tertiary service economy, where a great part of services requires higher skill levels (what Wren [2013] calls dynamic services required in ICT sectors). To reiterate, not all service jobs are high-skilled jobs, but generally speaking the skill demands of the service economy are higher than those of the industrial economy (but see the discussion below). The large sectoral changes were thus structurally connected to an increasing reliance on and economic demand for skills.

This becomes even clearer when zooming in on *occupational* change. Economists and sociologists focusing on labor markets usually distinguish three broad types of occupations with regard to the required skill levels: "routine" jobs are characterized by repetitive tasks that require medium-level (often vocational) skills; "non-routine manual" jobs (e.g., personal services, delivery, etc.) often require only low skills; and "non-routine cognitive" jobs, finally, have the highest skill demands. The latter can thus be used as one indicator of the spread of the knowledge economy, as an increasingly high share of non-routine cognitive workers would be an indication of an economy that places a lot of emphasis on high skills. Obviously, these categorizations have to remain somewhat rough and focus on "average skill levels," brushing over some substantial variation within the different categories. Yet, the argument goes (and empirics confirm) that these classifications are a sufficient approximation to empirical reality.

Unfortunately, it is rather difficult to get hold of high-quality data for many countries over time here. Accordingly, Figure 9.2 focuses on the richer "Western" democracies where high-quality data on occupational change is available. We distinguish eight country groups (again see Garritzmann et al. 2022c for details) and show data covering these countries over almost three decades (1991–2019). The left side of Figure 9.2 shows the share of the respective task groups over time, while the right side of the figure shows the same data but focuses on the differences between the start and end of the time series to highlight the major change that has happened over this period.

We highlight two takeaways. On the one hand, we see the same pattern in all country groups: Over time, there is a decrease in jobs characterized by "routine" tasks, while there is an increase in jobs characterized by "non-routine cognitive" tasks, but also some increase (at least in many countries) of "non-routine manual" jobs. The literature describes this phenomenon as "polarized upgrading" (Spitz-Oener 2006) as there is an increased reliance on higher skills ("upgrading"), but simultaneously also an increase of employment in low-skilled jobs and a decline of middle-skilled, routine-based jobs. This is a common pattern, at least across the richer democracies (as mentioned, other data is harder to get hold of). In this sense, the knowledge economy is spreading, but it is not "the only game in town" as simultaneously the low-skill sector is growing as well.

On the other hand, we also find some interesting variation across country groups, as this common trend is not uniform across contexts. Figure 9.2 shows, for example, that the share of people working in high-skill-reliant "non-routine cognitive" jobs is the largest group in the Anglo-Saxon countries, in Nordic and Continental Europe as well as in the Baltics. In contrast their shares are much lower in Southern Europe, the Visegrád countries, and in North-East Asia – while the trend is similar in these countries as well, the levels are still much lower as many people are still employed in jobs with "routine" tasks and there remains a lot of informal work, especially by women in households. Thus, while the knowledge economy is spreading, it is doing so quite unevenly.

Again, we can thus take away that while there is a common global trend towards the use of high skills (which we have shown empirically here only for the richer democracies), there is substantial variation across countries in the degree and timing of these changes. Thus, while all countries seem to develop towards knowledge economies, they have done so to different degrees and at different points in time.

Welfare states, growth regimes, and the emergence of the knowledge economy 133

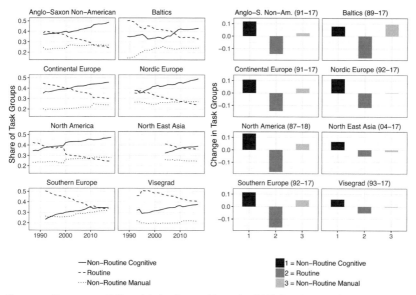

Note: Data source: ILO modeled estimates, November 2019 (Employment by sex and occupation [thousands], annual).
Source: Figure taken from Garritzmann et al. (2022c: 266).

Figure 9.2   Occupational change across countries

9.3 WHY THE EMERGENCE OF KNOWLEDGE ECONOMIES CHALLENGES DIFFERENT WELFARE STATES DIFFERENTLY: THE ROLE OF WELFARE LEGACIES AND GROWTH MODELS

We have seen in the previous section that (1) the knowledge economy is spreading, but (2) unevenly so across different contexts. In what is next, we argue that as a consequence these global trends challenge different welfare regimes differently, pointing towards differences in countries' preexisting welfare regimes and growth regimes. Generally speaking, we argue – in line with historical institutionalism – that policy-making always happens in specific contexts and we need to take these contexts seriously in order to understand the respective political dynamics. More specifically, we argue that (at least) two types of contexts are important in order to understand how and why the emergence of the knowledge economy challenges policy-makers in different contexts differently: welfare legacies and growth regimes.

On the one hand, we argue that the type of preexisting welfare state plays a key role. While it is impossible to mark a concrete date as the starting point of the knowledge economy, scholars agree that knowledge and skills have become increasingly important over the course of the 20th century, particularly since the 1990s and 2000s (Hall 2021), related to the increasing tertiarization of education, the high-skill reliance on labor markets, as well as skill-biased and task-biased technological change. As is well known, the historical origins of most welfare states (in Europe, North-East Asia, and the Americas), however, date back to the (late) 19th century. When we talk about "preexisting" welfare regimes, we have in mind the welfare states that were existing for decades already in the 1990s and 2000s. We argue below that, and why, the type of welfare state plays an important role for the respective challenges arising from the emergence of the knowledge economy.

On the other hand, building on a newer literature on "growth models" (Baccaro & Pontusson 2016) and "growth regimes" (Hassel & Palier 2021), we argue that countries' respective type of growth regime also moderates the effect of the emergence of the knowledge economy on current challenges. Growth regimes matter, because countries with different comparative institutional advantages are challenged differently by this new "Great Transformation."

We develop these arguments in turn.

9.3.1 Welfare Legacies

Welfare states differ starkly across countries, e.g., in terms of the size, generosity, degree of decommodification, kind of stratification, and distributive patterns of their welfare states. While we lack the space here to systematically review this literature (see for example Esping-Andersen 1990; Haggard & Kaufman 2008; Huber & Stephens 2001; Segura-Ubiergo 2007), we simplify the complex reality by distinguishing only two dimensions of welfare effort: the degree to which countries engage in *social compensation* (i.e., compensating people for job or income losses through programs such as pensions, unemployment benefits, or health care) on the one hand and on the other hand *social investments* (i.e., here particularly educational investments and educational enrollments as shown above, but also more generally social investments such as childcare, reconciliation policies between work and family life, vocational education and training, and active labor market policies) that aim to prevent risks in the first place with the goal to "prepare rather than repair" (Morel et al. 2012). Schematically, we can think about countries as having either a high or low compensatory social policy legacy and either a high or low investment legacy, as displayed in Figure 9.3 (see Heidenheimer 1973 for an early version of this distinction; see also Beramendi et al. 2015).

Why is this distinction relevant? We argue that the shift towards the knowledge economy affects countries with different welfare legacies differently. To see this, think about a country that has a strong compensatory welfare legacy, but a weak legacy of social investments (the bottom-right corner of Figure 9.3). Empirically, Southern European countries and most welfare states of Latin America (especially the traditional "big spenders" Argentina, Brazil, Chile, Uruguay, and Costa Rica [see Segura-Ubiergo 2007]) fall in this box, but also North-East Asia (especially Japan). In these welfare states, workers – especially workers in the formal, often industrial sector (de facto mostly men) – are covered well by existing social compensatory programs. These welfare states are relatively well equipped to cover the risks of the industrial society (at the cost of high gender inequality, though), but are challenged starkly by the emergence of the knowledge economy. This is so for several reasons. First, we saw above that the knowledge economy relies – among other things – on the supply of and demand for high skills. In the compensation-heavy but investment-poor countries, it is difficult to transition to this high-skill equilibrium, since investments are missing to create a high-skilled workforce and existing compensatory commitments limit policy-makers' fiscal leeway to adapt to the challenges of the knowledge economy. Moreover, these countries' growth models and comparative advantages (we come back to these points) do not rely on a high-skill strategy and accordingly there is rather limited economic demand for or pressure towards a high-investment strategy. Finally, and relatedly, especially Latin American countries could be argued to have fallen into a "low-skill (bad jobs) trap," since neither workers, companies, nor policy-makers have a substantial interest in investing in skills (at the expense of higher taxation or cutbacks in other areas) (Snower 1994; Schneider 2013). Countries with this combination of high compensation and weak investment thus struggle the most with the post-industrial "Great Transformation."

The opposite constellation appears in countries with a weak compensatory legacy but comparatively strong investments (the top-left corner of Figure 9.3). Empirically, we find this constellation most clearly in several Anglo-Saxon countries (e.g., the US, the UK, Ireland, New Zealand). The strong investment legacy prepares the ground for these countries to transition to the knowledge economy more easily, since they already invest substantially in skill developments. On the other hand, because of the weak compensatory legacy in these countries, economic losers of the "Great Transformation" are at risk since the social safety net is less generous (Esping-Andersen 1990). The resulting risk is that the transition to the knowledge economy might result in increasing inequalities.

In a third scenario, the knowledge economy appears in a context where countries are characterized by a strong welfare legacy of social compensation *and* social investments. This is the case in Denmark, Sweden, Finland, and Belgium, for example (see the top-right corner of Figure 9.3). These countries appear best prepared to transition to the knowledge economy, as they provide skill investments and a compensatory safety net. The socio-economic challenge in this scenario is the fiscal burden that the expansive welfare state creates. As Figure 9.3 indicates, these countries' welfare states are costly, consuming more than 25 percent of countries' GDP. This does not have to be a problem, but it creates a challenge since it is likely that there will be political debates about the substantial taxation (and potentially public debt) levels, raising questions about the sustainability of this model in the long term.

A final scenario is when the knowledge economy challenges countries with a weak compensatory and a weak investment legacy (the bottom left of Figure 9.3). This is the case in the economically less developed and state-capacity deprived Latin American and South-East Asian countries, for example. In this context, we anticipate two challenges. On the one hand, it will be difficult to transition to a knowledge economy in the first place, since these countries lack the necessary high skills to provide the basis for the knowledge economy. On the other hand, these countries struggle with substantial poverty problems, since the absence of public coverage leaves people reliant on market or family solutions, which for many will not work out. Consequently, the emergence

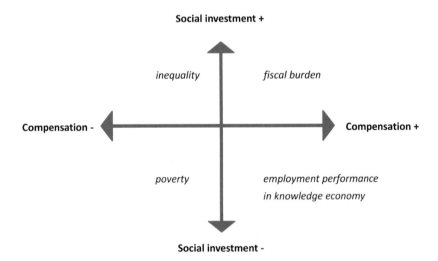

Source: Own depiction, based on ideas developed in Garritzmann et al. (2022a, 2022b).

Figure 9.3   *Two-dimensional welfare legacies*

of the knowledge economy will be slow in this context and be related to discourses about poverty reduction.

In sum, we argue that the "Great Transformation" towards the knowledge economy is related to different challenges in different countries, as their preexisting welfare legacies moderate this transition and affect the social, economic, and political challenges that are likely to arise.

9.3.2 Growth Regimes and Strategies

We argue that besides the respective welfare legacy, a second major moderating factor of the transformation towards the knowledge economy is countries' respective growth regimes and their associated economic strategies. The recent literature in political economy has argued that countries are characterized by different growth regimes, which are believed to have important implications for countries', actors', and firms' preferences, strategies, and behavior (Baccaro & Pontusson 2016; Hassel & Palier 2021). A growth regime is the way the economy is organized, with a particular set of institutions shaping economic and political actors' preferences and decisions. Amongst these institutions, as identified by Amable (2003), three can be related to welfare systems in a broad sense: labor market and industrial relations, skill-formation systems, and social protection institutions (the two other ones being product market regulation and financial systems).

Debate is ongoing on the nature and number of different growth regimes, on their internal logics, as well as their politics (Baccaro et al. 2022). Newer accounts (Hassel & Palier 2021) distinguish five types of growth regimes: Three export-led ones (focused either on dynamic services, or on high-quality manufacturing, or FDI-financed exports) and two domestic demand-led growth models (either financialization-based or wage- and welfare-based). Countries with different types of growth regimes face different challenges in the transformation towards knowledge-based economies. While some growth regimes are very much complementary to the knowledge economy, others are less so, resulting in larger challenges.

The knowledge economy appears complementary particularly to economies following a growth regime based on the export of dynamic services (e.g., the Nordic European countries or the Baltics) since these services employ a high-skilled workforce and these models have relied on the development of higher education for the majority of their youth. In the Nordic European countries, higher education is accessible and affordable and the welfare state provides a lot of support (grants and loans) to students, with no references to parents' income (Garritzmann 2016). It is also the case in countries with a financialization-based demand-led growth mode, where financialization is associated with a rise in ICT and digitalization, which itself requires more general high skills, which is traditionally provided by very high-level universities in these countries (Avlijaš et al. 2021). In countries with these regimes, the increasing economic reliance on a high-skill strategy reinforces the strategies of their growth regimes and the role played by social investment and/or higher education in their models.

In countries with other growth regimes, i.e., in export-led growth models focused on high-quality manufacturing or on FDI as well as in wage- and welfare-based domestic demand-led growth regimes, the knowledge economy creates many more challenges, since its emergence challenges key pillars of the existing models. The manufacturing-based regimes (like Germany) do rely on skills, but on specific vocational skills, which are less likely to be provided as a shift from vocational training towards academic higher education is clearly visible. Social and fiscal attractiveness being at the core of FDI export-led growth regimes, they do not have the institutions nor the means to invest heavily in higher education. The Southern European countries are largely based on domestic consumption and tourism, which neither provide incentives nor means for investing in high skills (Avlijaš et al. 2021).

9.4 CONCLUDING DISCUSSION: POTENTIAL WELFARE STATE REFORM SCENARIOS

We have seen so far in this chapter that the emergence of the knowledge economy has affected different welfare states differently, as effects are moderated by countries' welfare legacies and growth models. We close with a few reflections on how social policy-makers could respond to these challenges. What could policy-makers do in terms of social policy to help with the transition towards the knowledge economy or to cushion the negative consequences of this transition?

We argued elsewhere (Garritzmann et al. 2022a, 2022b) that generally speaking policy-makers can choose among four main welfare reform scenarios: social investments, social protectionism, market liberalism, and basic income strategies. *Social investments* are policies that aim at creating, preserving, or mobilizing human skills (ibid.) – with their focus on skills and capabilities, this policy approach thus appears to be the most "natural ally" of the skill focus of the knowledge economy. A closer look reveals though, that social investment policies come in many forms and shapes, as they can aim at different functions (skill creation, skill preservation, and skill mobilization) and with different distributive profiles (inclusive, stratified, targeted) which have different socio-economic effects and different political dynamics (ibid.). While we do find traces of social investment policies in most countries around the globe, countries differ tremendously in the degree to which they rely on social investments and the kinds of social investment strategy they develop (ibid.).

A second social policy approach is to focus on social compensation in order to protect workers from the potentially negative side effects of the knowledge economy. Accordingly, we call this strategy *social protectionism*. Empirically, this strategy is most prevalent in the dependent market economies in the Central-European Visegrád countries, as their compensation-heavy welfare legacies and their FDI-focused growth regime also creates incentives to follow this road. If we assume that the knowledge economy continues to spread and to intensify (which appears plausible), the question arises to what degree the social protectionism strategy will be viable in the long term. This remains to be seen.

A third strategy is *market liberalism*. The idea here is to keep public solutions at a minimum and to focus on creating and maintaining strong and functioning markets where people and firms could buy the skills and social insurances that they prefer (at least for those having the means to do so). Different degrees of liberalism would be possible, from a very passive state to a state that aims to guarantee equality of opportunity on the market. The obvious challenge for this model is inequality – market forces are likely to create and widen existing inequalities (in terms of wages, wealth, and education, potentially also gender and race), which might not only raise concerns about equality but also about economic growth and sustainability in the longer term.

Finally, policy-makers could chose a *basic income* strategy. Theoretically speaking, this could be a viable option since it would fully decouple people's wellbeing from their labor market participation, so that concerns about the negative effects of the knowledge economy on labor market participation could be mitigated. Empirically, no country has hitherto tried this approach yet (besides local and relatively meager policy experiments) and there are major concerns about the financability and political viability of this strategy.

Which of these different welfare reform strategies policy-makers choose is a political question. We argue and show elsewhere (Garritzmann et al. 2022a, 2022b) that this is crucially shaped by the interaction of legacies and socio-economic pressures, on the one hand, and socio-political coalitions, on the other hand. While we lack the space to develop this argument here in full we can briefly sketch some core insights. Our and our colleagues' worldwide analyses show, for example, that legacies and socio-economic challenges are crucial to understand what *functions* of social investment countries focus on, i.e., whether they develop skill creation, skill mobilization, and/or skill preservation policies. These policies' *distributive profiles*, however, are shaped by the respective socio-political coalition, where especially the size of the new educated middle class plays a crucial role on the micro level and the strength of new left parties on the macro level. In short: Politics is at the heart of different welfare reform scenarios and shapes the strategies that countries choose to address (or not!) the challenges of today's knowledge economies.

NOTES

1. The chapter is based on and expands our previous work in the WOPSI-project (Garritzmann et al. 2022a, 2022b, particularly Garritzmann et al. 2022c).
2. See http://www.barrolee.com.

REFERENCES

Amable, Bruno. *The Diversity of Modern Capitalism*. Oxford: Oxford University Press, 2003.

Ansell, Ben W., & Lindvall, Johannes. *Inward Conquest: The Political Origins of Modern Public Services*. Cambridge: Cambridge University Press, 2021.

Autor, David H., Levy, Frank, & Murnane, Richard J. "The Skill Content of Recent Technological Change: An Empirical Investigation." *Quarterly Journal of Economics* 118 (2003): 1279–1333.

Avlijaš, Sonja, Hassel, Anke, & Palier, Bruno. "Growth Strategies and Welfare State Reforms in Europe." In: *Growth and Welfare in Advanced Capitalist Economies*, edited by Anke Hassel & Bruno Palier, pp. 372–436. Oxford: Oxford University Press, 2021.

Baccaro, Lucio, & Pontusson, Jonas. "Rethinking Comparative Political Economy: The Growth Model Perspective." *Politics & Society* 44, no. 2 (2016): 175–207.

Baccaro, Lucio, Blyth, Mark, & Pontusson, Jonas. *Diminishing Returns: The New Politics of Growth and Stagnation*. Oxford: Oxford University Press, 2022.

Beramendi, P., Häusermann, S., Kitschelt, H., & Kriesi, H. *The Politics of Advanced Capitalism*. Cambridge: Cambridge University Press, 2015.

Bonoli, Giuliano. "Time Matters: Postindustrialization, New Social Risks, and Welfare State Adaptation in Advanced Industrial Democracies." *Comparative Political Studies* 40 (2007): 495–520.

Durazzi, Niccolo. "The Political Economy of High Skills: Higher Education in Knowledge- Based Labour Markets." *Journal of European Public Policy* 26, no. 12 (2019): 1799–1817.

Esping-Andersen, Gøsta. *The Three Worlds of Welfare Capitalism*. Princeton, NJ: Princeton University Press, 1990.

Esping Andersen, Gøsta, Gallie, Duncan, Hemerijck, Anton, & Myles, John. *Why We Need a New Welfare State*. Oxford: Oxford University Press, 2002.

Garritzmann, Julian L. *The Political Economy of Higher Education Finance: The Politics of Tuition Fees and Subsidies in OECD Countries, 1945–2015*. Basingstoke: Palgrave, 2016.

Garritzmann, Julian L., Häusermann, Silja, & Palier, Bruno. *The World Politics of Social Investment (Volume I): Welfare States in the Knowledge Economy*. Oxford: Oxford University Press, 2022a.

Garritzmann, Julian L., Häusermann, Silja, & Palier, Bruno. *The World Politics of Social Investment (Volume II): The Politics of Varying Social Investment Strategies*. Oxford: Oxford University Press, 2022b.

Garritzmann, Julian L., Häusermann, Silja, Kurer, Thomas, Palier, Bruno, & Pinggera, Michael. "The Emergence of Knowledge Economies: Educational Expansion, Labor Market Changes, and the Politics of Social Investment." In: *The World Politics of Social Investment (Volume I): Welfare States in the Knowledge Economy*, edited by Julian L. Garritzmann, Silja Häusermann, & Bruno Palier, pp. 251–281. Oxford: Oxford University Press, 2022c.

Haggard, Stephan, & Kaufman, Robert R. *Development, Democracy, and Welfare States*. Princeton, NJ: Princeton University Press, 2008.

Hall, Peter A. "How Growth Strategies Evolve in the Developed Democracies." In: *Growth and Welfare in Advanced Capitalist Economies*, edited by Anke Hassel & Bruno Palier, pp. 57–97. Oxford: Oxford University Press, 2021.

Hassel, Anke, & Palier, Bruno. *Growth and Welfare in Advanced Capitalist Economies: How Growth Regimes Evolve*. Oxford: Oxford University Press, 2021.

Heidenheimer, Arnold J. "The Politics of Public Education, Health and Welfare in the USA and Western Europe: How Growth and Reform Potentials have Differed." *British Journal of Political Science* 3, no. 3 (1973): 315–340.

Hemerijck, Anton. *Changing Welfare States*. Oxford: Oxford University Press, 2012.

Holliday, Ian. "Productivist Welfare Capitalism: Social Policy in East Asia." *Political Studies* 48 (2000): 706–723.

Huber, Evelyne, & Stephens, John D. *Development and Crisis of the Welfare State: Parties and Policies in Global Markets*. Chicago: University of Chicago Press, 2001.

Kim, Mason S. *Comparative Welfare Capitalism in East Asia*. Basingstoke: Palgrave Macmillan, 2016.

Lee, Jong-Wha, & Lee, Hanol. "Human Capital in the Long-Run." *Journal of Developmental Economics* 122 (2016): 147–169.

Morel, Nathalie, Palier, Bruno, & Palme, Jakob. *Towards a Social Investment State? Ideas, Policies and Challenges*. Bristol: Policy Press, 2012.

Oesch, Daniel. *Occupational Change in Europe: How Technology and Education Transform the Job Structure*. Oxford: Oxford University Press, 2013.

Polanyi, Karl. *The Great Transformation*. New York: Farrar & Rinehart, 1944.

Powell, Walter W., & Snellman, Kaisa. "The Knowledge Economy." *Annual Review of Sociology* 30 (2004): 199–220.

Schneider, Ben Ross. *Hierarchical Capitalism in Latin America: Business, Labor, and the Challenges of Equitable Development*. Cambridge: Cambridge University Press, 2013.

Segura-Ubiergo, Alex. *The Political Economy of the Welfare State in Latin America: Globalization, Democracy, and Development*. Cambridge: Cambridge University Press, 2007.

Snower, Dennis J. "The Low-Skill, Bad-Job Trap." *CEPR Discussion Paper Series*, No. 999, Center for Economic Policy Research (CEPR), London, 1994.

Spitz-Oener, Alexandra. "Technical Change, Job Tasks, and Rising Educational Demands: Looking Outside the Wage Structure." *Journal of Labor Economics* 24, no. 2 (2006): 235–270.

Wren, Anne. *The Political Economy of the Service Transition*. Oxford: Oxford University Press, 2013.

10. Allies or enemies of the welfare state? Welfare support and critiques from (left-wing) protesters in Europe

Femke Roosma

INTRODUCTION

Historically, welfare states have advanced under the pressure of social movements. From the 19th century onwards, popular movements and unions have stirred up political decision making about education, health and social insurance schemes (Barker & Lavalette, 2015). In the past decade, social movements have engaged vividly with the welfare state again. After the financial crisis of 2008 and the following economic crisis, austerity policies became a contested and much debated recipe in the European welfare states (Ólafsson et al., 2019). Anti-austerity movements have gained prominence, with the 15M movement in Spain in May 2011 and Occupy protests – that followed the Occupy Wall Street protest – all over Europe in the autumn of 2011 (Lobera, 2019; Peterson et al., 2015). Later on the Yellow Vest movement especially in France mobilized against the loss of social security (Lobera, 2019). These movements resisted the claim of several policymakers that there was no alternative to cutting spending and protecting the financial sector at the cost of the welfare state (Lobera, 2019). In the decade after the crisis many people engaged in some sort of protest and oftentimes, this protest focused on preventing a retrenchment of the welfare state. What do we know about protesters' welfare attitudes? And how did these attitudes change in this crucial time for European welfare states?

Welfare states rely on support from the public. Social legitimacy is essential for welfare states to be able to function efficiently and effectively (Roosma et al., 2013; Rothstein, 1998). Although support for welfare redistribution is usually high and a strong role for the government in providing social benefits and services is preferred by a large segment of the population, there are also substantial critiques on the performance of the welfare state; on its policy outcomes, its effect on the economy and on potential abuse and underuse of social provisions (Roosma et al., 2013). These different types of attitudes appear to be quite stable over time, when we look at the general population (Laenen et al., 2020; Roosma, 2021).

Thus, we already know quite a bit about welfare support and critiques from the general public and how this changed in about a decade after the financial crisis. But we lack knowledge about the public attitudes to welfare of specific subgroups within the population; specifically those groups who have a higher interest in the welfare state. People who join in social movement action repertoires (as protesting, signing petitions, sharing political content online) are more engaged in society. Social movement 'participation often emerges out of a sense of solidarity' (Hunt & Benford, 2004, p. 439). Therefore participants in social movement activities might not only be better informed about welfare policies or have stronger opinions about these policies, but also have more ability to influence welfare policies. Are these people engaged in protest allies of the welfare state or rather enemies? Their support for, but especially their critiques on, the welfare state are of substantial interest to understand more of the dynamic underlying welfare state legitimacy and social policy change.

In this chapter I look further into the welfare attitudes of people engaged in protest, since the turbulent times in the welfare state; the years after the financial crisis of 2008. My research questions are the following: Are people participating in protest more or less supportive of the welfare state compared to the general public and are they more or less critical of the welfare state? Does this differ for left-wing or other politically affiliated protesters? Have these welfare attitudes of (left-wing) protesters changed since 2008? And do these welfare attitudes of protesters change across different European regions?

In this chapter I analyse welfare state support and welfare state critiques among (left-wing) protesters using data from two waves of the European Social Survey in 2008/9 and 2016/17 for 17 European countries. In the next section I review the literature and formulate hypotheses. Afterwards I describe the data and methods used to analyse these hypotheses. In the results section the outcomes of the empirical analyses will be presented and I will end with a conclusion and discussion.

FROM WELFARE STATES UNDER PRESSURE TO SOCIAL MOVEMENT PARTICIPANTS AND THEIR WELFARE ATTITUDES

Welfare States Under Increasing Pressure

After years of expanding the welfare state, from the 1980s onwards, welfare states came under pressure from international competitiveness, cost constraints and the ideological demand for individual choice (Taylor-Gooby, 2002).

Globalization pushed governments to become more competitive and to lower taxes and benefit contributions (Korpi & Palme, 2003). Population aging and related increasing demands for old age pensions and health care provisions increased the cost constraints (Esping-Andersen, 2002), and also changing political ideas about the role of government and individual responsibility altered the objective of many provisions, usually framed as 'from welfare state to enabling state' (Gilbert, 2004). More individual responsibility, more obligations and sanctions were introduced to benefit schemes to activate people to the labour market (Immervoll & Scarpetta, 2012). The pressure to reform has resulted in steady adaptations of the welfare state over the course of decades. At the same time, public opinion data continues to show critiques on potential welfare abuse and negative consequences of the welfare state for economic competitiveness among the general public (Roosma et al., 2016; Van Oorschot et al., 2012).

However, more serious challenges for the welfare state came after the 2008 financial crisis followed by a worldwide economic crisis. European welfare states were hit in diverging ways. Some countries were severely exposed to the initial crisis of the financial sector (Great Britain and Iceland). Other European states suffered more from the Eurocrisis that followed after (Greece, Ireland, Spain and Portugal), or by the worldwide economic downturn (Hungary and Estonia) (Farnsworth & Irving, 2012), and many countries faced high levels of GDP contraction and rising unemployment rates (Ólafsson et al., 2019). Welfare states responded differently to these challenges. Eastern and Southern European countries had few possibilities to soften the impact of the crisis with stimulus packages and were more or less forced to turn to welfare retrenchment and austerity measures (Blyth, 2013; Ólafsson et al., 2019). Other countries had room to manoeuvre but the elected right-wing governments chose austerity measures as a political option (Blyth, 2013). Ólafsson et al. (2019) conclude that harsh austerity measures were implemented in countries like Spain, Portugal, Greece, Great Britain, Ireland and also Hungary, Poland, Estonia and Slovenia. Milder austerity measures were taken for instance in the Netherlands, Belgium, France, Finland and the Czech Republic, while more balanced policy responses were implemented in Norway, Sweden, Germany and Switzerland. The Southern European countries and Ireland were among the hardest hit countries (Lobera, 2019). Opinion poll data continues to show critical evaluations of welfare policy performance as well. Especially in Eastern and Southern European countries people are very dissatisfied with the standard of living of the unemployed and perceive the underuse of benefits (Roosma et al., 2014). However, among the general public these critical attitudes have been remarkably stable (Laenen et al., 2020; Roosma, 2021).

Social Movement Responses

Although the steady welfare state transformation from the 1980s onwards attracted resistance, often led by labour unions and left-wing political parties, social movement activity focused on the welfare state was modest. This was very different in the years after the financial and economic crisis. The aftermath of these crises caused a social climate of increasing fear and distress about the future and came together with a severe loss of trust in political institutions and elites (Lobera, 2019). It led to the mobilization of protesters in anti-austerity movements across Europe, focused on material deprivation and social inequality (Lobera, 2019). Protests began to take shape in 2010 when the effects of austerity policies on daily lives became very evident. Starting in Greece, which had been heavily affected by the Eurocrisis, protests spread across Spain, Portugal and later on the rest of Europe (Lobera, 2019; Peterson et al., 2015). Peterson et al. (2015) describe three different types of mobilization that occurred in the wave of anti-austerity protests. First, national and local trade unions have played a very important role in mobilizing against austerity policies (Larsson, 2014). Peterson et al. (2015) (based on a typology developed by Císař (2013)) label this as *membership activism*; protesters mobilized primarily through union membership. Trade union demonstrations and strikes have taken place all across Europe, with most sizable mobilizations in Spain, Italy, Greece, Belgium and Great Britain, however strongly focused on national and local policies (Pianta & Gerbaudo, 2015). Second, a new group of protesters, not usually engaged in protest activities has been mobilized by new groups of civic organizers. These social movements were labelled as the Indignados (15M movement) and Occupy movements, and spread from Spain and Greece into Italy and France but also other European countries. In Great Britain, Occupy London was the main spin-off of the US Occupy Wall Street movement whose main claim was that wealth should be more fairly distributed from the most wealthy 1 per cent to the other 99 per cent of the citizenry (Peterson et al., 2015). These types of mobilizations were labelled as *episodic mass mobilizations*; mobilizations with many participants, no organizations prominently involved and with few events (Císař, 2013; Peterson et al., 2015). Finally, in a few Southern European countries small radical unions and parties were able to organize large and often confrontational protests against austerity measures. These were labelled as *radical mass activism* (Císař, 2013; Peterson et al., 2015).

Movement Participants

Peterson et al. (2015) show that there were important differences among the participants in the three types of anti-austerity movements, but also one important similarity. The participants in *membership activism* (mobilized by trade unions) were overall somewhat older, lower educated and more often employed. People participating in the *episodic mass mobilizations* (mobilized by the Occupy/Indignados movements) instead, were younger, higher educated, more often unemployed and students. Participants of *radical mass activism* have profiles lying in between these two. Moreover, participants mobilized by trade unions and radical left groups define themselves more as working class, while participants mobilized by the Occupy/Indignados movements define themselves more as middle class. There is one similarity clearly standing out; participants in all types of anti-austerity movements identify themselves as politically 'left' on ideological self-placement scales (Peterson et al., 2015).

The Occupy and Indignados movements are described as unique in their ability to mobilize a new younger, higher educated public, not on post-materialist, but on materialist issues (Langman, 2013). However, in anti-austerity protests not only the young and higher educated were mobilized. The role of trade unions in anti-austerity and pro-welfare protests on the national level must not be underestimated (Peterson et al., 2015). All in all, anti-austerity movements have mobilized a very broad segment of the population, distinguishing themselves from traditional 'old' and 'new' social movements that had more specific participant compositions (Peterson et al., 2015). Left-wing political ideology however, is a strong allying factor that should be taken into account in analysing protesters' attitudes towards the welfare state.

Hypotheses

Based on the findings from previous studies mentioned above, I expect that people participating in protest are more solidaristic (Hunt & Benford, 2004), more engaged and therefore have more concerns about budget cuts in social policy and welfare retrenchment. In general they might be more caring for the social system and be more in favour of the welfare state, and at the same time more concerned about economically vulnerable people like the unemployed and people on benefits. Therefore I expect that:

H1:   People participating in protest are more supportive of redistribution and have stronger welfare critiques compared to people not participating in protest.

However, it can be expected that among social movement participants and activists there are different ideological motivations and ideas to engage in protest. Moreover, in the years 2008/9 and 2016/17 austerity, redistribution and welfare protection were not the only concerns among people engaging in protest. Unfortunately, the used dataset offers no opportunities to find the aim of the protest people report to be engaged in. However, as Peterson et al. (2015) have shown, protesters in anti-austerity movements identified themselves clearly as ideologically left. Therefore, I relate to political orientation and assume that protesters on the political left are more concerned with the welfare state than protesters on the political right or political centre or people not engaging in protest at all.

H2:   Left-wing protesters are more supportive of redistribution and have more welfare critique compared to right-wing protesters, centre protesters and people not participating in protest.

As it is assumed that left-wing protesters are most concerned with the welfare system and more in favour of its perseverance or restoration, I expect that these attitudes have become stronger in the years after the crisis, when the mobilization of protesters emerged and anti-austerity movements gained more traction (Lobera, 2019).

H3: Left-wing protesters are more supportive of redistribution and have more welfare critique compared to right-wing protesters, centre protesters and people not participating in protest, and these effects are stronger in 2016/17 compared to 2008/9.

Finally, as studies have shown, the impact of the financial and economic crises and also social movement activity differed for different European countries and regions. I expect that especially in countries where the crisis has hit the hardest and social movements were the most active, protesters show stronger support for redistribution and stronger welfare critiques. Previous studies (Lobera, 2019; Ólafsson et al., 2019) have shown that this was mostly the case in Southern European (Spain and Portugal) countries and the Anglo-Saxon European countries (Great Britain and Ireland).

H4: Left-wing protesters are more supportive of redistribution and have more welfare critique compared to right-wing protesters, centre protesters and people not participating in protest, and these effects are stronger in Southern and Anglo-Saxon European countries.

In the next section I describe the data and methods used to test these hypotheses before turning to the results of the analyses.

DATA AND METHODS

To test the hypotheses I will use data from the European Social Survey wave 4 (2008/9) and wave 8 (2016/17). I include 17 European countries (see Table 10.1) that appear in both waves. These datasets both include a broad module on welfare attitudes, with repeated questions over two waves. In addition information on participation in social movement action repertoires is available from these surveys.

In analysing support for the welfare state I make use of an often used variable that measures *support for redistribution* by the government on a scale from 1 to 5. The variable was recoded, so that a higher score indicates more support for redistribution. To measure welfare critiques, I use two different variables related to the feared and/or perceived consequences of austerity measures; a worse situation for those on benefits and/or with the lowest incomes. The first variable asks respondents how they evaluate the *standard of living of the unemployed* in their country, on a 11-point scale running from 'extremely bad' to 'extremely good'. The variable was recoded, so that a higher score indicates a more critical view on the situation of the unemployed. The second variable measures the perceived underuse of benefits on a scale from 1 to 5, a higher score indicates more perceived underuse. It asks respondents whether they believe that 'many people with very low incomes *get less benefit* than legally entitled to'. It indicates to what extent the welfare state is able to redistribute to those deserving and entitled.

To measure engagement in protest I use four variables in which respondents have indicated if they have 'worn or displayed campaign *badge/sticker* in the last 12 months', '*signed a petition* in the last 12 months', 'taken part in a lawful *public demonstration* in the last 12 months' and if they have '*boycotted certain products* in the last 12 months'. I created a dummy variable in which all respondents who have indicated at least one of these four types of *protests* are assigned a value of 1 and respondents who have not participated in any type of protest receive the value 0. Table 10.1 gives an overview of the percentage of respondents indicating each type or any type of protest for the two survey waves. Overall there is a slight increase in engagement in protest between 2008/9 and 2016/17.

By combining respondents' ideological affiliation with their engagement in protest I create four variables. In addition to the variable protest mentioned above, I use left–right self-placement: respondents indicate on an 11-point scale their placement on a left (0) to right (10) scale. The first measures *left-wing protesters*, i.e. respondents engaging in any type of protest and indicating that they are on the left side of the political spectrum (score from 0 till 3) (11 per cent of the sample). The second indicates *right-wing protest-*

ers, respondents engaging in any type of protest and being right wing on the political spectrum (score from 7 till 10) (9 per cent of the sample). The third indicates *centre protest*, protesters with a score from 4 till 6 (18 per cent), and finally, *people not engaging in protest* (62 per cent of the sample). I use *centre protesters* as a reference category in the analyses.

As control variables on the individual level I include *education in years*, *subjective income* (asking respondents how they cope on their present income on a four-point scale), whether a respondent indicated to be *unemployed* or not, their *age* and *gender*. I also include *left–right self-placement* to control for the ideological affiliation of the non-protesters.

In order to analyse the differences among country groupings I create five country groupings: Northern, Eastern, Western, Southern and Anglo-Saxon European countries. See Table 10.1 for the countries in each grouping.

The analyses will proceed in the following steps. First I will present descriptive statistics of the percentage of protesters in the different country groupings and the relation between levels of engagement in protest and mean support for redistribution and both welfare critiques at the country level. Next I will present results of the multilevel random intercept models to analyse the effects of engagement in protest in general and left-wing protest in particular on the three outcome variables. Furthermore I analyse the moderation effect with the year of the survey and country groupings to see how effect sizes differ across years and European regions.

RESULTS

Descriptive Results

First, I look at the descriptive results. Table 10.1 gives an overview of the percentage respondents engaged in protest per country, in 2008/9 and 2016/17. We see substantial differences between countries. Eastern European countries exhibit relatively low levels of protest, with percentages around 10 to 20 per cent. Northern European countries show the highest levels of engagement in protest instead, with percentages running from over 50 to even 70 per cent in Sweden. Western European countries are somewhere in the middle, with higher levels of engagement in Switzerland, France, Germany and Great Britain and lower levels in the Netherlands, Belgium and Ireland. More remarkable is the situation of Southern European countries; these show relatively low levels of respondents engaged in protest in 2008/9, but there had been a strong increase in participation in 2016/17 (Portugal from 9 to 32 per cent, Spain from 27 to 43 per cent).

Looking at the relation with countries' mean support for government redistribution, uncontrolled for population composition but taking into account

Table 10.1　Percentage of respondents involved in any type of protest in 2008 and 2016 overall, per type and per country

Overall	2008	2016
Any of the four types	35	40
- Worn a badge or sticker	8	9
- Signed a petition	24	27
- Participated in demonstration	6	8
- Boycotted products	17	20
Country	**2008**	**2016**
Northern European countries		
Finland (FI)	52	61
Norway (NO)	55	62
Sweden (SE)	64	70
Eastern European countries		
Czech Republic (CZ)	20	24
Estonia (EE)	15	21
Hungary (HU)	12	7
Poland (PL)	13	18
Slovenia (SI)	14	26
Western European countries		
Belgium (BE)	35	38
Switzerland (CH)	49	50
Germany (DE)	48	55
France (FR)	49	49
Netherlands (NL)	30	38
Southern European countries		
Spain (ES)	27	43
Portugal (PT)	9	32
Anglo-Saxon European countries		
Great Britain (GB)	47	49
Ireland (IE)	35	29

design and population weights, we see a negative relation (corr. −0.319) as depicted in Figure 10.1. Eastern and Southern European countries are among those with the highest levels of support for government redistribution and the lowest levels of engagement in protest. When we look at critiques on the welfare state we see a negative relationship between the perceived bad standard of living of the unemployed and engagement in protest (corr. −0.647) and a negative relationship between the perceived underuse of benefits and engagement in protest (−0.356). These relationships are depicted in Figures 10.2 and 10.3 respectively. We see a mirroring pattern with support for redistribution: Eastern and Southern European countries show the highest levels of critique on the welfare state and the lowest levels of engagement in protest, while for the Northern and to lesser extent the Western European countries the pattern is the opposite.

Based on these country-level analyses, you would conclude that more protest is associated with less support for and less critique on the welfare state. However, we will see in the next section that this relationship on the individual level is precisely the opposite. At the country level other mechanisms explain the relationship between the main variables of interest.

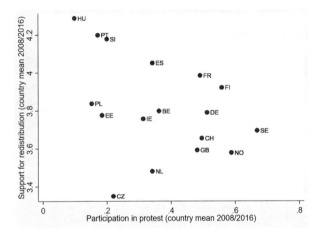

Source: European Social Survey waves 4 and 8. Own calculations. ESS design and population weights are applied.

Figure 10.1   *Support for redistribution and participation in protest (average country means of 2008 and 2016)*

152 *Welfare states in a turbulent era*

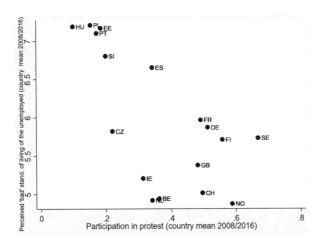

Source: European Social Survey waves 4 and 8. Own calculations. ESS design and population weights are applied.

Figure 10.2   Perceived 'bad' standard of living of the unemployed and participation in protest (average country means of 2008 and 2016)

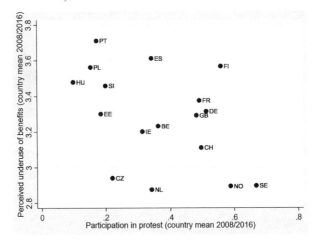

Source: European Social Survey waves 4 and 8. Own calculations. ESS design and population weights are applied.

Figure 10.3   Perceived underuse of benefits and participation in protest (average country means of 2008 and 2016)

Multivariate Analyses

In this next step I analyse the relationship between engaging in protest and welfare attitudes in a multivariate setting (Table 10.2). Model 1a looks at the effects on support for redistribution and includes the dummy for protest (engaging in any kind of protest) and controls for year of the survey, education, subjective income, unemployment, left–right self-placement, age and gender. Models 1b and 1c show the effects on the two welfare critiques outcome variables. Results show that, as expected, in general for the European population people engaging in protest are more supportive of redistribution and more critical towards the standard of living of the unemployed. There is however no significant effect of engaging in protest on the perceived underuse of benefits. The control variables show mostly expected effects; people with lower subjective incomes, people who are unemployed, more left-wing affiliated and older are more in favour of redistribution and more critical about the standard of living of the unemployed and see more underuse of benefits. Women are more supportive of redistribution and perceive a worse standard of living for the unemployed compared to men. However, there is no gender difference in perceived underuse. Lower educated people are more supportive of redistribution and see more underuse, however, they are less likely to perceive a bad standard of living for the unemployed. Moreover, results show that in general support for redistribution and the perceived underuse of benefits was higher in 2016/17, compared to 2008/9, while in 2008/9 respondents perceived a worse standard of living for the unemployed compared to 2016/17. The first hypothesis is partly confirmed.[1]

Next, I take a closer look to the type of protesters, as different attitudes from left- and right-wing protesters are expected. In Models 2a–c instead of the dummy for protest, the variable indicating left-wing protesters (people engaging in protest who indicated themselves as left wing), the variable indicating right-wing protesters, and the variable indicating people who are not engaged in protest are included. The reference category are people who are engaged in protest, but place themselves in the political centre. The predictors show substantial differences. There are strong effects for protesters with a left-wing affiliation; they are more supportive of redistribution and perceive a worse standard of living for the unemployed. Moreover, there is a significant effect of left-wing protesters perceiving the underuse of benefits. Right-wing protesters and people not protesting are instead less in favour of redistribution, compared to the reference category of centre-affiliated protesters. For the two welfare critiques there are less substantial differences between right-wing protesters, centre protesters and people not engaged in protest. All in all it shows that it is left-wing protesters who are more pro-welfare and more critical towards the welfare state. This confirms hypothesis 2.

Table 10.2 Multilevel regression analyses on three outcome variables

	Support for redistribution							Perceived bad standard of living for unemployed							Perceived underuse of benefits						
	Model 1a		Model 2a		Model 3a		Model 1b		Model 2b		Model 3b		Model 1c		Model 2c		Model 3c	
	Coef.	Std. Err.	Coef.	Std. Err.	Coef.	Std. Err.	Coef.	Std. Err.	Coef.	Std. Err.	Coef.	Std. Err.	Coef.	Std. Err.	Coef.	Std. Err.	Coef.	Std. Err.
Intercept	4.779***	.061	4.703***	.061	4.7109***	.062	6.716***	.199	6.720***	.200	6.7335***	.200	4.104***	.060	4.066***	.061	4.068***	.061
Year 2016	.041***	.008	.038***	.008	.024**	.008	-.242***	.015	-.244***	.015	-.254***	.015	.018*	.008	.017*	.008	.012	.008
Protest	.054***	.009					.125***	.017					.013	.009				
Protest categories (ref. centre protest)																		
Left-wing protest			.216***	.017	.149***	.022			.230***	.031	.181***	.040			.094***	.016	.066**	.021
Right-wing protest			-.188***	.017	-.189***	.017			-.063	.032	-.064*	.032			-.046**	.017	-.047***	.017
No protests			-.494***	.011	-.050***	.011			-.085***	.020	-.085***	.020			-.002	.011	-.002	.011
Left-wing protest * Year 2016					.126***	.022					.093	.048					.053*	.026
Education in years	-.019***	.001	-.020***	.001	-.020***	.001	.011***	.002	.010***	.002	.011***	.002	-.022***	.001	-.023***	.001	-.023***	.001
Subjective income	-.171***	.006	-.170***	.006	-.171***	.006	-.285***	.011	-.285***	.011	-.285***	.011	-.148***	.006	-.149***	.006	-.149***	.006
Unemployment	.090***	.019	.090***	.018	.089***	.018	.432***	.034	.430***	.034	.432***	.034	.098***	.018	.100***	.018	.100***	.018
Left-right self-placement	-.092***	.002	-.066***	.002	-.066***	.002	-.095***	.004	-.077***	.004	-.095***	.004	-.027***	.002	-.018***	.002	-.019***	.002
Age	.004***	.000	.004***	.000	.004***	.000	.010***	.000	.010***	.000	.010***	.000	.001**	.000	.001**	.000	.001**	.000
Gender (male is ref.)	.096***	.008	.095***	.008	.095***	.008	.068***	.015	.069***	.015	.068***	.015	.012	.008	.012	.008	.012	.008

	Support for redistribution	Perceived bad standard of living for unemployed	Perceived underuse of benefits
N country	17	17	17
N	56,244	55,673	51,847

Notes: *p<.05; **p<.01; ***p<.001.

In Models 3a–c hypothesis 3 will be tested. Model 3a shows a positive interaction effect between the year of the survey (2016/17) and left-wing protesters on support for redistribution. The positive effect of left-wing protesters almost doubles in 2016/17 compared to 2008/9. Left-wing protesters were more pro-welfare in the years after the crises. Model 3b shows an interaction effect of the year of the survey (2016/17) and left-wing protesters on the perceived bad standard of living of the unemployed in a positive direction, but the effect is borderline insignificant ($p= .051$). Model 3c presents a positive interaction effect of left-wing protesters and the year of the survey on the perceived underuse of benefits, which is here borderline significant. All in all there is a weak tendency that left-wing protesters are more critical about the welfare state performance in 2016/17 compared to 2008/9. Hypothesis 3 is largely confirmed.

Finally, the results of the moderation effects for the different country groupings are presented in Tables 10.3a and 10.3b. In Table 10.3a I look at the interaction effects of the five country groupings and left-wing protest on the support for redistribution. Results show a positive significant interaction effect in the Northern welfare states. Left-wing protesters are significantly more supportive of redistribution in these countries compared to left-wing protesters in other European countries. In Eastern European countries instead, left-wing protesters are less supportive of the welfare state. Other country groupings do not moderate the effect of left-wing protesters on support for government redistribution.

Tables 10.3b and 10.3c show the moderation effects for country groupings on the relation between left-wing protesters and welfare critiques. Again we see for the Eastern European country a deviating pattern; here left-wing protesters are less critical on their welfare state performance – both considering the perceived bad standard of living of the unemployed and the perceived underuse of benefits – compared to left-wing protesters in other European regions. In fact in Eastern European countries the effect of left-wing protesters on welfare critiques becomes insignificant. On the other end there is a positive interaction for Anglo-Saxon European countries on the relation between left-wing protesters and both the perceived bad standard of living of the unemployed and the underuse of benefits. In Anglo-Saxon European countries left-wing protesters are more critical on the welfare state. For other country groupings there are no significant interaction effects found. Hypothesis 4 can therefore only be partly confirmed. Only for Anglo-Saxon European countries are effects in the expected direction found and only for welfare critiques.

When patterns in the Eastern European countries are analysed in more detail (results are available from the author), results show that in Eastern European countries left-wing protesters are not significantly different from centre protesters and non-protesters in their support for redistribution and

Table 10.3a Multilevel regression models – moderation effects of country groupings on support for redistribution

Support for redistribution

	Model 4a		Model 5a		Model 6a		Model 7a		Model 8a	
	Coef.	Std. Err.	Coef.	Std. Err.	Coef.	Std. Err.	Coef.	Std. Err.	Coef.	Std. Err.
Intercept	4.705***	.067	4.684***	.071	4.733***	.070	4.679***	.062	4.718***	.064
Year 2016	.037***	.008	.037***	.008	.038***	.008	.038***	.008	.038***	.008
Protest categories (ref. centre protest)										
Left-wing protest	.175***	.018	.251***	.017	.208***	.020	.218***	.016	.213***	.017
Right-wing protest	−.185***	.017	−.188***	.017	−.188***	.017	−.188***	.017	−.188***	.017
No protests	−.052***	.011	−.055***	.011	−.050***	.011	−.050***	.011	−.049	.011
North EU	−.019	.014								
East EU			.080	.119						
West EU					−.102	.117				
South EU							.202	.161		
Anglo-Saxon EU									−.129	.165
Left-wing protest * NorthEU	.177***	.031								
Left-wing protest * EastEU			−.388***	.043						
Left-wing protest * WestEU					.019	.117				
Left-wing protest * SouthEU							−.021	.040		
Left-wing protest * AngloEU									.020	.040
Control variables added										

	Support for redistribution
N group	17
N	56,578

Notes: *p<.05; **p<.01; ***p<.001.

Table 10.3b Multilevel regression models – moderation effects of country groupings on the perceived bad standard of living of the unemployed

	Model 4b		Model 5b		Model 6b		Model 7b		Model 8b	
	Coef.	Std. Err.	Coef.	Std. Err.	Coef.	Std. Err.	Coef.	Std. Err.	Coef.	Std. Err.
Intercept	6.813***	.212	6.371***	.176	6.971***	.207	6.620***	.200	6.811***	.202
Year 2016	−.234***	.015	−.244***	.015	−.244***	.015	−.244***	.015	−.244***	.015
Protest categories (ref. centre protest)										
Left-wing protest	.237***	.034	.249***	.032	.244***	.038	.229***	.032	.193***	.032
Right-wing protest	−.064*	.032	−.063*	.032	−.063	.032	−.063*	.032	−.065*	.032
No protests	−.084***	.020	−.088***	.020	−.085***	.020	−.085***	.020	−.085***	.020
North EU	−.529	.489								
East EU			1.197***	.309						
West EU					−.857*	.368				
South EU							.846	.561		
Anglo-Saxon EU									−.778	.569
Left-wing protest * NorthEU	−.033	.058								
Left-wing protest * EastEU			−.210**	.081						
Left-wing protest * WestEU					−.032	.049				
Left-wing protest * SouthEU							.009	.075		
Left-wing protest * AngloEU									.299***	.074
Control variables added										

	Perceived bad standard of living of unemployed
N group	17
N	56,000

Notes: $*p<.05; **p<.01; ***p<.001$.

Table 10.3c Multilevel regression models – moderation effects of country groupings on the perceived underuse of benefits

Perceived underuse of benefits

	Model 4c Coef.	Std. Err.	Model 5c Coef.	Std. Err.	Model 6c Coef.	Std. Err.	Model 7c Coef.	Std. Err.	Model 8c Coef.	Std. Err.
Intercept	4.085***	.065	4.053***	.070	4.098***	.069	4.032***	.060	4.065***	.064
Year 2016	.017*	.008	.017*	.008	.017*	.008	.018*	.008	.017*	.008
Protest categories (ref. centre protest)										
Left-wing protest	.092***	.018	.103***	.017	.096***	.020	.095***	.017	.083***	.020
Right-wing protest	−.046**	.017	−.046**	.017	−.046**	.017	−.046**	.017	−.047**	.017
No protests	−.002	.011	−.003	.011	−.002	.011	−.002	.011	−.002	.011
North EU	−.108	.138								
East EU			.045	.117						
West EU					−.111	.115				
South EU							.280	.152		
Anglo-Saxon EU									.004	.166
Left-wing protest * NorthEU	.009	.031								
Left-wing protest * EastEU			−.106*	.044						
Left-wing protest * WestEU					−.003	.026				
Left-wing protest * SouthEU							−.011	.040		
Left-wing protest * AngloEU									.088*	.039
Control variables added										

	Perceived underuse of benefits
N group	17
N	52,126

Notes: *p<.05; **p<.01; ***p<.001.

in their welfare critiques. This could be explained by the fact that left–right self-placement does not apply well to Eastern European countries (Lipsmeyer & Nordstrom, 2003). Other country groupings confirm the overall pattern, with one exception; in Southern European countries both left-wing protesters as well as right-wing protesters are most critical on the standard of living of the unemployed (compared to non-protesters and centre protesters), and a similar pattern occurs for the perceived underuse of benefits, although here the positive effect for right-wing protesters is insignificant. An explanation could be that in Southern welfare states the situation of the unemployed is such a pressing issue that the critique on the welfare state is carried by left- and right-wing protesters alike.

CONCLUSION AND DISCUSSION

In this chapter I have analysed the welfare attitudes of a specific subgroup of the population; people engaging in protest. Welfare attitude research is usually focused on welfare opinions among the general population, while largely ignoring the fact that specific subgroups have not only a higher stake in welfare policies, but are also more likely to influence these policies. In the wake of the financial and economic crises after 2008, anti-austerity movements mobilized large segments of the population to stand up against the severe retrenchment of the welfare state and supporting more redistribution of wealth (Lobera, 2019). Although this study was not able to unravel whether people participating in these *specific* protests are more supportive of the welfare state and more critical about its performance at the same time, it has shown that this is the case for people participating in protests in general and in particular for left-wing protesters. (Left-wing) protesters, more than non-protesters (or otherwise politically affiliated protesters) are more concerned about the outcomes of welfare policies and are more supportive of welfare redistribution by the state. Moreover, they are more so of this opinion in 2016/17 than compared to 2008/9. It reveals that indeed this specific subgroup of the population, that engages actively in public debate by different means of protest, has a stronger position and stronger concerns about the welfare state. These protesters might be seen as 'allies' of the welfare state, as they support its main goal of redistribution, however, when it comes to formulating critiques towards that same welfare state, they might rather be considered as 'enemies'.

At the country level, we see interesting things happening. Differences in engaging in protest activities are very large; participation rates differ between 7 per cent in Hungary and 70 per cent in Sweden. Northern, Anglo-Saxon and Western European countries have high to moderately high participation rates, while Eastern European countries show very low levels. Also the steep increase in participation levels in Southern European countries between

2008/9 and 2016/17 is worth noticing, especially because in these countries anti-austerity movements were very prominent. The relationship with welfare support and critiques is reversed at the country level. It would clearly be an ecological fallacy to conclude that these country-level patterns equal individual-level relations. Expectations regarding regional differences are only partly confirmed. It found that left-wing protesters are more supportive of redistribution in Nordic countries and show more critiques on the welfare state in Anglo-Saxon countries, compared to left-wing protesters in other European countries. However, results in Eastern European countries, on the individual level, differentiate the most with the general overall pattern in Europe. This is probably the case because left–right self-placement is a problematic predictor of ideological positions in these countries (Lipsmeyer & Nordstrom, 2003).

Of course there are several limitations to this study. First, the dataset does not contain specific information about the type of protest respondents were engaged in. On the one hand this is less relevant as the main interest of this chapter is the welfare attitudes of more engaged citizens, not related to a particular protest. On the other hand, however, it would have informed us better about different types of protesters within this group. Dividing protesters into left- and right-wing groups only partly solves this issue, but at the same time shows that the political position of protesters matters. Second, distinguishing between only left, right and centre protesters neglects that supporters of the radical right are often more concerned with the welfare state and supportive of redistribution compared to the liberal and conservative right. Unfortunately the available measure does not have the ability to make distinctions between different categories of right-wing political affiliation. Third, only two survey years are available for measuring welfare attitudes and protest activity in this turbulent welfare state decade. The year 2016/17 is relatively late as the peak of the anti-austerity movement was merely in the year 2013. Information for more years would be necessary to paint the full picture of the impact of anti-austerity protests on welfare attitudes among protesters. Still the remarkable change in protest activity in the Southern European countries suggests that something has happened in engaging citizens in protest in the years after the economic crisis. Finally, the low rate of protest activity and the deviating patterns in political protesters' attitudes towards the welfare state in the Eastern European countries, remain a puzzle that needs to be studied further in future research.

In conclusion, protesters exhibiting different attitudes towards the welfare state than the general population is an interesting finding, that suggests that those engaged more with society are not only the most supportive but also the strongest critics of welfare policies: acting both as enemies as well as allies of the welfare state.

NOTE

1. As a robustness check I have run the models for the four separate indicators that are part of the overall variable 'protest'; wearing a batch, signing a petition, boycotting products and participating in protests. I found that for the three different outcome variables effects were all in similar directions, but effects differ in size. With regard to the outcome variables 'support for redistribution' and the 'perceived standard of living of the unemployed' I found that for all four indicators effects are not only in the same direction, but also all effects are significant. With regard to the outcome variable 'underuse' – for which the main effect is positive but insignificant – I found positive and significant effects for wearing a badge and boycotting products (both borderline significant) and for participating in a demonstration (strong and significant). There is an insignificant effect for signing a petition for the outcome variable underuse. In conclusion, robustness checks show that attending a demonstration gives the strongest effects on all outcome variables, while the effects for the other variables is somewhat smaller and depends on the outcome variable. So, from an empirical point of view there are differences in types of protest, but not substantial and they do not alter the conclusions presented in this chapter. The results of this robustness check can be obtained from the author.

REFERENCES

Barker, C., & Lavalette, M. (2015). Welfare changes and social movements. In D. della Porta & M. Diani (Eds.), *The Oxford handbook of social movements* (pp. 711–728). Oxford University Press. https://doi.org/http://doi. org/10.1093/oxfordhb/9780199678402.013

Blyth, M. (2013). *Austerity: The history of a dangerous idea*. Oxford University Press.

Císař, O. (2013). A typology of extra-parliamentary political activism in post-communist settings: The case of the Czech Republic. In K. Jacobsson & S. Saxonberg (Eds.), *Beyond NGO-ization: The development of social movements in Central and Eastern Europe* (pp. 139–169). Ashgate.

Esping-Andersen, G. (Ed.). (2002). *Why we need a new welfare state*. Oxford University Press.

Farnsworth, K., & Irving, Z. (2012). Varieties of crisis, varieties of austerity: Social policy in challenging times. *Journal of Poverty and Social Justice*, *20*(2), 133–147. https://doi.org/10.1332/175982712X652041

Gilbert, N. (2004). *Transformation of the welfare state: The silent surrender of public responsibility*. Oxford University Press.

Hunt, S. A., & Benford, R. D. (2004). Collective identity, solidarity, and commitment. In D. A. Snow, S. A. Soule, & H. Kriesi (Eds.), *The Blackwell companion to social movements* (pp. 433–458). Blackwell Publishing Ltd.

Immervoll, H., & Scarpetta, S. (2012). Activation and employment support policies in OECD countries: An overview of current approaches. *IZA Journal of Labor Policy*, *1*(9), 1–20. https://doi.org/10.1186/2193-9004-1-9

Korpi, W., & Palme, J. (2003). New politics and class politics in the context of austerity and globalization: Welfare state regress in 18 countries, 1975–95. *American Political Science Review*, *97*(3), 425–446. https://doi.org/http://dx.doi.org/10.1017/S0003055403000789

Laenen, T., Meuleman, B., & van Oorschot, W. (2020). *Welfare state legitimacy in times of crisis and austerity: Between continuity and change*. Edward Elgar Publishing.

Langman, L. (2013). Occupy: A new new social movement. *Current Sociology*, *61*(4), 510–524. https://doi.org/10.1177/0011392113479749

Larsson, B. (2014). Transnational trade union action in Europe. *European Societies*, *16*(3), 378–400. https://doi.org/10.1080/14616696.2013.813958

Lipsmeyer, C. S., & Nordstrom, T. (2003). East versus West: Comparing political attitudes and welfare preferences across European societies. *Journal of European Public Policy*, *10*(3), 339–364. https://doi.org/http://dx.doi.org/10.1080/1350176032000085342

Lobera, J. (2019). Anti-austerity movements in Europe. In C. Flesher Fominaya & R. A. Feenstra (Eds.), *Routledge handbook of contemporary European social movements* (pp. 267–283). Routledge.

Ólafsson, S., Daly, M., Kangas, O., & Palme, J. (2019). *Welfare and the Great Recession: A comparative study*. Oxford University Press.

Peterson, A., Wahlström, M., & Wennerhag, M. (2015). European anti-austerity protests: Beyond 'old' and 'new' social movements? *Acta Sociologica*, *58*(4), 293–310. https://doi.org/10.1177/0001699315605622

Pianta, M., & Gerbaudo, P. (2015). In search of European alternatives: Anti-austerity protests in Europe. In M. Kaldor & S. Selchow (Eds.), *Subterranean politics in Europe* (pp. 31–59). Palgrave Macmillan.

Roosma, F. (2021). The social legitimacy of European welfare states after the age of austerity. In B. Greve (Ed.), *Handbook on austerity, populism and the welfare state* (pp. 110–129). Edward Elgar Publishing. https://doi.org/10.4337/9781789906745

Roosma, F., Gelissen, J., & Van Oorschot, W. (2013). The multidimensionality of welfare state attitudes: A European cross-national study. *Social Indicators Research*, *113*(1), 235–255. https://doi.org/http://dx.doi.org/10.1007/s11205-012-0099-4

Roosma, F., Van Oorschot, W., & Gelissen, J. (2014). The preferred role and perceived performance of the welfare state: European welfare attitudes from a multidimensional perspective. *Social Science Research*, *44*, 200–210. https://doi.org/http://dx.doi.org/10.1016/j.ssresearch.2013.12.005

Roosma, F., Van Oorschot, W., & Gelissen, J. (2016). The Achilles' heel of welfare state legitimacy: Perceptions of overuse and underuse of social benefits in Europe. *Journal of European Public Policy*, *23*(2), 177–196. https://doi.org/http://dx.doi.org/10.1080/13501763.2015.1031157

Rothstein, B. (1998). *Just institutions matter: The moral and political logic of the universal welfare state*. Cambridge University Press.

Taylor-Gooby, P. (2002). The silver age of the welfare state: Perspectives on resilience. *Journal of Social Policy*, *31*(4), 597–621. https://doi.org/http://dx.doi.org/10.1017/S0047279402006785

Van Oorschot, W., Reeskens, T., & Meuleman, B. (2012). Popular perceptions of welfare state consequences: A multilevel, cross-national analysis of 25 European countries. *Journal of European Social Policy*, *22*(2), 181–197. https://doi.org/http://dx.doi.org/10.1177/0958928711433653

11. Conflicting demands and financial abilities?
Bent Greve

11.1　INTRODUCTION

Voters want parties to support their preferences, including spending on specific elements in the welfare state, and parties want to attract voters in order to gain power. In a sense, this is part of a long-term struggle to get the median voter to support specific interventions (Romer and Rosenthal 1979), and thereby swing the voters towards a majority. In principle, this can take the form of support for both more or less money for specific welfare state challenges. The long view has been that voters have always asked for more welfare and, also as was shown more than 40 years ago, that combining the available economic resources with the demands has implied a crisis for the welfare states due to insufficient resources to meet the demands over at least the last 40 years (OECD 1981). The fact that pressure for more spending has an impact on welfare states' development is also a long-standing issue. Niskanen (1971) pointed to specific pressure groups such as the administrative and employed persons in the public sector. In order to get the welfare state to continue its development it has even, also historically, been an issue that support from the middle class has been important (Korpi and Palme 1998), and this could only be reached by including the delivery of welfare to the middle class and not only those the most in need. It has even further back, through the work of Keynes, been known that effective demand was necessary to cope with crisis as this could ensure jobs and activities (Carter 2021).

It is against this background that this chapter discusses the present challenges for the welfare states. This is done by looking into two separate, but interlinked issues. One is how to manage the development in welfare spending, including the use of evidence as a way of ensuring the best usage of scarce resources. The other, in combination herewith, is how to steer the public sector economy so that there is room for manoeuvring in times of crisis – such as the financial crisis of 15 years ago, the COVID-19 crisis, and now inflation and the crisis in Ukraine.

11.2 EXPECTATIONS OF THE WELFARE STATE

There will presumably never be sufficient resources to fulfil all expectations from voters (including also voters as part of various pressure groups). This implies that decision makers will have to prioritize scarce resources. This can take the form of the politician who wants to increase their chances of re-election by trying to attract the median voter by spending on activities with higher support from voters. However, a risk here is that the median voter does not necessarily have single peaked preferences, and different voters have varied types of preferences, for example, young voters might have stronger preferences for environmental issues, whereas elderly voters prefer long-term and health care. Change in preferences over the life-course is in many ways logical, without arguing that the electorate do not have variations herein, and that support for services across generational issues is possible. Still, the implication is that even if this is the case, it is also the case that preferences change over time, as indicated in Figure 11.1.

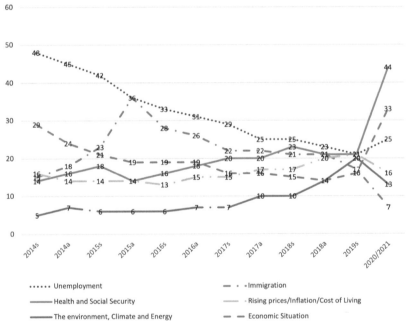

Source: Figure 12.1 in Greve (2020b) and updated with data from EUROBAROMETER 94.2, accessed 2 February 2022.

Figure 11.1   Core important national issues for EU citizens since 2014

Thus, voters' perception of what is important changes over time and not only due to demographic changes such as an ageing population, but also, and presumably, especially in relation to a sudden crisis. This is exemplified in Figure 11.1, which shows that even a topic increasing in importance such as the environment declined strongly after the outbreak of COVID-19, with health and the economy increasing as issues which are then more important for voters. The same was the case after the financial crisis, when the economy and employment were very central and important for citizens. Thus, to focus only on voters' attitudes might be shortsighted, albeit seemingly natural for those wanting re-election. The perception on where to spend money in welfare states can thereby change rapidly, albeit over time voters especially seem to favour welfare spending in relation to health care as well as on old age.

The variation of what people find should be supported and attract more spending also varies across countries, as is shown in Table 11.1.

Table 11.1 shows clearly that pensions, long-term and health care are the most supported elements from citizens for higher spending across the OECD, and thereby this also means that political parties, especially in order to gain voters, are willing to support more spending on these welfare issues. There is not the same level of support for the different areas in all countries, presumably reflecting the differences in the actual level of benefits and services, demographic changes and historical development. The support for higher spending decreases when respondents are asked for their support if they have to pay an extra 2% of their income in taxes and social contributions. The same areas still have the highest support, but, for example, support for health decreases from 70.0% in Table 11.1 to 44.7%, support for pensions falls from 66.0% to 41.9% and long-term care falls from 69.0% to 34.4% (table 3.2 in OECD 2021b). Still, it indicates the clearly conflicting expectations for where the welfare states shall have a role, and even a stronger role than presently. This while also showing that the possible change in taxes and duties can have a modifying role on what citizens want. So, not only prioritizing on what and where to spend, but also balancing this with the willingness to pay for the welfare states can be central issues.

11.3 EVIDENCE-BASED POLICIES

The high expectation for more welfare increases the need to have good instruments to use when having to choose between types of expenditures and investment in the welfare states given that, as mentioned above, there will always be scarce resources. This raises the issues of having evidence-based policies and including in them the available knowledge about possible variations in the cost of providing the service. The length of this chapter does not make it possible to go into detail, however for a number of discussions including the possible

Table 11.1 Percentages in each country who want to spend more or much more on one or more areas, given this could influence level of taxes and benefits in EU countries and the OECD average

	Family support	Education	Employment support	Unemployment support	Income support	Housing support	Health support	Incapacity-related support	Pensions	Long-term care	Public safety
Austria	46.6	56.7	46.7	33.5	45.2	48.3	67.8	60.3	66.8	74.1	45.6
Belgium	32.6	46.5	38.5	27.3	39.8	31.1	64.7	47.1	61.1	60.2	47.1
Denmark	23.0	38.0	27.5	28.2	24.5	18.3	57.8	34.7	44.1	61.3	49.1
Estonia	55.7	47.8	50.3	54.1	57.7	47.6	71.2	68.3	72.2	70.9	35.5
Finland	33.2	43.3	37.8	31.0	31.5	25.7	57.4	42.2	51.9	64.1	52.3
France	35.9	50.0	47.5	27.3	24.1	33.8	65.3	57.5	66.4	64.1	60.9
Germany	48.4	64.5	43.2	38.3	53.5	50.4	63.2	55.5	74.1	70.8	59.3
Greece	70.8	78.7	74.2	76.8	72.1	68.0	86.2	76.3	75.3	74.4	63.6
Ireland	47.5	62.5	52.6	34.6	44.6	52.8	78.5	64.6	62.5	74.5	59.3
Italy	64.4	72.1	72.5	63.6	61.0	55.4	76.2	68.0	69.7	72.6	68.1
Lithuania	60.3	61.3	62.8	59.7	65.5	57.5	68.9	68.9	79.3	73.8	48.5
Netherlands	30.1	51.0	38.9	31.2	36.3	40.2	63.1	41.1	53.4	61.1	52.2
Poland	51.4	57.4	67.4	55.7	61.5	59.4	75.7	71.4	81.2	71.0	55.1
Portugal	71.5	72.4	67.1	59.9	35.6	56.8	85.9	80.2	72.0	81.3	66.7
Slovenia	55.3	51.2	57.2	49.8	51.8	61.2	72.1	70.9	78.4	77.7	33.5
Spain	56.9	75.0	66.4	61.1	54.4	59.0	82.4	71.7	70.7	78.3	52.0
Average	50.6	58.5	54.8	49.4	50.9	50.6	70.0	61.2	66.0	69.0	53.6

Note: The "Average" is the OECD average and only countries that are both members of the OECD and the EU are included in the table.
Source: OECD (2021b), table 3.1.

conflicting perspectives, also methodologically, in finding the evidence, see a number of chapters in Greve (2017), as well as in Greener and Greve (2013). Another issue is that it is not sufficient that one intervention is better than another, the marginal cost of improving the level and/or quality of services also needs to be taken into consideration when making a decision.

The issue of best practice further revolves around the fact that knowledge changes over time, and that it might be difficult to get good data, including also to know what the contrasting case is, e.g. what would have happened without the specific intervention. The rate of the discount factor, as is central in cost–benefit analysis, can by its choice hereof also strongly influence what to do, e.g. using a higher discount rate will reduce the willingness to invest, especially for projects having a long time to pay back the investment. Lastly, the value of life, often measured by Quality-Adjusted Life Year (QALY), is in itself a strongly contested issue. Ensuring that there is a randomized control test can also be an issue, including how to collect these data in a solid way. Thus, in a way, this increases the risk that policy makers only use the results they like. Still, it can be a way of informing decision makers as well as the general public on how evidence might help in prioritizing resources. There is, in fact, knowledge on the best practice to use in many welfare areas.

It is thus clear that, for example, spending on the quality of life for children when growing up can be important (Heckman 2006), although the result has been criticized (Rea and Burton 2018). Reducing the number of children growing up in poverty, not only very young children, but also in their teenage years seems to be important, including also improving the position of those not growing up in poverty in relation to education and labour market attachment (Lesner 2018).

However, even if a decision from a strict economic point of view is the most optimal way of using scarce resources, this can be in conflict with ethical considerations. For example, in relation to treatment and care for elderly people, using economic metrics might implicitly imply a less positive evaluation of intervention for elderly people (Greve 2017). It can furthermore also be in conflict with the perspective of the voters, and thereby be a risk for those in power if they neglect these viewpoints, even if they have evidence that spending on other issues can be more important.

At the same time, it is still the case that using evidence when comparing interventions to solve one specific issue can be very important, as this can ensure using the most effective of the possible types of interventions. This can also, as an example, help in reducing the pressure on health care costs, as a new intervention which cannot be proved to be more effective will not be implemented. Even if one intervention is only marginally better than another, one can still compare this with the extra cost and use this as a criterion for making the decision of whether or not to implement the possible instrument. See, for example, how this is done in the UK (NICE – the National Institute for Health and Care Excellence).

Decisions might often be "easier" where it has been possible to test and carry out randomized control experiments on existing types of treatment, rather than introducing new types of treatment related to, for example, care for the elderly and children. This can be more difficult as the decisions are also related to the personal interaction between staff and users. Professional norms and the understanding of who best knows what to do in a situation might also imply that the implementation of changes in especially care-related activities might be difficult.

All in all, this implies that even if there is and will be difficulties in ensuring the existing evidence is of high quality, this kind of information can help in steering the public sector economy, as it can prove to be a useful instrument in order to help in making the most out of the available resources. This should then be a way of reducing the tension between different demands for changes in the welfare states and to inform citizens about the cost and benefits of making specific changes.

11.4 STABLE PUBLIC SECTOR FINANCING

Overall, on average, welfare states in Europe cannot be argued to have been in a state of permanent austerity, retrenchment or crisis (Greve 2020a). This is not to neglect the fact that both the financial crisis and the COVID-19 pandemic have had a profound effect on the welfare states (see among others Williams 2016; Taylor-Gooby, Leruth, and Chung 2017; Stanley 2016; Cotofan et al. 2021; Greve et al. 2021).

The variation in the ability to cope with a crisis includes variations in the welfare state's structure, and also the situation with public sector debt, which has seemingly been a hindrance as this has reduced the ability to finance not only the increased pressure on the health care system, but also the short-term decline (at the least) in economic growth and increased the need for welfare state benefits.

A deficit during a crisis can be high, such as in many OECD countries in the wake of the COVID-19 pandemic it was around 10 percentage points of GDP in 2020 (OECD 2021a), and in the financial crisis it even reached around one-third of GDP in Ireland. In order to be able to finance such a dramatic change, without the risk of getting too high a level of public sector debt, is part of the question of how to steer societal development. This has been less of a problem with the low levels of interest in recent years, however with a higher level of inflation interest rates will increase, which can be more burdensome for countries with high levels of debt.

This chapter does not enter into the debate on how and where to set the level of public sector deficit and debt which can ensure sustainable development (Skidelsky and Fraccaroli 2017; Reinhart and Rogoff 2010). However, it is more important to show that countries with a high level of debt and deficit seemingly have had more difficulties in financing expenditure after the financial crisis as well as a reduced ability to cope with the change in economic options in the wake of the COVID-19 pandemic than those with strong public finances before the crisis. Whether the need for restructuring economies in especially Southern Europe was a consequence of the financial crisis or an imbalance with the criteria for membership of the Economic and Monetary Union is not the point here. This includes whether or not there should have been less strong demand for changes or accepting a reduction in the debt to the banks, especially, but also the public sector, the so-called haircut (Bussière et al. 2013). The point being there was a risk for these welfare states with high levels of public sector debt due to higher expenditures in order to pay the interest on the debts.

Whether the debt is due to high spending or to a lowering of the levels of taxation (as argued by trickle-down economics), which has a long history (Shiller 2019), is not the issue here, albeit seemingly that the argument of lowering taxes and duties should benefit all has implied a negative impact on welfare states' financial abilities (Greener 2018; Blyth 2013; Greve 2020b). However, coping with and reducing the risk that companies and others pay too little in tax can be an important issue, also witnessed among other things by the strong interest in the taxation of multinational companies and across borders of the activities in both the OECD and the EU (see for example https://www.oecd.org/tax/beps/, accessed 2 February 2022). The taxation of multinational companies is not the only issue. There is also the possible risk that work through platforms can imply both a lower quality of jobs and income for some, and that this increases the risk of a larger hidden economy, which then implies lower incomes for the welfare states. This further shows that reducing the size of the hidden economy might pave the way for financing the welfare states at a lower overall tax rate, while at the same time presumably increasing the level of equality (Barrios et al. 2017; Alstadsæter, Johannesen, and Zucman 2017).

Overall, the aim of this section is to show that saving for a rainy day can be an important issue in order to develop welfare states, and also in more turbulent times as countries with the lowest debt have a higher flexibility to increase spending in times of crisis. This can naturally imply both tax increases or reductions in spending or a combination hereof can be necessary also in good times. The core aspect is that there should be a financial leeway to expand and ensure demand-driven changes in economic recovery after strong external shocks as without that the cost of doing so will be very high. This includes having sufficient automatic stabilizers within the public sector economy so that, even without active political decisions, this might reduce some of the negative impact on the overall activities in a society in the wake of change both in economic fluctuations and also, and especially, in relation to sudden and large economic crises.

11.5 SOLVING CONFLICTING DEMANDS

The conflict between ensuring support from voters and reaching the best possible distribution was also shown a long time ago by Korpi and Palme (1998) as targeting benefits and services towards the poor could risk reducing the support for the welfare states' continued development. Whether such a relatively simple causality actually holds can be questioned (Gugushvili and Laenen 2021), albeit still so that higher levels of welfare spending imply lower levels of those at risk of poverty and more equal societies. Thus, bribing the middle class, as it has been labelled, was important in one respect to ensure that the middle class would support the welfare state. However, with a declining middle class in Europe (Derndorfer and Kranzinger 2021), as well as a declining number of working-class votes (Gingrich and Häusermann 2015), this could pose new problems for the welfare states, including how to prioritize scarce resources. The increase in votes for populist parties also poses the issue of where to spend the limited resources, given the often more chauvinistic approach to welfare state development of these parties (Greve 2019). The preference for redistribution also varies and is influenced not only by the perceived or actual economic position of individuals, but also their ideological position (Weisstanner and Armingeon 2021). Even during the COVID-19 crisis there were differences in support for different social groups, i.e. the interpretation of who is deserving (Gandenberger et al. 2022). Thus, not only is increasing demand an option, but there is also a balance as to who are seen as legitimate receivers of welfare state benefits.

Further, the issue is not only who is deserving, but also that there are different perceptions of what being at risk means. Therefore, the risks that are less visible are assumed to be less risky and therefore get less support. This due to the fact that "[s]uch misperceptions can affect policy, because some governments will allocate their resources in a way that fits with people's fears rather than in response to the most likely dangers" (Thaler and Sunstein 2021, location 807).

At the same time, meeting the demand from specific voter groups could be costly and implying a need for more resources in the years to come, including that if one group gets more then it can be the case that other groups might also expect to get more and better services. Furthermore, people tend to adapt to their circumstances in what has been labelled the hedonic treadmill (Kahneman 1999). This also implies that political parties will need to promise new goods and services in order to attract voters because they have got used to what they have and are therefore more willing to vote for parties promising them new elements. Adaptation in combination with loss aversion also implies that it might be difficult to reduce spending where, perhaps, it is less needed than it was when first enacted.

Adaptation and loss aversion can imply a conflict on how to be able to finance the welfare states. This conflict is less strong in growing economies, but is due to the same reasons, i.e. spending not necessarily being possible in times of fewer resources, such as when crisis occurs, and other demands are pressing on the public sector spending. There has also been a conflict from some wanting tax cuts, even with the arguments that this would help to increase economic growth and labour supply, while a reduction in spending could imply a higher public sector debt, which then could be a reason later for a reduction in services and benefits, as already shown a long time ago (Pierson 1994). The Southern European welfare states in Europe, as an example hereof, have seen the consequences of public sector debt in the wake of the last financial crisis (Zartaloudis 2014; Petmesidou and Guillén 2014).

An issue also in welfare states is who shall produce and deliver different types of services and benefits. This is often a debate on the role and division of responsibilities between state, market and civil society. However, it can be argued that this is a false dichotomy (Greve 2022), as the public sector is dependent on the market, and the private sector is dependent on the public sector (at least related to issues such as safety, infrastructure, education, etc.). This shows, as also indicated in Section 11.2, that using evidence can be important, but also that social investment can be central for resolving conflicting demands (Ronchi 2018; Plavgo and Hemerijck 2020; Morel, Palier, and Palme 2012). Using a social investment perspective might therefore be one way to muddle through the competing demands, while naturally also ethical issues can be important so that different generations can have access to the welfare state, which continues to be legitimate.

This argument indicates the strong importance of a continuation of the generational contract, i.e. that one generation pays for the previous generation, with the expectation that the next will pay for them. Presumably, this also implies the need for the level of, and conditions for receiving, benefits being seen as legitimate among the citizens, and a continued balance between and an understanding of what is seen as legitimate among voters.

This also shows that "governments proactively strengthen their resilience to future risk" (OECD 2021a, p. 23), or even clearer (p. 48): "Stimulus packages and public investment are essential for the recovery, but when the time is appropriate, governments will eventually need to rebuild fiscal buffers to safeguard their ability to provide financial support in future crises."

However, ensuring fiscal buffers while at the same time mediating across generations, expectations from voters and changes in demand for welfare services as a consequence of demographic and technology changes might be strong challenges for all welfare states in Europe.

11.6 CONCLUSIONS

Welfare states are central for the good life of citizens in many countries. Still, there is also pressure and the need for restructuring in a number of countries as a consequence of changes in a number of issues such as demography, new technology, globalization and labour markets. These all have an impact on the welfare state's ability to finance and deliver welfare to its citizens in the years to come. Ensuring the taxation of multinational companies and the hidden economy can be important in order to generate the appropriate income from them.

However, as is also shown in economic history, there will be bubbles in economies, such as the Wall Street Crisis in 1929 as well as later in the financial and housing markets, and the dot.com bubble early in this century. Bubbles are not new – the Tulip bubble in 1637 is apparently the first such bubble. Besides this, other crises can pop up (such as recently witnessed by the COVID-19 pandemic and climate change). This can also have an impact on the abilities of welfare states to help citizens in the way they expect. Welfare states, if wanting to continue to have legitimacy, must be prepared for such rapid changes and the need for state intervention. Thus, to put it simply, there can be a need for reducing public sector debt in good times in order to have money for bad times, and even more in times of unexpected crisis. Countries with a buffer as well as an ability to combine the use of strong automatic stabilizers together with an ability to rapidly change direction and/or implement new instruments in times of crisis will be those best able to cope with crisis and ensure the most stable welfare to its citizens.

The use of evidence to ensure the best use of scarce resources can also be important despite the fact that it does not by itself solve the conflict between different groups' pressure, ideological positions and expectations of what the welfare state will be able to deliver and finance in the years to come.

LITERATURE

Alstadsætter, A., N. Johannesen, and G. Zucman. 2017. "Tax Evasion and Inequality." National Bureau of Economic Research Working Paper No. 23772.
Barrios, S. et al. 2017. "Measuring the Fiscal and Equity Impact of Tax Evasion: Evidence from Denmark and Estonia." JRC Working Papers on Taxationa and Structural Reforms, Sevilla.

Blyth, Mark. 2013. *Austerity: The History of a Dangerous Idea*. Oxford, UK: Oxford University Press.
Bussière, Matthieu, Jean Imbs, Robert Kollmann, and Romain Rancière. 2013. "The Financial Crisis: Lessons for International Macroeconomics." *American Economic Journal: Macroeconomics* 5 (3): 75–84.
Carter, Zachary D. 2021. *The Price of Peace: Money, Democracy, and the Life of John Maynard Keynes*. New York: Random House Trade Paperbacks.
Cotofan, Maria, Jan-Emmanuel De Neve, Marta Golin, Micah Kaats, and George Ward. 2021. "Work and Well-Being during COVID-19: Impact, Inequalities, Resilience, and the Future of Work." In *World Happiness Report*, edited by Helliwell, John F., Richard Layard, Jeffrey Sachs, and Jan-Emmanuel De Neve, 153–190. https://worldhappiness.report/ed/2021/.
Derndorfer, Judith, and Stefan Kranzinger. 2021. "The Decline of the Middle Class: New Evidence for Europe." *Journal of Economic Issues* 55 (4): 914–938.
Gandenberger, Mia K., Carlo M. Knotz, Flavia Fossati, and Giuliano Bonoli. 2022. "Conditional Solidarity: Attitudes towards Support for Others during the 2020 COVID-19 Pandemic." *Journal of Social Policy*, 1–19.
Gingrich, Jane, and Silja Häusermann. 2015. "The Decline of the Working-Class Vote, the Reconfiguration of the Welfare Support Coalition and Consequences for the Welfare State." *Journal of European Social Policy* 25 (1): 50–75.
Greener, Ian. 2018. *Social Policy After the Financial Crisis: A Progressive Response*. Cheltenham, UK and Northampton, MA, USA: Edward Elgar Publishing.
Greener, I., and B. Greve. 2013. *Evidence and Evaluation in Social Policy*. Cheltenham, UK and Northampton, MA, USA: Edward Elgar Publishing. https://doi.org/10.1002/9781118816530.
Greve, B. (ed.). 2017. *Handbook of Social Policy Evaluation*. Cheltenham, UK and Northampton, MA, USA: Edward Elgar Publishing. https://doi.org/10.4337/9781785363245.
Greve, B. 2019. *Welfare, Populism and Welfare Chauvinism*. Bristol: Policy Press.
Greve, B. 2020a. *Austerity, Retrenchment and the Welfare State: Truth of Fiction?* Cheltenham, UK and Northampton, MA, USA: Edward Elgar Publishing.
Greve, B. 2020b. *Myths, Narratives and Welfare States*. Cheltenham, UK and Northampton, MA, USA: Edward Elgar Publishing.
Greve, B. 2022. *The Role of the Public Sector: Economics and Society*. Cheltenham, UK and Northampton, MA, USA: Edward Elgar Publishing.
Greve, B., Paula Blomquist, Bjørn Hvinden, and Minna van Gerven. 2021. "Nordic Welfare States: Still Standing or Changed by the COVID-19 Crisis?" *Social Policy & Administration* 55 (2): 295–311. https://doi.org/https://doi.org/10.1111/spol.12675.
Gugushvili, Dimitri, and Tijs Laenen. 2021. "Two Decades after Korpi and Palme's 'Paradox of Redistribution': What have we Learned so Far and Where do we Take it from Here?" *Journal of International and Comparative Social Policy* 37 (2): 112–127.
Heckman, J. 2006. "Skill Formation and the Economics of Investing in Disadvantaged Children." *Science* 30: 1900–1902.
Kahneman, Daniel. 1999. "Objective Happiness." In *Well-Being: The Foundations of Hedonic Psychology*, edited by Kahneman, Daniel, Ed Diener, and Norbert Schwarz, 3–25. New York: Russell Sage Foundation. https://doi.org/10.1007/978-3-540-68540-1_1.

Korpi, W., and J. Palme. 1998. "The Paradox of Redistribution and Strategies of Equality: Welfare State Institutions, Inequality and Poverty in the Western Countries." Paper No. 174, LIS Working Paper Series, Luxembourg.

Lesner, Rune V. 2018. "The Long-Term Effect of Childhood Poverty." *Journal of Population Economics* 31 (3): 969–1004. https://doi.org/10.1007/s00148-017-0674-8.

Morel, N., B. Palier, and J. Palme (eds.). 2012. *Towards a Social Investment Welfare State? Ideas, Policies and Challenges*. Bristol: Policy Press.

Niskanen, Jr., William A. 1971. *Bureaucracy and Representative Government*. New York: Aldine-Atherton.

OECD. 1981. *The Welfare State in Crisis*. Paris: OECD.

OECD. 2021a. *Government at a Glance 2021*. Paris: OECD. https://doi.org/https://doi.org/https://doi.org/10.1787/1c258f55-en.

OECD. 2021b. *Main Findings from the 2020 Risks That Matter Survey*. https://doi.org/https://doi.org/https://doi.org/10.1787/b9e85cf5-en.

Petmesidou, Maria, and Ana M. Guillén. 2014. "Can the Welfare State as We Know It Survive? A View from the Crisis-Ridden South European Periphery." *South European Society & Politics* 19 (3): 295–307. http://10.0.4.56/13608746.2014.950369.

Pierson, P. 1994. *Dismantling the Welfare State? Reagan, Thatcher and the Politics of Retrenchment*. Cambridge Studies in Comparative Politics. Cambridge: Cambridge University Press. https://doi.org/DOI: 10.1017/CBO9780511805288.002.

Plavgo, Ilze, and Anton Hemerijck. 2020. "The Social Investment Litmus Test: Family Formation, Employment and Poverty." *Journal of European Social Policy*, 0958928720950627.

Rea, David, and Tony Burton. 2018. "Does an Empirical Heckman Curve Exist?" Paper No. 18/3, Institute for Governance and Policy Studies.

Reinhart, Carmen M., and Kenneth S. Rogoff. 2010. "Growth in a Time of Debt." *American Economic Review* 100 (2): 573–578. https://doi.org/10.1257/aer.100.2.573.

Romer, Thomas, and Howard Rosenthal. 1979. "The Elusive Median Voter." *Journal of Public Economics* 12 (2): 143–70.

Ronchi, S. 2018. "Which Roads (If Any) to Social Investment? The Recalibration of EU Welfare States at the Crisis Crossroads (2000–2014)." *Journal of Social Policy* 47 (3): 459–478. https://doi.org/10.1017/S0047279417000782.

Shiller, Robert J. 2019. *Narrative Economics: How Stories Go Viral and Drive Major Economic Events*. Princeton, NJ: Princeton University Press.

Skidelsky, Robert, and Nicoló Fraccaroli (eds.). 2017. *Austerity vs Stimulus: The Political Future of Economic Recovery*. Cham: Palgrave Macmillan. https://doi.org/10.1007/978-3-319-50439-1.

Stanley, Liam. 2016. "Legitimacy Gaps, Taxpayer Conflict, and the Politics of Austerity in the UK." *British Journal of Politics & International Relations* 18 (2): 389–406. http://10.0.4.153/1369148115615031.

Taylor-Gooby, P., B. Leruth, and H. Chung. 2017. *After Austerity: Welfare State Transformation in Europe after the Great Recession*. Oxford: Oxford University Press.

Thaler, Richard H., and Cass R. Sunstein. 2021. *Nudge: The Final Edition*. London: Penguin.

Weisstanner, David, and Klaus Armingeon. 2021. "Redistributive Preferences: Why Actual Income is Ultimately More Important than Perceived Income." *Journal of European Social Policy*, 09589287211037912.

Williams, Fiona. 2016. "Critical Thinking in Social Policy: The Challenges of Past, Present and Future." *Social Policy & Administration* 50 (6): 628–647. http://10.0.4.87/spol.12253.

Zartaloudis, S. 2014. "The Impact of the Fiscal Crisis on Greek and Portuguese Welfare States: Retrenchment before the Catch-Up?" *Social Policy and Administration* 48 (4): 430–449. https://doi.org/10.1111/spol.12069.

12. Effective and fair labour markets: more and focused active labour market policy?

Henri Haapanala

12.1 INTRODUCTION: ALMP, AMBIGUITY AND CONTROVERSY

The intersection of labour markets and social policy is central to the welfare state. Unemployment and inactivity are not only harmful to people's quality of life, but also threaten the social and economic prosperity of countries struggling with ageing populations and declining working-age cohorts. In the labour market, we observe a concerning dualisation between the 'haves' and 'have-nots' as skill-biased technological change, digitalisation and the proliferation of non-standard employment have made it ever more difficult for people with characteristics such as low education, routine manual skills or a migrant background to find decent work (Standing 2013). As jobseekers are facing a more precarious environment, policies must adapt to find the best ways of addressing these challenges and facilitating transitions into high-quality, sufficiently paying employment.

In recent decades, active labour market policies (ALMPs) have become ubiquitous following highly positive experiences in certain European countries. For instance, the EU strategy of 'flexicurity' celebrated the Danish and Dutch models of ALMP which facilitated labour market transitions with extensive public employment services and high rates of part-time and flexible employment (European Commission 2007). More recently, the European Pillar of Social Rights proclaims the right to 'active support to employment' in order to promote equal and effective access to the labour market (European Commission et al. 2017). The appeal of ALMPs is in their promise to deliver both 'flexibility' and 'security': allowing employers to react to market conditions with rapid adjustments to the labour force while guaranteeing a base level of employment security for workers. In contrast, 'passive' labour market policies such as unemployment benefits are often criticised for disincentivising jobseekers from accepting work, although estimates of the size of this effect in economic literature are notably small (Schmieder and Trenkle 2020). Nonetheless, countries often justify ALMPs with a need to reduce the risk of moral hazard inherent in passive labour market policies (Fossati 2018).

However, ALMPs have attracted a wealth of scholarly debate over their effectiveness and potential bias against specific groups of jobseekers in unemployment or inactivity (hereafter referred to as ALMP participants). They are often criticised for 'Matthew effects', or an inegalitarian allocation of participants with the greatest re-employment potential into the most effective programmes (Bonoli and Liechti 2018; Auer and Fossati 2020; Im and Shin 2022). Instead of serving their intended purpose as enabling and capacitating policy instruments, findings point to ALMPs reproducing labour market inequalities for vulnerable individuals such as low-educated and immigrant workers. This trend is concerning for policy-makers who want to facilitate effective, fair and equal access to labour markets.

In this chapter, I assess the use and effectiveness of ALMPs in Europe over the period from 2008 to 2022. Through the lens of process-tracing, I outline how ALMPs were applied during a time characterised by two substantive social-economic crises. First, during the Great Financial Crisis of 2008–2012 ALMPs fell short of their potential for countering the labour market shock, particularly in the worst-affected countries where the necessary economic resources were depleted by austerity. Second, the COVID-19 pandemic of 2020–2021 produced an unprecedented labour market response as ALMPs intertwined with new and large-scale passive income support measures. Finally, I assess the potential of ALMPs to achieve the objectives of active inclusion in the future from the perspectives of technological change, Matthew effects, and employer engagement with ALMP participants.

12.2 VARIETIES OF ALMP: FROM SOCIAL INVESTMENT TO WORKFARE

While this chapter focuses on recent developments in ALMP, I set the stage with a brief overview of history and definitions. The origins of ALMP are usually traced back to post-World War II Sweden where the system of state-sponsored retraining and mobility subsidies helped achieve low inflation and full employment by facilitating the flexible movement of employees between jobs and industries (Molinder 2021).[1] However, ALMPs in the context of a male full-employment society played a much narrower social role than they do today. Bonoli (2013: 167) posits that whereas the Swedish model focused on moving established workers from less to more successful firms, post-industrial ALMPs lean more towards the labour market accession of vulnerable, precarious or inactive groups such as the unemployed, migrants, low-skilled and low-educated. This makes contemporary ALMPs into *social policy* instruments whereas the Swedish model primarily focused on *economic policy*.

Following the decades of stagflation which ended the Keynesian full-employment paradigm, ALMPs truly proliferated in the 1990s and early 2000s. At a time when the ideas of social investment and 'Third Way' social democracy held power in European capitals, this brand of labour market policy with a distinctive dual focus on individual capacity-building and active participation in society found a natural ideological home (Bonoli 2013: 48ff.). It is indeed commonplace to view ALMPs as social investment policies delivering social gains through the empowerment of individuals (Hemerijck 2018). According to this perspective, ALMPs are central to an enabling and capacitating welfare state whose key focus is on supporting individuals and families through life transitions.

Research assessing the effectiveness of ALMPs usually distinguishes between different subtypes. Most of these distinctions are based on either one (e.g. Torfing 1999; Auer and Fossati 2020; Haapanala 2022) or two dimensions (e.g. Bonoli 2010, 2013; Dinan 2019). The most common one-dimensional framework draws an axis from human capital building ALMPs to incentives-based ALMPs looking to achieve 'workfare' or welfare through work (Torfing 1999). The two-dimensional frameworks supplement this axis with another, such as proximity to the labour market (Bonoli 2013) or supply/demand side targeting (Dinan 2019). Viewed through the theoretical lens of typologies, it becomes easier to understand the depth and complexity of ALMPs. They demonstrate that public expenditure on ALMPs is not a sufficient indicator for evaluating the effectiveness and socio-economic impacts of activation, but we also need to consider the specific details of the policy intervention.

According to the widely used typology of Bonoli (2013), ALMPs can be divided into four subtypes. First, *incentive reinforcement* includes measures that encourage re-employment by making benefit payments to ALMP participants conditional upon compliance with personalised employment plans, job search efforts or caseworker advice. Second, *employment assistance* covers measures delivered by public employment services that aim to improve the participant's employability such as job search assistance, personalised counselling or subsidised employment. Third, *upskilling* includes more direct or comprehensive education services such as vocational training leading to a formal qualification. Fourth, there are *occupation* schemes such as direct job creation in the public sector. During the 2000s and particularly after the Great Financial Crisis, the share of incentive reinforcement ALMPs has substantively increased (Dinan 2019). On the other hand, the use of occupation ALMPs has declined as evidence suggests they fail to produce long-term gains in employability (Card et al. 2018). Auer and Fossati (2020) suggest that public sector job creation can even be detrimental to employability as private-sector employers avoid hiring jobseekers with a history of supported employment in non-market occupations.

A large strand of research has emerged to analyse the effectiveness of ALMPs over the short, medium and long term, and their success in lifting people out of precarity – that is, whether the participants are able to remain in unsubsidised market employment after the policy intervention, or return to the cycle of unemployment and ALMPs soon after programme completion (Martin 2015; Wulfgramm and Fervers 2015; Bengtsson et al. 2017; Card et al. 2018). Two concerning observations emerge from this literature. First, despite concerns that a one-dimensional typology of ALMPs risks setting up a false dichotomy between 'good' human capital building and 'bad' coercive policies, reviews consistently find these subtypes to perform very differently in terms of short- and long-term effectiveness (Card et al. 2018). Upskilling policies, specifically labour market training or vocational education, deliver positive employment effects visible around 2–3 years after programme completion. Incentive-oriented policies such as job search assistance, monitoring and sanctions deliver positive employment effects more rapidly, within one year of programme completion, but this effect dissipates over time (Card et al. 2018: 909–911). Therefore an excessive focus on coercive over human capital building ALMPs risks trading off long-term gains for short-term improvements in employment rates, and vice versa.

Second, the expansion of incentive reinforcement ALMPs has taken place in parallel with the increasing privatisation and marketisation of public employment services. Following the principles of new public management theory, ALMPs have been on the front line of privately provided public services (Maron 2021). Caseworkers' performance is assessed in several countries with quantitative targets such as the number of participants successfully re-employed, and public employment services have been partially or fully privatised in countries including Denmark, Ireland, the Netherlands, the United Kingdom and Israel (Bredgaard and Larsen 2008; Maron 2021). However, contracting out public services to caseworkers who are considered employees under private law blurs the boundary between the state and the market. In the case of politically unpopular or controversial policies, this can be intentional. Incentive reinforcement ALMPs are indeed controversial since they are strongly disliked by ALMP participants, people at risk of unemployment, and often also left-wing parties and trade unions (Vlandas 2013; Fossati 2018; Bledow and Busemeyer 2021). Governments applying coercive or disciplinary ALMPs to achieve employment targets may want to protect their public image by contracting out their implementation. In the words of an

Israeli private-sector caseworker, 'someone has to do the dirty work' (Maron 2021: 9).

12.3 ALMPS AS CRISIS INSTRUMENTS: THE FINANCIAL CRISIS AND ITS LESSONS

From 2008 to 2012, the Great Financial Crisis and subsequent Eurocrisis led to skyrocketing unemployment and an urgent need to manage the labour market transitions of dismissed workers. The main line of defence against the collapse of the global financial system was fiscal and monetary, with policies going far beyond the conventional counter-cyclical strategies of public spending on unemployment benefits, public sector employment or job retention. In the labour market, the European Commission strongly encouraged the use of ALMPs to speed up re-employment and minimise structural unemployment (Martin 2015). Heyes (2013) identifies two distinct 'phases' of labour market policy during the crisis: in the first phase, governments countered the unemployment shock with high levels of public spending and fiscal stimulus including employment subsidies, reductions in employers' social insurance contributions, and ALMPs focused on training, lifelong learning and job search assistance. In the second phase, as the financial crisis morphed into the Eurozone sovereign debt crisis, public spending turned from an asset to a liability. Accordingly, the policy focus shifted from costly and slow-moving human capital building ALMPs into workfare-style instruments and an overall cut in ALMP spending: decisions intended to save public expenditure by spending less on labour market policies altogether and directing the limited spending towards measures with more immediate effects.

While the economics of public expenditure weighed strongly against member states during the sovereign debt crisis, critics argue that the shift from human capital building ALMPs towards workfare and austerity was amplified by the deregulatory, neoliberal attitudes characterising European socio-economic governance at the time (Rubery 2011). Indeed, workfare ALMPs intending to breathe life into a sclerotic labour market through the rapid re-entry of jobseekers were called for by both the Troika (European Commission, ECB and IMF) and the Commission acting through the European Semester process of socio-economic policy coordination (Heyes 2013; Barnard 2014). However, the ability of workfare to produce its intended outcomes was crippled by the issue of budget discipline. Marques and Hörisch (2020) posit that austerity had a two-fold impact on skyrocketing youth unemployment, particularly in the worst-hit Mediterranean countries subject to the Troika: the economic clampdown both depressed consumer demand and brought ALMP expenditure to such low levels that public employment services were unable to cope with the number of jobseekers regardless of the type of intervention.

The use of ALMPs in the 2008–12 period was characterised by a shift towards workfare, conditionality, and the overarching aim of economising on public expenditure. However, as the case of the Mediterranean countries demonstrates, this strategy resulted in a questionably weak labour market recovery at a substantive political cost. Public grievance with the EU's handling of the crisis, which largely centred around the sense that the Union cared more about the rights of the economy and businesses than those of citizens, undoubtedly played a role in the 'socialisation' of EU socio-economic governance and the upcoming Commisson's political emphasis on Social Europe (Zeitlin and Vanhercke 2018). After the acute crisis period, the focus of ALMPs in 2014–19 turned back towards the goals of social investment with a greater emphasis on the quality of employment and labour market transitions alongside the speed and flexibility of re-employment (Bekker 2018).

The launch of the European Pillar of Social Rights (EPSR) in 2017 was an important milestone for Social Europe. Characterised as the most significant EU social policy document in two decades, the EPSR became the flagship policy of the Juncker Commission and the main mechanism for implementing the social dimension of European integration (Carella and Graziano 2022). However, this initiative is widely understood to be a compromise between the interests of the left and right, workers and employers, and social and economic lobbies – in effect setting up a road map and a list of preferences for future social legislation rather than a binding set of social rights enjoying a 'hard law' status on par with the EU Treaties, the EU Charter of Fundamental Rights or ILO Conventions (Garben 2018).

A more critical interpretation would suggest the emergence of the EPSR and the post-crisis reorientation towards social investment ALMPs reflected an environment with greater room for manoeuvre, as unemployment and inactivity fell from existential threats to more manageable levels. During the height of the crisis, several governments justified austerity and workfare ALMPs with the narrative of TINA – 'there is no alternative' – and breaking from the narrative midway through would have made the previous cuts seem in vain (Séville 2017). The same appears to hold at EU level. Crespy (2020) posits that the 'social retrenchment' following from austerity was the result of a Commission and European Central Bank steadfastly committed to the neoliberal mission of market liberalisation and deregulation. Consequently, the post-crisis reorientation towards the EPSR and inclusive social policies formed part of a larger reaction to the Eurosceptic and anti-austerity movements gaining substantive ground in the European Parliament. This demonstrates that politics and civil society are never far away from the implementation of social policy.

On the topic of ALMPs, the EPSR has aspirations for both social investment and workfare. The right to active support to employment (§4) calls for human capital building ALMPs, specifically 'timely and tailor-made assistance to improve employment or self-employment prospects [such as] support for job search, training, and re-qualification' (European Commission et al. 2017). However, the right to unemployment benefits (§13) implies the need for incentive reinforcement ALMPs to balance the risk of moral hazard. Specifically, the unemployed should be provided with 'adequate activation support from public employment services' while noting that benefits 'shall not constitute a disincentive for a quick return to employment'. The right to minimum income (§14) is also conditional on labour market re-entry, as it requests combining the benefits of 'those who can work ... with incentives to (re) integrate to the labour market'. In explicitly encouraging people able to work to return to paid employment, this principle expresses a strong preference for individual responsibility through workfare. Overall, the Commission working through the EPSR sets a clear expectation for member states to deliver welfare and social rights through an effective labour market with a prominent role for ALMPs to incentivise (re-)entry to open-market employment.

12.4 POST-COVID LESSONS: NEW BALANCE OF WORKFARE AND WELFARE

Only 12 years after the Great Financial Crisis, considered a 'once-in-a-century' social and economic catastrophe,[2] the COVID-19 pandemic forced governments all around the world into action that can only be described with words such as 'massive' and 'unprecedented' (Béland et al. 2021). In order to reduce the spread of a highly infectious coronavirus, virtually every country in Europe and the world implemented some form of lockdown during March 2020. The initial and most stringent policy measures included border closures, stay-at home orders, limitations or bans on social interaction, and mandatory closures of establishments (Hale et al. 2021). After the first wave of COVID-19, blanket lockdowns were replaced with more targeted restrictions on 'non-essential' activities which particularly affected sectors such as tourism, hospitality and retail (Verick et al. 2022). The uniquely cross-cutting nature of the crisis necessitated policy responses with unprecedented scope, scale and stringency.

In Europe in particular, the political and economic fallout from the Great Financial Crisis underpinned the policy response to COVID-19. Amidst a general sense of acknowledgement that austerity had failed to support the working population in countries such as Portugal, Spain, Greece, Italy and Ireland, governments had a strong incentive to make the COVID-19 response as solidaristic and human-centred as possible (Béland et al. 2021; de la Porte and Jensen 2021; Verick et al. 2022). This was particularly visible in the labour market. During the acute phase of the crisis in the spring and summer of 2020, ALMPs gave way to measures aimed at job preservation, income maintenance, dismissal protection and the extension of protections to groups with notoriously patchy coverage such as non-standard and self-employed workers (Moreira and Hick 2021). However, the historic labour shortages accompanying the post-pandemic recovery of economic activity in 2022 indicate that neither active nor passive labour market policies were fully able to cope with changes specifically related to the pandemic, specifically labour market withdrawals and the rising bargaining power of workers in high-risk, low-paid, 'low-quality' occupations (OECD 2022b).

The short-term revival of income support and unemployment protection does not suggest that the economic context which motivated ALMPs in the first place has disappeared – on the contrary. As Moreira and Hick (2021) point out, the evolution of the COVID-19 pandemic from an acute crisis to a protracted strain on welfare systems closely resembles the Great Financial Crisis which unfolded in several phases with distinct policy priorities. Although in 2020 most governments were not afraid to ignore the conventional rules on deficits and public debt, the political and economic pressures to rebalance national budgets, service government debts, and enter a new era of austerity and workfare are only going to get stronger. From an employment perspective, the main challenge will be the labour market (re-)integration of unemployed and inactive people including those pushed into inactivity by the pandemic. Policies also need to take into account long-standing inequalities exacerbated by the pandemic, providing tailored support to vulnerable groups such as young, female, low-skilled, migrant and non-standard workers (OECD 2021a, 2021c).

This indicates an enhanced role for ALMPs. While employment protection policies such as the EU's SURE fund[3] were widely credited for successfully keeping the unemployment shock in 2020–21 much less severe than expected given the contraction in GDP, these measures were designed to be exceptional and strictly time-limited (European Commission 2021b). Over the course of 2021, the attention of governments gradually shifted from crisis management back towards more ordinary labour market policies with a prominent role for education and training, active inclusion of vulnerable groups, and upskilling of workers to meet the demands of an increasingly digitalised and technologically advanced labour market (OECD 2021b). Research shows that timing is crucial for the effectiveness of ALMPs. Particularly human capital building measures, which require a long time commitment as participants complete their courses in education and training, are best initiated during a downturn when labour demand and the forgone income during the time in education are low (Card et al. 2018: 927). Several European countries applied human capital building ALMPs in their pandemic recovery strategies from autumn 2020, aiming to reskill dismissed workers and provide an effective use of time for people in part-time work, furlough or temporary unemployment (OECD 2022a).

At the EU level, the Commission Recommendation on Effective Active Support to Employment following COVID-19 pays great attention to job quality and human capital building ALMPs (European Commission 2021a). Member states are encouraged to develop ALMPs with a focus on hiring and transition incentives, upskilling and reskilling, and individually tailored support from public employment services. As an example of evidence-based policy, both the Commission and the OECD have in their post-COVID recommendations emphasised upskilling and employment incentive ALMPs over occupation schemes which have been found to be ineffective at increasing open-market employment (OECD 2021b: 11). Overall, the emphasis on upskilling, training, support of vulnerable individuals, and the integration of ALMPs with passive measures and social services reflects the breadth of policy learning in countries and international organisations. While some level of incentive reinforcement is necessary to encourage jobseekers to accept work, countries are determined not to repeat the mistakes of workfare-biased activation that came to characterise the response to the Great Financial Crisis.

The COVID-19 pandemic raised the need for an active and interventionist state on a scale rarely seen outside of wartime. As Castles (2010) points out, Western welfare states were created in the aftermath of world wars with the policy lessons from war recovery built into the institutions. However, a global pandemic remains one of the rare 'black swan' events with very few purpose-built response mechanisms or institutions. Therefore the response to COVID-19 required plenty of improvisation, innovative repurposing of existing institutions to new uses, as well as political opportunism from actors like the EU looking for a more prominent role in social and health policies. Most countries judged to have handled the pandemic well – Germany, Finland, Norway, Denmark, etc. – had the advantage of robust social and economic systems with low debt-to-GDP ratios, strong public services and comprehensive labour market institutions with experience in both active and passive policies. This contrasts in particular to the 'liberal' welfare states of Ireland and the UK who had extremely weak last-resort safety nets prior to the crisis and needed to adapt their pandemic response accordingly (McGann et al. 2020). As the cost-of-living crisis exacerbated by Russia's war in Ukraine has overtaken the COVID-19 pandemic as the overwhelming policy priority in Europe, public employment services are likely to face even greater pressure to facilitate the labour market recovery and re-integration of vulnerable groups. This will be the least difficult to accomplish in countries with strong and well-funded institutions (OECD 2021c).

12.5 ACHIEVING ACTIVE INCLUSION: THE ROLE OF TECHNOLOGICAL CHANGE, MATTHEW EFFECTS AND EMPLOYERS

In the age of digitalisation and skill-biased technological change, human capital building ALMPs are needed not only to tide over temporary labour market crises, but also to supplement the formal education system in upskilling and reskilling the working population. Labour market polarisation and the disappearance of routine, manual production work have undermined low-skilled occupations for decades, and the pandemic further accelerated the digital transformation with the rapid expansion of remote working (Eichhorst et al. 2020). These pressures combined with the rise of online social services have turned digital literacy into a basic citizenship skill. Indeed, the vast majority of today's occupations require at least basic computer skills (OECD 2021b). The Recommendation on Effective Active Support to Employment recognises the crucial role of ALMPs in supporting the digital transition, namely by providing individualised support and training to jobseekers in disadvantaged positions and facilitating the recognition of skills acquired outside of formal education (European Commission 2021a). Upskilling initiatives which are more flexible than the formal system of vocational education and training (VET) benefit especially jobseekers in a temporary state of labour market uncertainty. However, VET and ALMP should be coordinated so as to cultivate the skills most demanded by employers and industries.

The extent to which the active inclusion and social investment dimensions of ALMP are realised varies strongly between countries. As already discussed, countries with established mechanisms of ALMPs such as Finland, Sweden, Denmark, Germany, Belgium and the Netherlands are best able to combine high employment rates with support and protection for vulnerable groups (Marchal and van Mechelen 2017). In particular, the 'Nordic model' where VET and public employment services are closely integrated with the needs of industry is seen as a leading example despite having increased its emphasis on workfare (Bengtsson et al. 2017). Policies which consider both the needs of employers and the capacities of ALMP participants have the possibility to deliver win–win outcomes. However, research finds a concerning amount of 'Matthew effects' in the delivery of ALMPs.[4] In other words, it is unclear to what extent the policy interventions are able to reduce the inequalities faced by labour market participants from disadvantaged backgrounds.

Matthew effects in ALMPs largely arise from the personal characteristics of ALMP participants and how they affect the decision-making of caseworkers. When caseworkers are judged on performance targets such as the number of participants successfully (re-)employed, they have an incentive to allocate individuals who they consider to have the highest likelihood of employment into the most effective programmes (Bonoli and Liechti 2018). Participants with low education or weak cognitive skills also have a risk of self-selecting out of training programmes if they are pessimistic about their ability to pass or gain a long-term advantage (Im and Shin 2022). Cognitive characteristics are not the only source of bias. Auer and Fossati (2020) find that participants in Switzerland with immigrant, linguistic or religious minority backgrounds are likely to be 'parked' in the least effective ALMP programmes. While it is difficult to establish the direction of causality, the evidence of Matthew effects is concerningly widespread. Access biases exist even in countries which put considerable emphasis on egalitarian and human capital building ALMPs such as Finland (Im and Shin 2022). This shows the objectives expressed at European level in a new light. One must ask critically whether ALMPs are successful in 'providing equal opportunities in labour market transitions regardless of sex, racial or ethnic origin, religion or belief, disability, age, or sexual orientation' (European Commission 2021a: 4).

Lastly, labour demand has a crucial role in achieving fair and inclusive outcomes. The bulk of ALMP research focuses on programme effects on participants, but the motivation of employers to hire ALMP participants is an equally important part of the equation. The seminal paper on this subject compared employer participation in Denmark and the UK, finding that Danish firms belonging to an employers' association or centralised bargaining were more likely to interact with ALMPs and recruit for long-term, relatively high-skilled employment, whereas British employers largely utilised ALMP participants as cheap, unskilled labour (Martin and Swank 2004). A follow-up study by Valizade et al. (2022) reaffirms these differences. Inclusive and human capital building ALMPs are more common in Denmark than the UK, and the employers who are most likely to recruit ALMP participants tend to be actively engaged in industrial relations. That being said, the majority of employers even in Denmark conduct all their hiring through the open market with less than a third hiring either temporary or permanent workers through public job centres (Bredgaard 2018: 373). This suggests that several challenges lie in the way of truly realising the aims of active inclusion. In addition to providing comprehensive ALMP services such as upskilling and labour market training on equal and non-discriminatory terms, greater attention needs to be paid to expand the pool of employers willing to hire ALMP participants into long-lasting, high-quality employment.

12.6 CONCLUSION

Active labour market policies are central instruments for post-industrial welfare states. They reflect a vision of an enabling and capacitating 'social investment' state where everyone able to work receives the necessary support for finding productive, high-quality employment. During the last two decades, policy learning from two socio-economic crises of historical proportions has led the EU institutions and member states to prioritise upskilling and incentive reinforcement ALMPs which are the most effective at providing long-term gains in human capital or speeding up the transition to employment. However, experiences of the Great Financial Crisis and COVID-19 pandemic demonstrate that ALMPs cannot do it all alone. Policies which exclusively prioritise the speed and quantity of (re-)employment risk exacerbating inequalities for jobseekers from disadvantaged backgrounds and distorting the hiring incentives of employers. Matthew effects must be taken seriously in order to build more inclusive labour markets with equitable treatment of jobseekers and workers regardless of employment contract, sex, age, education, race, religion, migrant status or any other personal characteristic.

In addition, workfare ALMPs enable a rapid return to employment but they risk exacerbating precarious work. Even in Denmark, which is considered the model country for ALMPs, the vast majority of employers hire permanent workers through the open market and ALMP participants are often hired for reasons of cost or flexibility. Future research could elaborate on employer perceptions of ALMP participants or the extent to which ALMPs succeed in reducing the stigmatising effect of long-term unemployment. Human capital building, upskilling ALMPs seem as necessary as ever to help countries produce highly skilled labour forces compatible with the demands of technologically advanced and digitalised economies.

NOTES

1. This is known as the Rehn–Meidner model after its creators Gösta Rehn and Rudolf Meidner, economists at the Swedish Trade Union Confederation (LO).
2. The famous 'once-in-a-century' quote comes from the testimony of Alan Greenspan, chair of the Federal Reserve, to the US House of Representatives on 23 October 2008.
3. European Instrument for Temporary Support to Mitigate Unemployment Risk in an Emergency (SURE), Council Regulation (EU) no. 2020/672.
4. Matthew effects describe the accumulation of advantage, named after a verse in the Gospel of Matthew (13:12): 'Whoever has will be given more, and they will have an abundance. Whoever does not have, even what they have will be taken from them.'

REFERENCES

Auer D and Fossati F (2020) Compensation or Competition: Bias in Immigrants' Access to Active Labour Market Measures. *Social Policy & Administration* 54(3): 390–409.

Barnard C (2014) EU Employment Law and the European Social Model: The Past, the Present and the Future. *Current Legal Problems* 67(1): 199–237.

Bekker S (2018) Flexicurity in the European Semester: Still a Relevant Policy Concept? *Journal of European Public Policy* 25(2): 175–192.

Béland D, Cantillon B, Hick R, et al. (2021) Social Policy in the Face of a Global Pandemic: Policy Responses to the COVID-19 Crisis. *Social Policy & Administration* 55(2): 249–260.

Bengtsson M, de la Porte C and Jacobsson K (2017) Labour Market Policy under Conditions of Permanent Austerity: Any Sign of Social Investment? *Social Policy & Administration* 51(2): 367–388.

Bledow N and Busemeyer MR (2021) Lukewarm or Enthusiastic Supporters? Exploring Union Member Attitudes Towards Social Investment and Compensatory Policy. *Journal of European Social Policy* 31(3): 267–281.

Bonoli G (2010) The Political Economy of Active Labor-Market Policy. *Politics & Society* 38(4): 435–457.

Bonoli G (2013) *The Origins of Active Social Policy.* Oxford: Oxford University Press.

Bonoli G and Liechti F (2018) Good Intentions and Matthew Effects: Access Biases in Participation in Active Labour Market Policies. *Journal of European Public Policy* 25(6): 894–911.

Bredgaard T (2018) Employers and Active Labour Market Policies: Typologies and Evidence. *Social Policy and Society* 17(3): 365–377.

Bredgaard T and Larsen F (2008) Quasi-Markets in Employment Policy: Do They Deliver on Promises? *Social Policy and Society* 7(3): 341–352.

Card D, Kluve J and Weber A (2018) What Works? A Meta Analysis of Recent Active Labor Market Program Evaluations. *Journal of the European Economic Association* 16(3): 894–931.

Carella B and Graziano P (2022) Back to the Future in EU Social Policy? Endogenous Critical Junctures and the Case of the European Pillar of Social Rights. *Journal of Common Market Studies* 60(2): 374–390.

Castles FG (2010) Black Swans and Elephants on the Move: The Impact of Emergencies on the Welfare State. *Journal of European Social Policy* 20(2): 91–101.

Crespy A (2020) The EU's Socioeconomic Governance 10 Years after the Crisis: Muddling through and the Revolt against Austerity. *Journal of Common Market Studies* 58(S1): 133–146.

de la Porte C and Jensen MD (2021) The Next Generation EU: An Analysis of the Dimensions of Conflict behind the Deal. *Social Policy & Administration* 55(2): 388–402.

Dinan S (2019) A Typology of Activation Incentives. *Social Policy & Administration* 53(1): 1–15.

Eichhorst W, Hemerijck A and Scalise G (2020) *Welfare States, Labor Markets, Social Investment and the Digital Transformation.* IZA Discussion Paper No. 13391. Bonn: Institute of Labor Economics (IZA).

European Commission (2007) *Towards Common Principles of Flexicurity: More and Better Jobs Through Flexibility and Security.* Brussels: European Commission COM(2007) 359.

European Commission (2021a) *Commission Recommendation of 4.3.2021 on Effective Active Support to Employment following the COVID-19 crisis (EASE).* Brussels: European Commission COM(2021) 1372.

European Commission (2021b) The SURE Instrument: Key Features and First Assessment. *Quarterly Report on the Euro Area* 20(2): 41–49.

European Commission et al. (2017) *European Pillar of Social Rights.* Luxembourg: EU Publications Office.

Fossati F (2018) Who Wants Demanding Active Labour Market Policies? Public Attitudes Towards Policies that put Pressure on the Unemployed. *Journal of Social Policy* 47(1): 77–97.

Garben S (2018) The European Pillar of Social Rights: Effectively Addressing Displacement? *European Constitutional Law Review* 14(1): 210–230.

Haapanala H (2022) Carrots or Sticks? A Multilevel Analysis of Active Labour Market Policies and Non-Standard Employment in Europe. *Social Policy & Administration* 56(3): 360–377.

Hale, T, Angrist, N, Goldszmidt, R, et al. (2021). A Global Panel Database of Pandemic Policies (Oxford COVID-19 Government Response Tracker). *Nature Human Behaviour*, 5(4): 529–538.

Hemerijck A (2018) Social Investment as a Policy Paradigm. *Journal of European Public Policy* 25(6): 810–827.

Heyes J (2013) Flexicurity in Crisis: European Labour Market Policies in a Time of Austerity. *European Journal of Industrial Relations* 19(1): 71–86.

Im ZJ and Shin Y-K (2022) Who Gets Labour Market Training? Access Biases of Social Investment in Finland. *Journal of European Social Policy* 32(1): 3–18.

Marchal S and van Mechelen N (2017) A New Kid in Town? Active Inclusion Elements in European Minimum Income Schemes. *Social Policy & Administration* 51(1): 171–194.

Maron A (2021) Public Service, Private Delivery: Service Workers and the Negotiation of Blurred Boundaries in a Neoliberal State. *Work, Employment and Society*, online first.

Marques P and Hörisch F (2020) Understanding Massive Youth Unemployment during the EU Sovereign Debt Crisis: A Configurational Study. *Comparative European Politics* 18(2): 233–255.

Martin CJ and Swank D (2004) Does the Organization of Capital Matter? Employers and Active Labor Market Policy at the National and Firm Levels. *American Political Science Review* 98(4): 593–611.

Martin JP (2015) Activation and Active Labour Market Policies in OECD Countries: Stylised Facts and Evidence on their Effectiveness. *IZA Journal of Labor Policy* 4(1): 1–29.

McGann M, Murphy MP and Whelan N (2020) Workfare Redux? Pandemic Unemployment, Labour Activation and the Lessons of Post-Crisis Welfare Reform in Ireland. *International Journal of Sociology and Social Policy* 40(9/10): 963–978.

Molinder J (2021) How Effective are Mobility Subsidies in Targeting the Unemployed? Lessons from the Swedish Model, 1965–1975. *Economic and Industrial Democracy*, online first.

Moreira A and Hick R (2021) COVID-19, the Great Recession and Social Policy: Is This Time Different? *Social Policy & Administration* 55(2): 261–279.

OECD (2021a) Scaling Up Policies that Connect People with Jobs in the Recovery from COVID-19. *OECD Policy Responses to Coronavirus (COVID-19).* Paris: OECD Publishing.

OECD (2021b) Designing Active Labour Market Policies for the Recovery. *OECD Policy Responses to Coronavirus (COVID-19).* Paris: OECD Publishing.

OECD (2021c) Building Inclusive Labour Markets: Active Labour Market Policies for the Most Vulnerable Groups. *OECD Policy Responses to Coronavirus (COVID-19).* Paris: OECD Publishing.

OECD (2022a) Supporting Transitions and Securing Jobs. *OECD Policy Responses to Coronavirus (COVID-19).* Paris: OECD Publishing.

OECD (2022b) *The Post-Covid-19 Rise in Labour Shortages.* OECD Economics Department, Working Paper No. 1721. Paris: OECD Publishing.

Rubery J (2011) Reconstruction amid Deconstruction: Or Why We Need More of the Social in European Social Models. *Work, Employment and Society* 25(4): 658–674.

Schmieder JF and Trenkle S (2020) Disincentive Effects of Unemployment Benefits and the Role of Caseworkers. *Journal of Public Economics* 182: 104096.

Séville A (2017) From 'One Right Way' to 'One Ruinous Way'? Discursive Shifts in 'There Is No Alternative'. *European Political Science Review* 9(3): 449–470.

Standing G (2013) *The Precariat: The New Dangerous Class.* London: Bloomsbury.

Torfing J (1999) Workfare with Welfare: Recent Reforms of the Danish Welfare State. *Journal of European Social Policy* 9(1): 5–28.

Valizade D, Ingold J and Stuart M (2022) Employer Participation in Active Labour Market Policies in the United Kingdom and Denmark: The Effect of Employer Associations as Social Networks and the Mediating Role of Collective Voice. *Work, Employment and Society*, online first.

Verick S, Schmidt-Klau D and Lee S (2022) Is This Time *Really* Different? How the Impact of the COVID-19 Crisis on Labour Markets Contrasts with that of the Global Financial Crisis of 2008–09. *International Labour Review* 161(1): 125–148.

Vlandas T (2013) Mixing Apples with Oranges? Partisanship and Active Labour Market Policies in Europe. *Journal of European Social Policy* 23(1): 3–20.

Wulfgramm M and Fervers L (2015) Unemployment and Subsequent Employment Stability: Does Labour Market Policy Matter? *Socio-Economic Review*, 13(4): 791–812.

Zeitlin J and Vanhercke B (2018) Socializing the European Semester: EU Social and Economic Policy Co-Ordination in Crisis and Beyond. *Journal of European Public Policy* 25(2): 149–174.

13. Mass migration due to climate change? A critique of the security focus on climate mobilities

Meltem Yilmaz Sener

INTRODUCTION

According to many analysts, climate change[1] is the major challenge of the 21st century. There is increasing evidence which demonstrates that global climate is changing largely due to human influences (Karl & Trenberth 2003; McMichael & Haines 1997; IPCC 2007; Monbiot 2007; Rosa et al. 2015). There is now a scientific consensus that the world is getting warmer and it will have important consequences in terms of how societies are governed (IPCC 2013). This human-induced modern climate change is already having adverse impacts on humans all over the world because of the changes in eco-systems and increased frequency and magnitude of natural disasters (Cameron 2009). However, it would be wrong to claim that humans contribute to global climate change equally; there is global carbon inequality. As stated in an Oxfam Study (Gore 2015: 1), "the poorest half of the global population are responsible for only around 10% of global emissions yet live overwhelmingly in the countries most vulnerable to climate change – while the richest 10% of people in the world are responsible for around 50% of global emissions." Therefore, the poorest people are the least responsible for and the most vulnerable to climate change. An increasing number of environmentalists and government experts also stress the racially unequal impacts of carbon emissions via climatic changes (Ahuja 2016). The analysis by Kartha et al. (2020) of the future scenarios of global carbon inequality also demonstrates that this inequality will be passed on to future generations. Other scenarios also indicate that the world's richest 1% will have per capita consumption emissions in 2030 which will be 30 times higher than the global per capita level according to the goal of the Paris Agreement (Gore 2021).

Human mobility is said to be one of the major social consequences of climate change. A causal linkage between the two is taken for granted and constantly repeated in public discourses, policy debates, and certain strands of the academic literature.[2] Concepts like environmental migrant, eco-migrant, environmental refugee, climate refugee, and climate change-induced displacement have become a part of policy agendas during the last decades. These arguments also frequently carry alarmist tones, warning against mass migration from the Global South to Global North due to climate change and the consequent risk of increasing conflicts. These arguments also become the basis for international migration and climate policy. Although such discourses have almost gained the status of truth for many, they are misleading. As Boas et al. (2019: 901) state, "although the potential for climate change to disrupt livelihoods and threaten lives is real, these policies reinforce a false narrative that predicts large numbers of climate refugees." With such framing, mobility due to climate change is presented as a security crisis. With a "security turn" in climate discourse, climate change has increasingly been framed as a security issue (Oels 2014).

This chapter aims to critically review the literature that discusses climate migration. After an initial review, there will be a discussion of the misleading claims, gaps, and assumptions about this linkage in the literature. Finally, the chapter will discuss the necessary components of a research agenda on climate migration or "climate mobilities" that does not depend on problematic assumptions and that advances our understanding of the connection between climate change and human mobility.

LITERATURE ON CLIMATE MIGRATION AND CLIMATE REFUGEES: FAULTY ESTIMATES

The policy framework on the question of whether people migrate because of environmental/climate changes dates back to a 1985 study for the UN Environment Programme (UNEP) by El-Hinnawi (Daoudy et al. 2022). In this study, El-Hinnawi (1985: 4) defined environmental refugees as people "who have been forced to leave their traditional habitat, temporarily or permanently, because of a marked environmental disruption ... that jeopardized their existence and/or seriously affected the quality of their life." Since then, many studies have been published on the subject, although the terminology that they used differed and alternated between "climate change-induced displacement, environmental migrants, environmental-induced migrants, eco-migrants, displaced migrants or crisis migrants" (Ferris 2017: 113) as well as "climate/ environmental refugees" to refer to the forced nature of this type of migration.

Norman Myers is a scholar whose works are widely cited in the literature on *environmental refugees*. Starting from the late 1980s, Myers wrote several papers where he discussed the "growing phenomenon" of *environmental refugees* and *eco-refugees* (Myers 1986, 1993, 1994, 1997, 2002, 2005; Myers &

Kent 1995). Myers (1993: 752) defines environmental refugees as "people who can no longer gain a secure livelihood in their erstwhile homelands because of drought, soil erosion, desertification, and other environmental problems." He also specifically refers to the impacts of global warming on the emergence of environmental refugees. In his works, Myers gives estimates and predictions of the numbers of people who will be displaced because of environmental change. As Gemenne (2011) discusses, the numbers in his works became the most influential and controversial figures discussed in public debates. For instance, in Myers (1993), the total number of environmental refugees foreseen in a "greenhouse-affected world" circa 2050 is calculated as 150 million. Here, Myers also reminds the "strains generated for receiver nations today when they have to face throngs of refugees fleeing from drought, famine, floods, and other disasters" (p. 759). He concludes with a warning about the consequences of 150 million environmental refugees, apparently for the receiving nations in the North: "It requires a leap of the imagination to envisage 150 million destitutes abandoning their homelands, many of them crossing international borders. They would be all the more disruptive in a world struggling to cope with a plethora of environmental problems" (p. 759).

In another report by Myers and Kent (1995), there is the argument that there were 25 million people displaced because of environmental changes in 1995. This number seems to be based on a compilation of different regional and country reports, some of which were conducted by Myers and others by other researchers. The figure of 25 million includes 5 million displaced people in the Sahel, 7 million in other parts of Africa, 6 million internal migrants in China, 2 million in Mexican cities, and 1 million people displaced by public works projects (Gemenne 2011). In a later work (Myers 2002: 610), Myers talked about the 1995 estimate of 25 million environmental refugees as "cautious and conservative." He also argued that the number of environmental refugees "could well double by the year 2010 and increase steadily for a good while thereafter as growing numbers of impoverished people press ever harder on overloaded environments" (Myers 2002: 609).

Gemenne (2011) makes an assessment of the estimate of the number of environmental refugees by Myers and argues that it does not rely on any specific methodology:

> ...for each region of the world, the number of internally displaced people is considered. On the basis of these figures, Myers makes an estimate of the proportion that could have been displaced because of environmental disruptions. This estimate is based on reports and observations of environmental degradation in the considered region, but no attention is given to an examination of the linkages between environmental change and migration behavior. In an essentialist fashion, Myers assumes that all people displaced in an area affected by environmental changes have been displaced solely because of these changes. ... Myers rules out the possibility that

some could have been displaced outside of their country – international migration is not considered in his estimate. (Gemenne 2011: S43)

Gemenne (2011) also emphasizes that despite these limitations, the estimate by Myers (25 million) has been extensively used in public debates and in some reports and documents that aimed to raise awareness about environmental refugees. The problem that Gemenne points out is not limited to Myers' estimates. About the literature that aims to predict the numbers of climate refugees, Biermann and Boas (2010: 67) state that "all current predictions are fraught with numerous methodological problems and caveats." They also state that these methodological problems usually lead to pessimistic estimates. We can also say that these pessimistic estimates feed alarmist discourses, although these discourses on climate refugees are at odds with contemporary research on the impact of climate change on migration (Bettini 2017: 34). In the literature, there is also no agreement on the definition of climate or environmental refugees, which makes it difficult to compare their results. As many studies operate with very broad definitions of climate or environmental refugees, their estimates end up being large numbers (Suhrke 1994). Moreover, many of these estimates depend on assumptions about human behavior such as the assumption that people will flee from affected areas, although we don't know whether and how many individuals will have migration as their main strategy. Additionally, although climate change is one reason to migrate, it is usually not the only or the main cause. Therefore, the prediction of numbers of climate or environmental refugees is difficult (Biermann & Boas 2010).

Gemenne (2011) argues that although many of the estimates of climate/environmental refugees were published in the gray literature, rather than academic journals, with little attention to methodological issues and received with skepticism in the scholarly community, they created great interest in the media and policy-making circles. They have had a significant impact on public debates as they were considered as a warning against an approaching human catastrophe. They have shaped the ways in which the public and policymakers approach the issue.

SECURITIZATION

The debate about the possible results of climate change on migration developed during the 1980s and 1990s, and it was especially steered by environmental scientists who were concerned about the impacts of climate change on populations. As I have discussed above, the estimates of the numbers of potential migrants were a major component of these studies. As exemplified by the quotations from the work of Myers above, such migration was also represented as a potential disaster. These estimates of potential migrants were used by campaign groups to highlight and call attention to the possible impacts of these issues (Geddes 2015). The assumption that large numbers of people will migrate from vulnerable areas due to climate change has been accompanied by a perspective that sees climate migration as a security challenge. Being framed by a security perspective, it was argued that environmental/climate change could increase conflicts (Homer-Dixon 1991). Accordingly, climate change would encourage migration from vulnerable areas of the world to the developed regions and increase conflict, which would result in insecurity everywhere. Apocalyptic narratives were produced which predicted massive and unavoidable flows of climate refugees (Bettini 2013). As Geddes (2015) argues, the projection of potential mass migration had crucial impacts on the EU political system given the existing fears about the effects of large-scale migration. These projections reinforced the security-driven understanding of the "migration problem" (see for instance Greenhill 2010a, 2010b). Climate change has been characterized as a threat to national, international, and human security (Oels 2012). When the issue of climate migration is perceived as a foreign and security policy issue, the emphasis has been on controls to prevent large-scale migration.

As Daoudy et al. (2022) discuss, analysts have focused on different objects of security (state, international community, communities/individuals, eco-system), different actors that will deal with threats (military, multilateral organizations, communities, individuals), and different kinds of threats (scarcity, climate variability, conflict, etc.). They emphasize that "making assumptions about 'security' without identifying a referent object leads to misunderstandings over the nature of climate insecurity and how it operates on political, social, and ecological levels" (Daoudy et al 2022: 3). Similarly, McDonald (2013) also demonstrates that the link between climate change and security has been conceptualized in several different ways. Accordingly, climate security might refer to climate change as a national security threat, a human security threat, an international security threat, and an ecological security threat. These different understandings of security can legitimize different practices with different implications for climate change policy. However, as McDonald (2013) discusses, these different understandings of climate security have not been equally prominent. National and international security discourses have dominated with their focus on conflict, sovereignty, stability, and economic interests. This kind of focus has consequences like presenting victims as a threat:

> the national and international security discourses orient around the preservation of some notion of the status-quo: either the preservation of the sovereignty/territorial integrity of nation-states or the preservation of an international society of states ... the logic of these discourses can encourage perverse political responses that not only

fail to respond effectively to climate change but may present victims of it as a threat. (McDonald 2013: 49)

In the literature on climate migration, there are several examples for works that hold national and international security perspectives. For instance, in their article titled "Europe's Twenty-First-Century Challenge: Climate Change, Migration, and Security", Werz and Hoffman (2016) refer to climate change as an important contributing factor to migration. They write about how vulnerable regions such as sub-Saharan Africa, the Middle East, South Asia, and South-East Asia will face the consequences of climate change in the coming decades, and that the "destabilizing effects" of these changes will also have impacts for the foreign and economic interests of the EU. They stress that "given the current influx of refugees, time is running out" (p. 147). According to them, the migratory trends combined with the projected rapid population growth in Sahel and West Africa will affect Europe. Their proposed solution in the face of these trends is an enlarged conception of national security: "Europe, in concert with the US, should broaden its conception of national security to encompass the underlying trends which threaten the stability of the rules-based international order, which is the foundation of our own security and prosperity" (p. 150).

In an article on the security implications of climate change, Podesta and Ogden (2008) start by stating that developing nations will be the most negatively affected by climate change. In those countries, interwoven crises will drive human migration which will create food shortages in new regions. According to them, climate-induced migration will create the biggest geopolitical challenges in South Asia, Africa, and Europe. In this article, human migration is characterized as a threat, a challenge, a factor that can increase the risk of pandemic, and an issue that contributes to political and economic turmoil and exacerbates existing conflicts. With respect to the "challenges" that climate migration will bring to Europe, Podesta and Ogden (2008) write that "there will be a likely surge in the number of Muslim immigrants to the European Union, which could exacerbate existing tensions and increase the likelihood of radicalization among members of Europe's growing and often poorly assimilated Islamic communities" (p. 120). Elsewhere (Podesta & Ogden 2007: 8), they claimed that the "most worrisome" problems related to climate change will be from large-scale migrations of people. According to them, the movements of people will possibly create disruptions and these disruptions will create security concerns and regional tensions. "Uncontrolled migration" is named among potential problems "that are more likely to overwhelm the traditional instruments of national security" (p. 10).

In his article, Busby (2008) asks the question of whether climate change is a national security threat to the US. He answers this question affirmatively claiming that it constitutes a national security threat in terms of both direct threats and larger extraterritorial interests. He argues that governments of poor countries may use the "strategic threat of migration" if the governments of rich countries do not respond to climate change (Busby 2008: 489). He discusses that climate change may make violent conflict more probable and that environmental refugees is a potential cause of violent conflict.

In these examples and many others, climate-induced mass migration from the more vulnerable poor or developing countries to the developed ones is considered as a major threat to national security for the latter group of countries. This focus on national security of the developing countries and the accompanying worries seem to shape the direction of the debates on climate change to a large extent. Finally, these discourses on climate migration as a security threat also have racialized connotations (Ahuja 2016; Baldwin 2013, 2016). Such discourses feed into the already existing nationalist fears and exclusionist discourses about migrant groups that originate from developing countries or about Muslim migrants, as exemplified by Podesta and Ogden's (2008) scenario.

The media representations of climate change-induced migration have a major role to play in the securitization of this type of human mobility. Sakellari (2021) argues that the way the media presents migrating people because of climate change is similar to the ways in which they present migrants and refugees in general. Media, especially in the developed host countries, show climate migrants as victims who had to leave their homes or as a potential threat to the order of the host country (Sakellari 2021: 65). Methmann (2014) also shows that in news media, migrating people are portrayed as racialized and passive victims of a changing climate within US, UK, and German newspaper articles. There are contradictory elements in this type of this discourse in the sense that while they are portrayed as victims of climate change on the one hand, they are also represented as a source of threat for the countries where they are migrating. This type of portrayal as victim and threat leads to the framing of those people to be perceived as a single, unified group composed of passive but dangerous individuals. As the research shows, media often use discursive strategies of threat and urgency to portray climate change-induced migration.

CRITIQUES OF THE CLIMATE MIGRATION THESES

Especially in debates on migration, the uncritical use of certain categories by policymakers, media, and scholars can lead to an inaccurate understanding of migration phenomena. In some cases, there are widespread discourses which present deceptive portrayals of the scale, nature, and reasons of migration processes. The discourses that present climate change as a major driver of the massive movement of climate refugees from South to North is a major example for this (De Haas et al. 2019).

Human mobility is influenced by several socio-economic, cultural, political, and climate-related factors at the same time. It is not accurate to link it solely to climate change. It is important to recognize that migration in the context of climate change is multi-causal (Baldwin & Fornalé 2017: 322). Moreover, as all these factors come into play in influencing migration, it is difficult to be precise about to what extent climate change has an impact on it. In that sense, making a distinction between climate migrants/refugees and other migrants/refugees as distinguishable groups is not possible in many cases. This also makes most predictions about climate-related migration flawed. Although it is about environmental change in general, the major conclusions of the Foresight report *Migration and Global Environmental Change* (2011) are also relevant for climate migration. According to the report, environmental change will continue affecting migration in the future through its impact on economic, political, and social factors. However, the interactions between these factors are complex, so it will not really be possible to distinguish between migrants whose migration has been driven by environmental change and the other migrants. Additionally, the political, economic, and social factors behind migration will lead to the continuation of migration regardless of environmental change.

The report recognizes that the influence of environmental change on migration will increase in the future. When environmental change threatens people's livelihoods, migration comes into the picture as a traditional response. However, it is equally possible that environmental change can make migration less probable for the reason that migration (especially international migration) is expensive. Those individuals who are exposed to the impacts of environmental change may experience a decrease in the capitals (economic, social, cultural) which will be necessary for their move. The concept of *trapped populations* is used to refer to those people who are prevented from mobility due to environmental/climate change. Hence, the report emphasizes that, in the future, millions of people will be unable to move from those areas which are tremendously vulnerable to environmental change.[3] Although the "masses" who will migrate due to environmental/climate change are a major concern for policy today, "trapped populations" can also become a main policy concern (Black et al. 2011; Geddes et al. 2012; Ayeb-Karlsson et al. 2018; Zickgraf 2019; Cattaneo et al. 2020; Cundill et al. 2021). As Burzyński et al. (2022) argue, under the existing migration laws and policies, only a small portion of people who are affected by climate change can move beyond their homelands. The Foresight report concludes that "preventing or constraining migration is not a 'no risk' option. Doing so will lead to increased impoverishment, displacement, and irregular migration in many settings" (Foresight 2011: 9).

As I discussed in the previous section, another major characteristic of debates on climate mobility is linking this type of mobility to national security. In an early work, Deudney (1990) aimed to challenge the tendency to link climate/environmental change with national security making three major claims. He argued that it is analytically wrong to think of environmental degradation as a national security threat, as the focus of national security does not have much in common with environmental problems or their solutions. Moreover, he claimed, using the emotional power of nationalism to mobilize environmental awareness can be counterproductive as it can weaken globalist feelings. Finally, he stated that it is not likely that environmental degradation will cause interstate wars. Daoudy et al.'s (2022) warning about climate-conflict narratives is also crucial. They argue that especially the governments in the Global South may be considered as passive actors and victims of nature according to this kind of narrative. Focusing on climate as a major factor behind conflict may lead to neglecting other drivers of conflict including regime policies and authoritative systems. "Indeed, leaders may invoke the climate-conflict thesis to justify repressive measures to stop human mobility at the domestic and international levels, feeding perceptions of the culpability of 'environmental migrants' in triggering social and political unrest, while overlooking the responsibility of authoritarian or developmentally failed regimes" (Daoudy et al. 2022: 3). The links between climate change, migration, and conflict are complex and these complex links cannot be explained using simple and sensationalist accounts (Brzoska & Fröhlich 2016). Finally, we can also consider McDonald's (2013) argument that the dominance of national and international security discourses implies a tendency towards preserving the status quo. In fact, when we consider the scale of the challenges that we are faced with today due to climate change, what we need is a new way of thinking about our relationship to the world rather than trying to preserve the status quo.

A NEW RESEARCH AGENDA ON CLIMATE MOBILITIES

An overview of the recent debates on climate-induced migration demonstrates that we are not close to having progressive approaches to this kind of human mobility. Climate migration is mostly considered as a problem to be solved (Bettini 2017). It is important to push back against discourses that portray migrants as a source of fear or an issue that needs to be dealt with (Bryne 2018). Bettini's study is worth mentioning here. Bettini (2013) identified four major climate change discourses, which are scientific, capitalist, humanitarian, and radical discourses, and in his study, these discourses are exemplified by the IPCC Assessment Report 2007, the Stern Review of 2007, Christian Aid's "Human Tide: The Real Migration Crisis" in 2007, and the Agreement at the People's Conference on Climate Change and the Rights of Mother Earth Cochabamba, Bolivia respectively. He demonstrates that although these are conflicting discourses on climate change, they all converge into apocalyptic narratives. In other words, although these discourses frame climate change in different ways and do not share common goals, they establish a "discursive coalition" around apocalyptic narratives. Such narratives foresee an ultimate threat and mobilize a sense of fear and urgency. Moreover, dramatization of the climate issue as such does not necessarily ignite any struggle against it.

Boas et al. (2019) present six research priorities which can help climate migration policy to move beyond its current security focus: First, funding should be given to research that questions and examines the assumption that climate change leads to migration, not necessarily to research that supports that assumption. Second, as the concept migration does not cover the variety of ways in which humans might move in response to climate change, they propose the use of the term *climate mobilities*, rather than climate migration. Third, climate mobilities should be considered as the new normal, rather than an exception in new research. Fourth, policy should be based on research that takes into consideration the non-linear complexity of mobility in the context of climate change and social change. Fifth, research on climate mobilities should better include affected populations. Finally, climate mobilities research should also focus on destination areas, not only on the sending areas.

Bettini's (2017) recommendation that "there should be no space for the concept of climate refugees" is also crucial. As he argues, although the concept can easily attract attention, it cannot contribute to progressive agendas on climate and migration; it is a flawed concept. Moreover, climate migration should not be seen as a problem to be solved. As he argues, this kind of perspective relies on an understanding of migration as pathological. Although we need to talk more about climate change and migration, we should do it in the framework of climate justice, rather than as a security crisis (Bettini 2017: 37).

CONCLUSION

As Farbotko and Lazrus (2012) state, climate change is both a material phenomenon and also a narrative, and making sense of climate change necessitates comprehensive conceptualizations that both include multiple voices and also recognize the agency of vulnerable populations. On the one hand, there is growing consensus about some climate change effects like sea-level rise. However, on the other hand, there are also discourses about the impacts of climate change especially for humans, which are debatable to a large extent. Some of these discourses gained popularity especially in policy circles and public debates, being supported by certain strands of scholarship. The discussions about the impact of climate/environmental change on human mobility have largely been shaped by estimates and projections about mass migration. Consequently, it has been considered as a national and international security issue and the focus has largely been on preventing large-scale migration. Climate-induced migration has been approached as a destabilizing factor, a threat, and almost as a natural disaster. New research demonstrates that the projections about hundreds of millions of people being forced to migrate due to environmental and climate change are not well founded and they are misleading. Environmental/climate change should be understood as one driver of migration in addition to other political, economic, and social factors. Rather than being considered as a threat to national security, climate-induced migration can be perceived as an adaptation response to the impacts of climate change (Bardsley & Hugo 2010). Moreover, in addition to those who will migrate because of climate change, there will be many others who will be unable to move from those vulnerable areas. Immobility as well as mobility should be a policy concern if we are looking at the implications of climate change. We need a new research agenda that does not rely on assumptions rooted in national and international security agendas, and most important of all, we need a radical reexamination and transformation of our relationship to the world if we want to successfully deal with the challenges of climate change. As Faist and Schade (2013: 4) state, we need a reconsideration of the social construction of human–environment relationships, the inequalities behind the unsustainable exploitation of resources, the struggle of people who try to overcome those inequalities by mobility, and the part institutions play in overcoming or reproducing existing vulnerabilities to make sense of climate-induced migration.

NOTES

1. Although "climate change" will be the main concept used in this article, other concepts like "environmental change" will also be used while discussing other scholars' arguments in this area.
2. For a discussion on the strands of the climate migrant debate, see Faist and Schade (2013).
3. Benveniste et al. (2020) argue that there is no available estimate of the number of people who might be affected by the "trapping" effect. In this study, they claim to provide the first quantitative, global analysis of trapped populations due to resource depletion related to climate change. They show that "climate change can lead to decreases in emigration of lowest income levels – i.e. increases in trapped populations – by over 10% in 2100 for medium development and climate scenarios and by up to 50% for more pessimistic scenarios."

REFERENCES

Ahuja, Neel. "Race, human security, and the climate refugee." *English Language Notes* 54, no. 2 (2016): 25–32.

Ayeb-Karlsson, Sonja, Christopher D. Smith, and Dominic Kniveton. "A discursive review of the textual use of 'trapped' in environmental migration studies: The conceptual birth and troubled teenage years of trapped populations." *Ambio* 47, no. 5 (2018): 557–573.

Baldwin, Andrew. "Racialisation and the figure of the climate-change migrant." *Environment and Planning A* 45, no. 6 (2013): 1474–1490.

Baldwin, Andrew. "Premediation and white affect: Climate change and migration in critical perspective." *Transactions of the Institute of British Geographers* 41, no. 1 (2016): 78–90.

Baldwin, Andrew, and Elisa Fornalé. "Adaptive migration: Pluralising the debate on climate change and migration." *The Geographical Journal* 183, no. 4 (2017): 322–328.

Bardsley, Douglas K., and Graeme J. Hugo. "Migration and climate change: Examining thresholds of change to guide effective adaptation decision-making." *Population and Environment* 32, no. 2 (2010): 238–262.

Benveniste, Hélčne, Michael Oppenheimer, and Marc Fleurbaey. "Climate change increases trapped populations: When migration cannot be used as an adaptation solution." In *AGU Fall Meeting Abstracts*, vol. 2020, pp. GC036-08. 2020.

Bettini, Giovanni. "Climate barbarians at the gate? A critique of apocalyptic narratives on 'climate refugees'." *Geoforum* 45 (2013): 63–72.

Bettini, Giovanni. "Where next? Climate change, migration, and the (bio) politics of adaptation." *Global Policy* 8 (2017): 33–39.

Biermann, Frank, and Ingrid Boas. "Preparing for a warmer world: Towards a global governance system to protect climate refugees." *Global Environmental Politics* 10, no. 1 (2010): 60–88.

Black, Richard, W. Neil Adger, Nigel W. Arnell, Stefan Dercon, Andrew Geddes, and David Thomas. "The effect of environmental change on human migration." *Global Environmental Change* 21 (2011): S3–S11.

Boas, Ingrid, Carol Farbotko, Helen Adams, Harald Sterly, Simon Bush, Kees Van der Geest, Hanne Wiegel et al. "Climate migration myths." *Nature Climate Change* 9, no. 12 (2019): 901–903.

Bryne, Calvin. "Climate change and human migration." *UC Irvine Law Review* 8 (2018): 761–788.

Brzoska, Michael, and Christiane Fröhlich. "Climate change, migration and violent conflict: Vulnerabilities, pathways and adaptation strategies." *Migration and Development* 5, no. 2 (2016): 190–210.

Burzyński, Michał, Christoph Deuster, Frédéric Docquier, and Jaime De Melo. "Climate change, inequality, and human migration." *Journal of the European Economic Association* 20, no. 3 (2022): 1145–1197.

Busby, Joshua W. "Who cares about the weather? Climate change and US national security." *Security Studies* 17, no. 3 (2008): 468–504.

Cameron, Edward. "The human dimension of global climate change." *Hastings Environmental Law Journal* 15, no. 1 (2009): art. 1.

Cattaneo, Cristina, Michel Beine, Christiane J. Fröhlich, Dominic Kniveton, Inmaculada Martinez-Zarzoso, Marina Mastrorillo, Katrin Millock, Etienne Piguet,

and Benjamin Schraven. "Human migration in the era of climate change." *Review of Environmental Economics and Policy* 13, no. 2 (2020): 189–206.
Christian Aid. *Human tide: The real migration crisis*. Report, May 2007.
Cundill, Georgina, Chandni Singh, William Neil Adger, Ricardo Safra De Campos, Katharine Vincent, Mark Tebboth, and Amina Maharjan. "Toward a climate mobilities research agenda: Intersectionality, immobility, and policy responses." *Global Environmental Change* 69 (2021): 102315.
Daoudy, Marwa, Jeannie Sowers, and Erika Weinthal. "What is climate security? Framing risks around water, food, and migration in the Middle East and North Africa." *Wiley Interdisciplinary Reviews: Water* 9, no. 3 (2022): e1582.
De Haas, Hein, Stephen Castles, and Mark J. Miller. *The age of migration: International population movements in the modern world*. London: Bloomsbury Publishing, 2019.
Deudney, Daniel. "The case against linking environmental degradation and national security." *Millennium* 19, no. 3 (1990): 461–476.
El-Hinnawi, Essam. *Environmental refugees*. UNEP, Nairobi, 1985.
Faist, Thomas, and Jeanette Schade. *Disentangling migration and climate change*. Dordrecht, Heidelberg, New York and London: Springer, 2013.
Farbotko, Carol, and Heather Lazrus. "The first climate refugees? Contesting global narratives of climate change in Tuvalu." *Global Environmental Change* 22, no. 2 (2012): 382–390.
Ferris, Elizabeth. "The relevance of the Guiding Principles on Internal Displacement for the climate change–migration nexus." In B. Mayer and F. Crepeau (eds.), *Research handbook on climate change, migration and the law* (pp. 108–130). Cheltenham, UK and Northampton, MA, USA: Edward Elgar Publishing, 2017.
Foresight UK. *Migration and global environmental change: Final project report*. The Government Office for Science, London, 2011. https://www.gov.uk/government/uploads/system/uploads/attachment_data/file/287717/11-1116-migrationand-global-environmentalchange.pdf
Geddes, Andrew. "Governing migration from a distance: Interactions between climate, migration, and security in the South Mediterranean." *European Security* 24, no. 3 (2015): 473–490.
Geddes, Andrew, W. Neil Adger, Nigel W. Arnell, Richard Black, and David S. G, Thomas. "Migration, environmental change, and the 'challenges of governance'." *Environment and Planning C: Government and Policy* 30, no. 6 (2012): 951–967.
Gemenne, François. "Why the numbers don't add up: A review of estimates and predictions of people displaced by environmental changes." *Global Environmental Change* 21 (2011): S41–S49.
Gore, Timothy. *Extreme carbon inequality: Why the Paris climate deal must put the poorest, lowest emitting and most vulnerable people first*. Media Briefing, Oxfam International, 2 December 2015.
Gore, Tim. *Carbon inequality in 2030: Per capita consumption emissions and the 1.5C goal*. Study, Institute for European Environmental Policy, 5 November 2021.
Greenhill, Kelly M. *Weapons of mass migration: Forced displacement, coercion and foreign policy*. Ithaca, NY: Cornell University Press, 2010a.
Greenhill, Kelly M. "Weapons of mass migration: Forced displacement as an instrument of coercion." *Strategic Insights* 9, no. 1 (2010b): 116–159.
Homer-Dixon, T. "On the threshold: Environmental changes as causes of acute conflict." *International Security* 16 (1991): 76–116.

IPCC. *AR4 climate change 2007: The physical science basis*. Fourth Assessment Report, 2007.
IPCC. *AR5 climate change 2013: The physical science basis*. Fifth Assessment Report, 2013.
Karl, Thomas R., and Kevin E. Trenberth. "Modern global climate change." *Science* 302, no. 5651 (2003): 1719–1723.
Kartha, Sivan, Eric Kemp-Benedict, Emily Ghosh, Anisha Nazareth, and Tim Gore. *The carbon inequality era*. Joint Research Report, Stockholm Environment Institute and Oxfam International, 21 September 2020.
McDonald, Matt. "Discourses of climate security." *Political Geography* 33 (2013): 42–51.
McMichael, Anthony J., and Andrew Haines. "Global climate change: The potential effects on health." *BMJ* 315, no. 7111 (1997): 805–809.
Methmann, Chris. "Visualizing climate-refugees: Race, vulnerability, and resilience in global liberal politics." *International Political Sociology* 8, no. 4 (2014): 416–435.
Monbiot, George. *Heat: How we can stop the planet burning*. London: Penguin UK, 2007.
Myers, Norman. "The environmental dimension to security issues." *Environmentalist* 6, no. 4 (1986): 251–257.
Myers, Norman. "Environmental refugees in a globally warmed world." *Bioscience* 43, no. 11 (1993): 752–761.
Myers, Norman. "Eco-refugees: A crisis in the making." *People & the Planet* 3, no. 4 (1994): 6–9.
Myers, Norman. "Environmental refugees." *Population and Environment* 19, no. 2 (1997): 167–182.
Myers, Norman. "Environmental refugees: A growing phenomenon of the 21st century." *Philosophical Transactions of the Royal Society of London. Series B: Biological Sciences* 357, no. 1420 (2002): 609–613.
Myers, Norman. *Environmental refugees: An emergent security issue*. 13th Meeting of the OSCE Economic Forum, Prague, 23–27 May 2005.
Myers, Norman, and Jennifer Kent. *Environmental exodus: An emergent crisis in the global arena*. Washington, DC: Climate Institute, 1995.
Oels, Angela. "From 'securitization' of climate change to 'climatization' of the security field: Comparing three theoretical perspectives." In J. Scheffran, M. Brzoska, H. G. Brauch, P. M. Link, and J. Schilling (eds.), *Climate change, human security and violent conflict* (pp. 185–205). Berlin and Heidelberg: Springer, 2012.
Oels, Angela. "Climate security as governmentality: From precaution to preparedness." In J. Stripple and H. Bulkeley (eds.), *Governing the global climate* (pp. 197–216). Cambridge: Cambridge University Press, 2014.
Podesta, John, and Peter Ogden. *Global warning: The security challenges of climate change*. Center for American Progress, 5 November 2007.
Podesta, John, and Peter Ogden. "The security implications of climate change." *Washington Quarterly* 31, no. 1 (2008): 115–138.
Rosa, Eugene A., Thomas K. Rudel, Richard York, Andrew K. Jorgenson, and Thomas Dietz. "The human (anthropogenic) driving forces of global climate change." In R. E. Dunlap and R. J. Brulle (eds.), *Climate change and society: Sociological perspectives* (pp. 32–60). New York: Oxford University Press, 2015.
Sakellari, Maria. "Climate change and migration in the UK news media: How the story is told." *International Communication Gazette* 83, no. 1 (2021): 63–80.

Stern, Nicholas. *The economics of climate change: The Stern review*. Cambridge: Cambridge University Press, 2007.
Suhrke, Astri. "Environmental degradation and population flows." *Journal of International Affairs* 47, no. 2 (1994): 473–496.
Werz, Michael, and Max Hoffman. "Europe's twenty-first-century challenge: Climate change, migration and security." *European View* 15, no. 1 (2016): 145–154.
WPC. *People's Agreement: World People's Conference on Climate Change and the Rights of Mother Earth.* https://pwccc.wordpress.com/category/working-groups/06-climate-migrants/ (accessed 6 June 2022).
Zickgraf, Caroline. "Keeping people in place: Political factors of (im)mobility and climate change." *Social Sciences* 8, no. 8 (2019): art. 228.

14. The welfare state in turbulent times: a perspective from the United States
Alex Waddan

14.1 INTRODUCTION

The American welfare state has constantly lived in turbulent times with the value of government support for the public, both on a collective and individual basis, more contested than in other rich industrialized democracies. The United States is the archetype of Esping-Andersen's (1990) liberal welfare regime. In contrast even to other liberal regimes such as Canada and the United Kingdom, the U.S. lacks a truly universal national-level social welfare program (Béland and Waddan, 2017). Social Security and Medicare are social insurance programs that are effectively comprehensive in their scope, but these are targeted at the country's seniors and have not provided a model for the expansion of programs for working-aged Americans or the nation's children. In many areas of policy there is still a reliance on social assistance programs to provide benefits and services for the vulnerable, relying on bureaucracies that are fragmented and with eligibility criteria that are often designed to exclude rather than include potential recipients.

In the circumstances, the pressures of the financial crisis and the COVID-19 pandemic would seem likely to expose the fragilities and fragmentation of the existing social supports and leave many households facing significant economic vulnerability. As it is, the story of the U.S. government's response to these two, quite distinct but both hugely economically convulsive, crises has been more complex than might be expected from the stereotype of a minimalist welfare regime. In both cases there were significant expansions of social supports in order to protect households against the immediate economic pressures. To some extent the pressure to provide these supports was a function of the limited capacity of the pre-existing social welfare framework automatically to respond to increased demand. Yet, the scale of this policy reaction went beyond triage dealing with the immediate wounds as policymakers used the turbulence to justify attempting broader social policy restructuring. These efforts at more transformative change met with mixed success, but the efforts at short-term pain relief should not be neglected. In 2009 some of this assistance was hidden from explicit public view as much of the direct income support was enacted under the guise of a wider economic recovery package. That legislation was enacted largely on partisan lines with little Republican support for the measures, but in spring 2020 even conservatives were initially on board with pushing through an array of major expansions of social welfare programs.

This chapter will look at how policymakers responded to the Great Recession and the COVID-19 pandemic and will reflect on how the efforts to move beyond short-term measures to embed more permanent changes to U.S. social policy met with mixed success. First, it is important to establish the pre-existing parameters of the American welfare state.

14.2 THE AMERICAN WELFARE STATE

At the start of the new millennium the U.S. still lacked a universal health care system, a family allowance program and social policy instruments had been employed only sporadically to mitigate against rising market-based inequalities over the last generation (Taskforce on Inequality and American Democracy, 2004). Nevertheless, despite this compelling narrative that posits the U.S. as a relative welfare state "laggard" there are major welfare programs. Social Security and Medicare, which provide pensions and health insurance to the country's seniors, are popular (Newport, 2019) and have proved resilient in the face of efforts at direct retrenchment if otherwise vulnerable to "policy drift" (Béland and Waddan, 2012). Medicaid, providing health coverage to categories of low-income households, was established alongside Medicare in 1965 and grew beyond initial expectations, somewhat escaping the tag of "welfare medicine" (Olson, 2010).

In addition, if not generous in their payment levels, there are federally run cash or equivalent benefits that provide assistance on a means-tested basis. The Food Stamp Program, renamed as the Supplemental Nutrition Assistance Program (SNAP) in 2008, has served a greater and fewer number over time, but has acted as something of an automatic economic stabilizer for low-income households in recessions and has been expanded in scope, if temporarily, in times of acute crisis. Beyond these benefits and services, there is the so-called "hidden" or "submerged" welfare state (Howard, 1997; Mettler, 2011). This is primarily a series of programs that do not advertise as offering direct cash payments, but take the form of tax credits. Sometimes these are effectively cash programs. The Earned Income Tax Credit (EITC) is a refundable credit paid to low-income working families (Falk and Crandall-Hollick, 2016). The reference to "refundable" means that many beneficiaries do not just get back some of the tax they have paid but receive a payment beyond any taxes paid. In other cases, the measures are not readily identifiable as programs in themselves but act as subsidies enabling access to welfare services through the private sector. Most notably, employer-sponsored health insurance is not treated as a taxable in-kind benefit (Tax Policy Center, 2022). Hence, the government forfeits monies it would receive if it did treat these benefits as "salary."

If these hidden programs mean that there is more to the American welfare state than might immediately meet the eye, other aspects of its organization lead to fragmentation and inequities. Importantly, programs managed jointly by the federal and state governments can leave the latter with considerable discretion in the distribution of benefits and services. Medicaid, for example, is organized and funded by both federal and state governments. The federal government did impose some requirements on states for the latter to receive any federal monies but there was considerable state discretion in determining eligibility rules. In fact, when the Great Recession hit there were no two states with the same rules about coverage. Unemployment Insurance (UI) was another program with its governance divided between federal and state authorities. Again, this led to wide discrepancies in who received benefits. In 2019, the recipiency rate, measuring how many of the unemployed actually qualified for assistance, varied from New Jersey, where 59% of the unemployed got UI payments, to Florida where 11% did so (U.S. Department of Labor, 2022).

14.3 THE GREAT RECESSION

The fiscal crisis of 2008 that bled into the Great Recession hit a U.S. economy that had grown unevenly during the preceding years. As the recession took its toll on this already lumpy economy, the unemployment rate rose, peaking at 10.1% in October 2009 (U.S. Department of Labor, 2010). In aggregate "Real gross domestic product (GDP) fell 4.3 percent from its peak in 2007Q4 to its trough in 2009Q2, the largest decline in the post-war era" at that time (Rich, 2013).

These numbers show the scale and nature of the challenge that American socio-economic policymakers faced as the financial crisis quickly evolved into a deep recession. A revolution in economic policy was never likely to be the response to the vicissitudes of the downturn, but how would the framework of the U.S. welfare state, with its fragmented and sometimes piecemeal set of programs, respond to the rapidly emerged hardship imposed on so many households? While not heralding a revolution, the crisis did shift the political climate and add momentum to the campaign of "hope and change" of the Democrat presidential nominee Barack Obama, with Obama's victory in November 2008 leading to some considerable commentary suggesting that he might preside over a new New Deal (Skocpol and Jacobs, 2011). Shortly after the election *Time* magazine famously mocked up a picture of Obama as Franklin Roosevelt and during the transition incoming chief-of-staff Rahm Emanuel (2008) remarked: "You never want a serious crisis to go to waste. And what I mean by that, it's an opportunity to do things you think you could not do before." Did this mean that there was an opportunity to reinforce the American welfare state and add to the structures put in place in the 1930s and mid-1960s? And, if so, would the new administration, along with Democrat majorities in Congress, take advantage of the political opening resulting from economic turbulence to bring about policy change with a longevity beyond that turbulence?

The immediate evidence in fact suggests that the U.S. welfare state left many to flounder as the recession hit. Using the federal government's long-standing official poverty measure, the poverty rate rose from 12.5% in 2007 to 15.1% in 2010 (U.S. Census Bureau 2021). As noted by Fording and Smith at the end of Obama's first term (2012: 1162), "more people have become poor during Obama's first term in office than during any other presidential term for which we have data." As the authors go on to say, however, this snapshot gives a quite misleading summary of the full story. First, the scale of the downturn meant that many countries saw a real reduction in living standards for significant numbers of people. This was not an example of American exceptionalism. Second, it used a poverty measure that did not take into account some of the "hidden" welfare programs such as the EITC and hence the numbers cannot be taken at face value. Third, while even the most supportive historians are unlikely to frame the Obama era as matching the New Deal or Great Society for social policy innovation, the "opportunity" afforded by the turbulence of 2008 and 2009 was not unused by reformers. A series of measures were implemented that at least mitigated the consequence of the recession and in 2010 legislation was passed that saw the most significant reform of the U.S. health care system in 45 years.

A series of provisions were brought in at the start of 2009 as part of the American Recovery and Reinvestment Act (ARRA). While presented as a major stimulus package to combat the widespread economic damage, ARRA did contain a variety of targeted social policy measures to boost the spending power of low-income households. None of the measures were path-breaking innovations in terms of their inherent design, but they were expansive and to an extent effective.

First, ARRA contained provisions to extend the duration of UI. In normal economic times UI offers a relatively meagre degree of protection to workers suffering from unemployment. That meagreness is reflected both in terms of the percentage of the overall number of unemployed who actually receive UI and the level of benefits those deemed eligible end up receiving. In 2008, prior to the Great Recession about 35% of jobless workers received UI (McKenna and McHugh, 2016). The average weekly UI benefit paid across the U.S. amounted to 47% of the previous "normal" weekly wage of a UI recipient

(U.S. Department of Labor, 2022). The program was, however, regularly boosted by the federal government in recessions so that benefits would be paid for 39 weeks rather than the normal 26 weeks. ARRA further eased the rules so that states could more easily access those extra funds and in an unprecedented move the federal government paid an extra $25 per week to each recipient.

ARRA also provided extra monies for SNAP, both increasing the benefit levels and easing eligibility requirements. Overall, federal spending on SNAP, in current dollars, more than doubled between 2008 and 2013 (Spar and Falk, 2016: 9). As former senior advisor to President Clinton, Paul Starr (2018: 50) noted, SNAP served "one in four children and one in eight adults ... by 2010, as the program functioned, in effect, as a minimum basic income." In addition, one-off payments in May 2009 provided a $250 check to all Social Security and SSI beneficiaries.

Beyond these measures there was a further turn to the mechanisms of the "hidden" welfare state and, in particular, the use of tax credits to aid lower-income households. The EITC was expanded again, with an emphasis on helping families with more than two children. The Making Work Pay tax credit offered refundable tax credits of $400 for individuals and $800 for couples through 2009 and 2010 (Mettler, 2011). Finally the existing Child Tax Credit (CTC) was expanded to make its refundable share more generous, meaning that an increased number of families were eligible to get more back from government than they had paid in taxes.

Importantly, these various efforts did diminish the damaging impact of the Great Recession on low-income households. The Center on Budget and Policy Priorities (CBPP), using a refined poverty measure from the official one that did include the impact of programs such as the EITC, estimated that nearly 9 million people had been kept out of poverty due to this raft of measures (Sherman, 2016; for an analysis of alternative poverty measures, Fox et al., 2014). Therefore, U.S. policymakers had reacted to the turbulence of the economic crash with some alacrity as they expanded key elements of the welfare state's social assistance programs. In the end, however, these measures were not path-breaking. This was because they mostly built on existing frameworks and did not create new policy institutions. Moreover, the UI and SNAP expansions did not prove to be durable. Critically, the Democrats' congressional majorities proved to be short-lived. In the 2010 mid-term elections the Republicans gained control of the House and while the Democrats retained the Senate they could no longer set, never mind control, the legislative agenda.

This switch in partisan power was of particular consequence for many of the social policy initiatives in ARRA that had been designed as short-term responses to the immediate crisis and contained sunset clauses to draw them down over time. Hence, if they were to be extended beyond that crisis these welfare expansions required further legislation to renew them. In short, the institutional onus was on the need for positive action from supporters of the programs while inaction would be enough for welfare sceptics. From January 2011 the congressional votes were no longer there to sustain expanded UI or SNAP benefits. In contrast, the EITC expansion, reflecting the fact that it did have some bipartisan support was made permanent, albeit that this move received little publicity as it was part of a much bigger budget agreement painfully negotiated between the Obama White House and congressional Republican leaders at the end of 2015.

14.4 HEALTH CARE REFORM

For all these policy initiatives, Rahm Emanuel's comment about using a crisis as an opportunity for policy change was not widely interpreted to refer to these targeted and mostly time-limited measures. The passage of the Affordable Care Act (ACA), on the other hand, was, as expressed by Vice President Joe Biden at the 2010 signing ceremony, "a big ******* deal" (Stolberg and Pear, 2010). The travails of the American health care system have been well documented and this is a policy domain where American exceptionalism, and inefficiency, was indisputable (see, for example, Quadagno, 2006). In short, the U.S. managed to be an outlier amongst systems in rich nations in both leaving many residents without affordable access to care when they need it and consuming a proportion of GDP well beyond the norm. To a European eye, most shockingly, in 2008 14.9% of the population were without health insurance with many millions more underinsured. This persistent problem was despite the fact that the U.S. spent 16% of GDP on health care in 2008 compared to 11.2% of GDP in France, 10.5% in Germany and 8.7% in the United Kingdom (OECD, 2014). In itself, high spending on health care in a rich democracy might not seem problematic. Health care, after all, is a public good and the richer a country the more it tends to spend on health; but combining high spending with a lack of coverage demonstrates that this was a system beset with inefficiencies that went beyond any notion of inequalities that could be rationalized by reference to individual levels of "deservingness."

As it was, the road to the ACA was long and with many legislative potholes to negotiate and circumvent through 2009 and early 2010 (Jacobs and Skocpol, 2011). Along the way there were compromises with powerful provider interests, notably the pharmaceutical industry and hospitals, in order to soften their opposition to the emerging reform package. Moreover, the ACA was designed so that it did not challenge the fundamentals of the existing system. The preference of the left of the Democratic Party, to move to a single-payer system, was deemed politically impossible and was never given serious consideration in the White House. Employer-based insurance was to remain the primary source of insurance. The idea of introducing a so-called "public option" whereby a federal government-run scheme would compete with private insurers in the individual insurance market was discussed through the legislative process but was not included in the final legislation (Brasfield, 2011). Further, while health care providers were given new incentives to contain costs there was no effort to exert direct government control over their activities. In short, the ACA did not transform American health care into an NHS-lite.

Nevertheless, the ACA led to further government intervention on the financing side of care. There was a significant expansion of the Medicaid program and the initial intention was to set a new national floor for Medicaid eligibility whereby everyone in a household with an income at or below 138% of the federal poverty line would be covered by the program. In addition, the federal government provided subsidies, on a sliding scale, to people with incomes up to 400% of the poverty line in order to purchase insurance in the individual insurance market place (see Jacobs and Skocpol, 2010 for details).

The ACA also applied new pressures on private insurers. These were subject to new regulations requiring them to spend certain proportions of their turnover on care and people with pre-existing health conditions had to be offered affordable insurance plans. Further, in order to prevent insurers circumventing these new rules by offering cheap but flimsy plans, insurance packages had to provide cover against a prescribed list of illnesses and conditions. Finally, and causing the most controversy in the public realm, was the introduction of the so-called "individual mandate" whereby people were required to buy insurance unless they were in an exempt category (Kaiser Family Foundation, 2012). There was little public understanding of this measure, but the underlying logic was to collectivize risk by forcing younger and healthier individuals, who might choose to forego insurance, to participate in the insurance system thereby compensating the insurers that had been forced to offer protection to high-risk individuals.

The passage of the ACA did not lead to the smooth implementation of the law. Republicans maintained their opposition and since much of the responsibility for implementation had been passed on to state governments this provided a new forum for disputation (Béland, Rocco and Waddan, 2019). Further, at the federal level the GOP insisted that it would repeal the law when in an institutional position to do so. That moment seemed to have arrived in January 2017 as President Trump took over the White House accompanied by Republican control of Congress. Yet, the ACA survived, partially at least because in this case there had been positive feedback. This came not just from the millions who had secured care as a consequence of the law but from providers who had accommodated themselves to its provisions and now lobbied for maintaining its provisions (Béland, Rocco and Waddan, 2019).

As Joe Biden entered the White House it was reasonable to assume the ACA's place as the established law of the land, if in a politically battered and somewhat policy-bruised form. Passed in a time of crisis the law had then generated its own political and policy turbulence for almost a further decade. Through that period the ACA was diminished from its original scope. First, and most significantly, the expectation that all states would expand their Medicaid program was undone by a Supreme Court ruling that made it financially viable for states to opt out of that provision. Second, the Tax Cut and Jobs Act of 2017, primarily a piece of legislation cutting the corporate and some individual rate tax rates, reduced the penalty for individuals who did not buy insurance for themselves to $0. Widely reported as a repeal of the individual mandate (which was accurate in effect if not technically the case), there were anxieties that this would lead to a large drop in younger enrolees that would in turn destabilize the insurance market (Fiedler, 2017). Third, through its regulatory authority, the Trump administration made it easier for insurance companies to sell skimpy plans that left out key aspects required under the Obama administration's rules (Scott, 2020).

Despite these setbacks to a fulsome implementation of the ACA the law did help to reduce the number of uninsured Americans. In 2005 there were 41.2 million uninsured, which had risen to 48.6 million in 2010 as the Great Recession took its toll on employer-sponsored insurance. By Obama's last year in office that had dropped to 28.6 million and while the number did rise through the Trump years to 33.2 million in 2019, the figures stabilized after that despite the ravages of the pandemic (Statista, 2022). Moreover, the obligation on insurers to cover pre-existing medical conditions had become embedded in both political and policy worlds. Complaints remained that the premiums and deductibles in the individual insurance market were high but the early signs were that this market remained stable after the effective nulling of the individual mandate (Hall and McCue, 2021). One further evolution was that voters in a number of states took matters into their own hands, so to speak, and chose to expand their Medicaid programs by using the tools of direct democracy available in their state (Rocco, 2020). This included some strongly Republican states such as Idaho, Missouri, Oklahoma and Utah. Many states do not give voters the capacity to bypass elected officials in this way; for example, this is not a means to change policy available in Texas, the single state where Medicaid expansion to the ACA's standards would most reduce the number of uninsured. Nevertheless, the votes that have taken place to expand Medicaid do suggest a popular willingness to see greater government intervention to provide health cover for the most vulnerable households than is suggested by a narrative prioritizing the values of "rugged individualism."

14.5 THE COVID-19 PANDEMIC

Through his opening three years in office President Trump had been no friend to the American welfare state. As described above he had called for the repeal of the ACA and when this failed his administration had worked to make that law's provisions less effective. The administration's budgets, if never acted upon, had proposed cuts to an array of social welfare programs though it is difficult to conceive that Trump himself had much of a hand in developing those proposals. Interestingly, however, Trump's populism, to the extent that this had an identifiable core, meant that he eschewed some of the Republican social policy talking points of the previous two decades. In particular, and notably during the primary campaign for the Republican nomination, he rebuked the idea of privatizing or downsizing the U.S.'s two biggest welfare state programs, Social Security and Medicare (Waddan, 2019). These ideas, aimed at rolling back the parameters of the state, were best represented in the plans of the 2012 Republican Vice Presidential candidate, Congressman Paul Ryan of Wisconsin. While some small government conservatives hoped that a Trump second term might see the president move towards their preferences on these two programs, Ryan-style plans for voucherization of Medicare or a revival of President Bush's 2005 attempt to introduce personal savings accounts into the Social Security program were not put on the legislative agenda during his time in office.

Hence, as Trump entered the last year of his presidency, for all the traumatic political turbulence that had engulfed the country since his entry onto the political scene, there had not been a significant retrenchment of the welfare state. Furthermore, the advent of the COVID-19 pandemic and the realization of just how much economic chaos this would cause then led to some extraordinary policy innovation in the spring of 2020. The following two years saw wild social policy swings as normal partisan politics partially reasserted itself. At the start of 2021 the new Biden administration pushed through a wide-ranging package that fundamentally revamped the CTC, making that program a significant tool in reducing child poverty rates. As we will see, however, unlike the ACA that proved a short-lived extension of the U.S. welfare state.

In the 2018 mid-term elections the Democrats had won control of the House and were therefore in a strong position to help frame the policy response to the pandemic. The early months saw sweeping legislative action, most notably the Coronavirus Aid, Relief, and Economic Security (CARES) Act passed in a bipartisan manner. Importantly in the spring of 2020 the public, while still divided on questions of lockdowns and mask wearing, were supportive of extensive government intervention to maintain financial security for households hit by the fallout from the dramatic decline in economic activity (Pew

Research Center, 2020). A report by the Congressional Research Service (2021: 1) describes the magnitude of what happened: "The unemployment rate rose quickly in March 2020, and by April 2020 it had greatly surpassed its previous peaks observed during and just after the Great Recession. This rise in unemployment was caused by an unprecedented loss of 22.1 million jobs between January 2020 and April 2020."

The nation's UI system was simply inadequate to stabilize households in this catastrophic economic environment. The CARES Act, however, overhauled UI, if temporarily, in a way that dwarfed the changes made in ARRA 11 years previously. Three elements stand out. First, the normal recession-era extension of the duration of UI benefits was put in place. Second, the federal government increased weekly benefits by *$600 a week*, which did mean that many of the unemployed received more than when they were working. Third, the CARES Act also established the Pandemic Unemployment Assistance (PUA) program. This significantly expanded UI eligibility by making the benefit available to groups previously denied access "such as self-employed workers, independent contractors, and gig workers ... unable or unavailable to work due to COVID-19 related reasons" (U.S. Department of Labor, 2020). In order to get money quickly to households the CARES Act also authorized direct payments of $1,200 per adult and $500 per dependent child for everyone who had filed earnings of $75,000 or under in 2019 with the amounts tapering off after that figure. There was also a boost in federal funding to states to support the Medicaid program as its roles increased (Kliff, 2021).

The bipartisan support for the CARES Act soon fractured in predictable ways. Many Republicans began to worry that the generosity of the UI benefits would prove to be a disincentive to displaced workers returning to the labour force. In the lame-duck session of Congress in December 2020, further funding was authorized for UI benefits, SNAP and payments to individuals with incomes up to $75,000 (Barone, 2020). Soon afterwards, the switch in partisan control of the White House and Senate, giving the Democrats unified control of the Presidency and Congress, following Joe Biden's inauguration seemed to offer an opportunity to embed social welfare expansion more securely into the policy landscape.

As Obama took office at a time of crisis so too did Biden. The origins and nature of the two crises were quite distinct, but recession and disease had sown their own form of chaos, and, amidst chaos, some saw political opportunity for these new presidents to act in bold and innovative ways. Hence, just as Obama had entered office with commentators comparing the moment to the start of FDR's presidency, so too Biden was portrayed as a new president with a chance to pursue an audacious progressive agenda (Alter, 2020; Elving, 2021). The Biden administration, along with congressional Democrats, moved quickly to give apparent credibility to those comparisons. In March 2021 the

American Rescue Plan (ARP), a $1.9 trillion package, extended PUA and enhanced UI payments albeit at $300 rather than $600 per week. It also made a further direct payment to individuals of $1,400.

While these measures were assumed to be temporary adjustments to help people through the continuing pandemic turmoil, a further element of the ARP excited welfare state advocates. The law included changes to the CTC that significantly re-oriented that program (Marr et al., 2021). The maximum benefit increased by 50% from $2,000 to $3,000 for families per child, and to $3,600 for households with children younger than six years old. Even more fundamentally, the ARP changed the CTC's eligibility rules so that families that paid zero tax or even registered no earnings qualified for a newly fully refundable benefit. According to Luke Shaefer and Kathryn Edin (2021: 12), two prominent scholars of poverty in the U.S., these changes held out "the promise of dramatically cutting child poverty and eradicating its most extreme forms, nationwide." In its review of the evidence a Brookings Institute survey reported how recipient families used the new or extra monies to help pay for a variety of costs such as "routine expenses such as housing and utilities," "clothing or other essential items for children" or "purchasing more food for the family" (Hamilton et al., 2022: 3). In December 2021, the ARP's expansion of the CTC lifted an estimated 3.7 million children out of poverty (Center on Poverty and Social Policy, 2021).

The glitch in this apparent good news was that the expansion had been enacted on a one-year basis. Advocates had hoped that the evidence of the beneficial impact of the new policy would quickly establish a political dynamic demanding that the expansion become permanent, or at least further extended (Center for American Progress, 2021). That dynamic did not materialize. Unlike the Obama administration, which had worked with comfortable if not always fully cooperative Democratic majorities in Congress, the Biden White House faced a much trickier institutional balance. The original ARP passed on a strictly partisan basis, which had included using the Reconciliation process in Senate to bypass the filibuster. A year later, that trick fell foul to just two recalcitrant Democrat senators who prevented legislative movement.

14.6 CONCLUSION

To external observers the breakdown of the legislative process as the Biden administration and the vast majority of congressional Democrats sought to renew the CTC expansion, hinging on the actions of such a limited number of political actors, might seem bizarre. Yet, even as it quickly became evident that the end of the CTC expansion had caused a spike in child poverty (Parolin, Collyer and Curran, 2022), the obstacle put in place by these institutional arrangements proved insurmountable. Importantly this outcome should not be understood in isolation. The efforts of President Trump and the majority of congressional Republicans to repeal the ACA in 2017 were ultimately undone by the votes of three Republican Senators who allied with their Democratic counterparts. If those three had voted with their own party then the ACA would have been undone. Hence, since 2011 at least the permanent expansion and retrenchment of the U.S. welfare state has been decided by fine margins, contingent on the behaviour of one or two individual legislators.

If the CTC expansion had been made permanent alongside the ACA the U.S. would have emerged from the political, social and economic turbulence of the Great Recession and the COVID-19 pandemic with its welfare state significantly enhanced. As it is, the ACA did not resolve the riddle of American health care provision. Illness can still impose an immediate economic as well as health burden and the country remains an outlier in terms of its spending on care. In this context, the ACA largely built on rather than swept away existing policy legacies. Nevertheless, individual elements were more than incremental. Defining major policy change is itself a fraught task, but it is a legitimate interpretation of the evidence to say that the turbulence of the Great Recession created the political conditions to push through important, and durable, change to the American health care state. At the start of 2021, it appeared as if a similar dynamic might apply to family policy, but the radical re-orientation of the CTC proved transitory.

Hence, the U.S. retained its "laggard" status. The "hidden" state does mean that there is more government intervention than is sometimes apparent from a cursory viewing, but the evidence also suggests that the beneficiaries of this hidden activity do not perceive themselves as being helped by government and therefore do not give political credit to the architects of these policies (Shanks-Booth and Mettler, 2019). Furthermore, while the CARES Act suggests an understanding that in an emergency only the state has the capacity to intervene effectively, the normal patterns of partisan politics persisted and reasserted their logic. The ACA was enacted in a window of opportunity when the Democrats enjoyed large Congressional majorities; however, that window quickly closed and in a finely balanced political environment Republican opposition to expansive social policy initiatives thwarts efforts to reconstitute the New Deal. Progressive welfare state advocates do now have models that they can draw upon for future reform efforts, but the institutional impediments to enacting and implementing those reforms in a durable fashion are formidable.

BIBLIOGRAPHY

Alter, Charlotte. 2020. How Joe Biden is Positioning Himself as a Modern FDR. *Time*, October 28. https://time.com/5904569/joe-biden-fdr/

Barone, Emily. 2020. How the New COVID-19 Pandemic Relief Bill Stacks Up to Other Countries' Economic Responses. *Time*, December 21. https://time.com/5923840/us-pandemic-relief-bill-december/

Béland, Daniel, and Alex Waddan. 2012. *The Politics of Policy Change: Welfare, Medicare, and Social Security Reform in the United States*. Washington, DC: Georgetown University Press.

Béland, Daniel, and Alex Waddan. 2017. Why are There No Universal Social Programs in the United States? *World Affairs Journal*, 180 (1): 64–92.

Béland, Daniel, Philip Rocco, and Alex Waddan. 2016. *Obamacare Wars: Federalism, State Politics and the Affordable Care Act*. Lawrence, KS: University Press of Kansas.

Béland, Daniel, Philip Rocco, and Alex Waddan. 2019. Policy Feedback and the Politics of the Affordable Care Act. *Policy Studies Journal*, 47 (2): 395–422.

Brasfield, James. 2011. The Politics of Ideas: Where did the Public Option come from and Where is it Going. *Journal of Health Politics, Policy and Law*, 36 (3): 455–459.

Center for American Progress. 2021. Now is the Time to Permanently Expand the Child Tax Credit and Earned Income Tax Credit. https://www.americanprogress.org/article/now-time-permanently-expand-child-tax-credit-earned-income-tax-credit/

Center on Poverty and Social Policy. 2021. December Child Tax Credit Kept 3.7 Million Children from Poverty. https://www.povertycenter.columbia.edu/news-internal/monthly-poverty-december-2021

Congressional Research Service. 2021. Unemployment Rates During the Covid-19 Pandemic, CRS Report to Congress, R46554, https://sgp.fas.org/crs/misc/R46554.pdf

Elving, Ron. 2021. Can Biden Join FDR and LBJ in the Democratic Party's Pantheon? *NPR*, April 17. https://www.npr.org/2021/04/17/985980593/can-biden-join-fdr-and-lbj-in-the-democratic-partys-pantheon

Emanuel, Rahm. 2018. "The Opportunities of Crisis", YouTube, 19 November. https://www.youtube.com/watch?v=_mzcbXi1Tkk

Esping-Andersen, G. 1990. *The Three Worlds of Welfare Capitalism*. Oxford: Polity.

Falk, Gene, and Margot Crandall-Hollick. 2016. The Earned Income Tax Credit (EITC): An Overview. Congressional Research Service. https://fas.org/sgp/crs/misc/R43805.pdf

Fiedler, Matthew. 2017. Repealing the Individual Mandate Would do Substantial Harm. Brookings Institute, November 21. https://www.brookings.edu/blog/usc-brookings-schaeffer-on-health-policy/2017/11/21/repealing-the-individual-mandate-would-do-substantial-harm/

Fording, Richard, and Joseph Smith. 2012. Barack Obama's "Fight" to End Poverty: Rhetoric and Reality. *Social Science Quarterly*, 93 (5): 1161–1184.

Fox, Liana, Irwin Garfinkel, Neeraj Kaushal, Jane Waldfogel, and Christopher Wimer. 2014. Waging War on Poverty: Historical Trends in Poverty Using the Supplemental Poverty Measure. National Bureau of Economic Research Working Paper No. 19789, JEL No. I32. http://www.nber.org/papers/w19789.pdf

Hall, Mark, and Michael McCue. 2021. Expanding Consumer Health Insurance Options by Easing the Boundaries Between Individual and Small-Group Markets. Commonwealth Fund. https://www.commonwealthfund.org/publications/issue-briefs/2021/oct/expanding-insurance-options-boundaries-individual-small-group-markets

Hamilton, Leah, Stephen Roll, Mathieu Despard, Elaine Maag, Yung Chun, Laura Brugger, and Michal Grinstein-Weiss. 2022. The Impacts of the 2021 Expanded

Child Tax Credit on Family Employment, Nutrition, and Financial Well-being: Findings from the Social Policy Institute's Child Tax Credit Panel (Wave 2). https://www.brookings.edu/wp-content/uploads/2022/04/Child-Tax-Credit-Report-Final_Updated.pdf

Howard, Christopher. 1997. *The Hidden Welfare State: Tax Expenditures and Social Policy in the United States*, Princeton, NJ: Princeton University Press.

Jacobs, Lawrence, and Theda Skocpol. 2010. *Health Care Reform and American Politics: What Everyone Needs to Know*. New York: Oxford University Press.

Jacobs, Lawrence, and Theda Skocpol. 2011. Hard Fought Legacy: Obama, Congressional Democrats, and the Struggle for Comprehensive Health Care Reform. In Theda Skocpol and Lawrence Jacobs (eds.), *Reaching for a New Deal: Ambitious Governance, Economic Meltdown, and Polarized Politics in Obama's First Two Years*. New York: Russell Sage Foundation, pp. 53–104.

Kaiser Family Foundation. 2012. Data Note: A Snapshot of Public Opinion on the Individual Mandate. https://www.kff.org/wp-content/uploads/2013/01/8296.pdf

Kliff, Sarah. 2021. Medicaid Enrollment Surpassed 80 Million, a Record, During the Pandemic. *New York Times*, June 21. www.nytimes.com/2021/06/21/upshot/medicaid-enrollment-surpassed-80-million-a-record-during-the-pandemic.html

Marr, Chuck, Kris Cox, Stephanie Hingtgen, Katie Windham, and Arloc Sherman. 2021. *House COVID relief bill includes critical expansions of child tax credit and EITC*. Center for Budget and Policy Priorities. https://www.cbpp.org/sites/default/files/2-9-21tax.pdf

McKenna, Claire, and Rick McHugh. 2016. Share of Unemployed Receiving Jobless Aid Remained at Record Low in 2016. National Employment Law Project. https://www.nelp.org/blog/presidents-budget-proposes-unemployment-insurance-reforms-as-share-of-unemployed-receiving-jobless-aid-remained-at-record-low-in-2015/

Mettler, Suzanne. 2011. *The Submerged State: How Invisible Government Policies Undermine American Democracy*. Chicago: Chicago University Press.

Newport, Frank. 2019. Social Security and American Public Opinion. *Gallup*. https://news.gallup.com/opinion/polling-matters/258335/social-security-american-public-opinion.aspx

OECD. 2014. *OECD Health Data for 2013*. Directorate for Employment, Labour and Social Affairs. http://stats.oecd.org/Index.aspx?DataSetCode=SHA

Olson, Laura Katz. 2010. *The Politics of Medicaid*. New York: Columbia University Press.

Parolin, Zachary, Sophie Collyer, and Megan Curran. 2022. Absence of Monthly Child Tax Credit Leads to 3.7 Million More Children in Poverty in January 2022. Columbia University Center on Poverty and Social Policy. https://static1.squarespace.com/static/610831a16c95260dbd68934a/t/620ec869096c78179c7c4d3c/1645135978087/Monthly-poverty-January-CPSP-2022.pdf

Pew Research Center. 2020. Positive Economic Views Plummet: Support for Government Aid Crosses Party Lines. https://www.pewresearch.org/politics/2020/04/21/positive-economic-views-plummet-support-for-government-aid-crosses-party-lines/

Quadagno, Jill. 2006. *One Nation, Uninsured: Why the US has No National Health Insurance*. Oxford: Oxford University Press.

Rich, Robert. 2013. The Great Recession. Federal Reserve History. https://www.federalreservehistory.org/essays/great-recession-of-200709

Rocco, Philip. 2020. Direct Democracy and the Fate of Medicaid Expansion. *JAMA Health Forum*. https://jamanetwork.com/journals/jama-health-forum/fullarticle/2769873

Scott, Dylan. 2020. How Trump Gave Insurance Companies Free Rein to Sell Bad Health Plans. *Vox*. https://www.vox.com/2020/6/30/21275498/trump-obamacare-repeal-short-term-health-care-insurance-scam

Shaefer, Luke, and Kathryn Edin. 2021. How to End Extreme Child Poverty. *The Atlantic*, June, 11–14.

Shanks-Booth, Delphia, and Suzanne Mettler. 2019. The Paradox of the Earned Income Tax Credit: Appreciating Benefits but Not Their Source. *Policy Studies Journal*, 47 (2): 300–323.

Sherman, Arloc. 2016. *Obama's, and the Safety Net's, Anti-Poverty Achievement*. https://www.cbpp.org/blog/obamas-and-the-safety-nets-anti-poverty-achievement

Skocpol, Theda, and Lawrence Jacobs. 2011. *Reaching for a New Deal: Ambitious Governance, Economic Meltdown, and Polarized Politics in Obama's First Two Years*, New York: Russell Sage Foundation

Spar, Karen, and Gene Falk. 2016. *Federal Benefits and Services for People with Low Income: Overview of Spending Trends, FY 2008-FY2015*. Congressional Research Service.

Starr, Paul. 2018. Achievement without Credit. In Julian Zelizer (ed.), *The Presidency of Barack Obama: A First Historical Assessment*. Princeton, NJ: Princeton University Press, pp. 45–61.

Statista. 2022. Number of People Without Health Insurance in the United States from 1997 to June 2021. https://www.statista.com/statistics/200955/americans-without-health-insurance/

Stolberg, Sheryl Gay, and Robert Pear. 2010. Obama Signs Health Care Overhaul Bill, With a Flourish. *New York Times*, March 23. https://www.nytimes.com/2010/03/24/health/policy/24health.html

Taskforce on Inequality and American Democracy. 2004. *American Democracy in an Age of Rising Inequality*. Washington, DC: American Political Science Association. https://www.apsanet.org/portals/54/Files/Task%20Force%20Reports/taskforcereport.pdf

Tax Policy Center. 2022. *Key Elements of the U.S. Tax System*. https://www.taxpolicycenter.org/briefing-book/how-does-tax-exclusion-employer-sponsored-health-insurance-work

U.S. Census Bureau. 2013. *Health Insurance Historical Tables: Table HIB-4: Health Insurance Coverage Status and Type of Coverage by State All People: 1999 to 2012*. http://www.census.gov/hhes/www/hlthins/data/historical/HIB_tables.html

U.S. Census Bureau. 2021. *Income and Poverty in the United States*. https://www.census.gov/data/tables/2021/demo/income-poverty/p60-273.html

US Department of Labor. 2010. *Labor Force Statistics from the Current Population Survey*. http://data.bls.gov/PDQ/servlet/SurveyOutputServlet?data_tool=latest_numbers&series_id=LNS14000000

U.S. Department of Labor. 2020. *U.S. Department of Labor Publishes Guidance on Pandemic Unemployment Assistance*. https://www.dol.gov/newsroom/releases/eta/eta20200405

U.S. Department of Labor. 2022. *Employment and Training Administration, Recipiency Rates by State*. https://oui.doleta.gov/unemploy/Chartbook/a13.asp

Waddan, Alex. 2019. Trumpism, Conservatism and Social Policy. In Mara Oliva and Mark Shanahan (eds.), *The Trump Presidency: From Campaign Trail to World Stage*. London: Palgrave MacMillan, pp. 179–201.

15. The way welfare states can develop in turbulent times
Bent Greve

15.1 INTRODUCTION

This last chapter aims to sum up and combine the knowledge gained from all the chapters of the book in order to present how one could tentatively foresee the ability of welfare states to cope with the many and varied challenges they are having and most likely will continue to have. This includes not only an understanding of the possible challenges, but also how to cope with them.

It is not just a matter of trying to anticipate challenges and their extent, but also that there may be differences in expectations, legitimacy and ideological attitudes towards the welfare states, which may be influenced by whatever form the socio-economic development takes, and the possible crisis looming in the future. The factors that may affect opportunities are central to Section 15.2.

Prioritization will undoubtedly need to be continued in some welfare states, as well as being a significant challenge in order to ensure quality and equal access. Knowledge can contribute to the ability to make good decisions, but not necessarily on its own to solving challenges. This point is central to Section 15.3, including that given there are individual preferences, the balancing of these can be difficult because not all wishes – just like at Christmas – will be fulfilled.

Based on the chapters in the book, Section 15.4 takes a closer look at what can be expected to be the biggest challenges for the welfare states, including how and in what way there may be contradictions between different goals and expectations for the role of the welfare states.

Lastly, Section 15.5 concludes. Given that this chapter to a large degree builds upon the previous chapters, fewer references than normal are used.

15.2 WHAT ARE THE OPPORTUNITIES?

The opportunities for welfare states in the coming years will depend on a large number of factors, the central ones being the combination of challenges, which are discussed in more detail in Section 15.4, and the economic opportunities available for developing the welfare state.

The economic opportunities depend not only on the development of the macroeconomic conditions, but also on how economic growth can be combined with wishes for, for example, how environmental challenges are to be tackled, see also Chapter 6. Less growth will be able to influence the level of CO_2 emissions, but at the same time it will reduce the opportunities for providing more and new welfare services. In the same way, lower economic growth in many countries will imply that there will be citizens who cannot have the same standard of living as others. The latter could theoretically be addressed through a stronger economic redistribution, but there will be a high risk that there will not be sufficient voter support for this, with it being even more difficult to get support for a more progressive taxation of the highest income earners. Differences in prospects for the individual's private consumption can thus become a problem for the growth of public consumption. This is because if private consumption is increased for some and not for others, then those who don't get more individual consumption might be less willing to finance public sector spending.

Overall economic growth can thus be an important indicator of whether there are more or fewer opportunities available for the welfare states to develop. This also includes whether there is support for using the state as the means to be able to steer economic development using a Keynesian economic approach, see more in Chapter 7, to ensure the necessary demand in order also to have the possibility of as low an unemployment rate as possible.

The opportunities in the individual countries will also depend on whether in better economic times money is set aside for bad times, or at least to ensure that public debt is reduced so that there is room for manoeuvre to cope with the exogenous effects of welfare state opportunities in new crises.

Therefore, the opportunities will also be affected by the economic policy being organized in such a way that there will be an opportunity for extraordinary financial intervention in the event of new challenges, such as COVID-19, the crisis in Ukraine or new economic crises, see more in Chapters 5 and 12, or in relation to the climate crisis, Chapter 6.

At the same time, challenges increase the need to be able to prioritize and make systematic choices between different types of efforts, and for evidence-based knowledge to largely be used to decide between different types of activities, so that scarce resources are used in the best possible way, see further in Section 15.3. This can also be a way to cope with voters' expectations and the legitimacy of the welfare state, see also Chapter 5.

New technology will also be one of the ways that can help to create opportunities for welfare states. This is because in some areas it can contribute to more efficient production by carrying out new types of services and thus be able to better satisfy the citizens' wishes. It will be difficult for new technology to be implemented without several problems also occurring, see more in Section 15.4, such as on the labour market, see more in Chapter 3.

At the same time, new technology may bring the risk that welfare services that become expensive, such as gene therapy, become available only for the group that can afford to pay for these services themselves. Health services are important, including also that health itself – in the context of the changing demographic composition – is important, see more in Chapter 8. The welfare state's ability to create equality in access to a number of important welfare and health care services, and not only formally, but also in real terms, is thus an important element, which also requires economic opportunities for it to be ensured.

15.3 IS IT POSSIBLE TO PRIORITIZE?

In practice, everyday decisions are made which, albeit while not always being openly presented as such, imply prioritization among different activities and projects and where to spend the welfare state's scarce resources. This does not imply that the decisions are always based on the best available knowledge, which might also be difficult to obtain (Greve 2017). So, even decision makers might prioritize, albeit while not framing it as a choice between different options.

Still, the pressure from voters, interest groups and, related hereto, the ability to ensure re-election, as well as keeping the legitimacy of the welfare states begs the question of how to do this, given the expected change in societies in the years to come, see also Chapters 5 and 10.

The use of evidence-based knowledge can be a way forward. This includes, just to exemplify, that new medicine is used first only when it can be documented that the gain in quality of life is above a certain threshold, and also that when comparing interventions, the one being the most effective per invested sum of money is the one used for the purpose.

Still, even though this might be possible within one area, how to prioritize across areas is still very difficult. How shall one prioritize between income transfers to those in need (without a discussion on how to define and measure need) with spending on reducing climate change? Or, even if there is evidence that one intervention gives the most value for money, does this then imply that spending on health care for the elderly – who have typically left the labour market – shall not be prioritized as they have fewer healthy years left, and an intervention will only yield a limited number of QALYs? Thus, ethical and normative issues in relation to the understanding of justice and equality can be issues to be aware of (see also in relation to migration – Chapter 14; in relation to climate – Chapter 6; in relation to labour market policy – Chapter 12; and in relation to education – Chapter 9). Thus, even if the use of the best available knowledge is possible, there will still be room and the need for making prioritizations.

Voters' expectations are typically for a constant source of more and better services, which, as a consequence of the development of available resources, might not be possible to fulfil. At the same time, promises by politicians in order to be re-elected, in combination with voters' expectations, imply a risk that many find that there are fewer resources available than earlier (the austerity debate) without this in fact being the case (Greve 2020a, 2021), including that voters do not necessarily know the level of benefits (Geiger 2018; Greve 2020b). Thereby, the ability to prioritize will also be influenced by electoral promises, in combination with the fact that it will be natural for interest groups to try to get better and more resources covering their specific needs.

15.4 WHAT ARE THE LARGEST CHALLENGES?

Many of the current challenges are not new in this respect, but they have been exacerbated by the stronger integration of countries' economies in the global economy, and by the fact that difficulties in one country can quickly spread to another or, in fact, many countries at the same time. Also, this is a reason for arguing that despite the need for welfare states, they are also here in turbulent times.

This does not change the fact that demographic change, see more in Chapter 2, towards more older people and fewer younger people is a challenge, although it is modified by the fact that we not only live longer but are also healthier for more years than before. The challenge is a combination of a possible pressure in the field of health, see more in Chapter 8, and that elderly care can also be affected by these changes. In addition, if it leads to a smaller labour supply, there will also be the risk that it will create new challenges, including the need to ensure high levels of education (Chapter 11).

However, these new challenges will largely depend on how technological development will affect the need for labour, including also what types of skills will be needed in the coming years. If there are strong technological changes it will place greater demand on the organization of the labour market and labour market policy, see more in Chapters 8 and 12, to ensure a better balance between supply and demand, but also because the new technology with jobs on platforms and more and more precarious conditions challenge the cohesion of a welfare state.

This pressure can be exacerbated by the fact that new technology, especially the use of AI technologies, may create a bias in who gets the opportunity to get help in the event, for example, of unemployment. Thus, the principle of equality in who can have welfare state benefits is reduced through the continuation of existing types of bias in who gets what from the welfare state.

At the same time, new technology increases the risk that it may become difficult to finance the welfare state. This is partly because capital can easily be moved from one country to another, but also to a much greater extent that it can be difficult to assess where a product, especially a service product, is actually produced, and when the place of production is not clear, then it can be more difficult to determine where taxes are to be paid to finance welfare states. The risk of cheating to avoid paying taxes and duties and activities in the hidden economy are also increasing. Thus, technology can be a positive game changer, as well as an example of the risk of poorer and more insecure working conditions for many, and perhaps no job at all for numerous people.

However, these challenges are not the only ones that can be predicted; there can be, of course, bubbles in the economy, such as in the housing or financial markets, but also completely unexpected crises such as the COVID-19 pandemic, and the consequences of the Ukraine crisis for both Ukraine and Russia and also for the world economy, including inflation having a stronger impact on some groups than others. It is still unclear how long each crisis will be able to have an impact. These unexpected crises, as argued earlier in the chapter, mean that welfare states must be assumed to need resources to cope with such upheavals to avoid them leading to less strong welfare states with reduced services and rising inequality, and not just economic inequality, but also broader forms of inequality. The resources will also be necessary in order to secure a financial safety net in the event of a new crisis.

This growing inequality is also a challenge, as it means that societies are less closely connected socially, and in reality this also contributes to creating a breeding ground for more populist approaches to, and understandings of, the role of welfare states.

The climate crisis is increasing the need for public intervention to counteract the speed of climate change, and at the same time to be able to reduce CO_2 emissions, see also Chapter 6. But in addition, if significant public resources are to be used to help resolve the crisis, there may be a risk that fewer funds will be available to address other pressures on the welfare states. At the same time, it can increase the risk of conflict between different perceptions of whether, for example, climate or health policy is the most important, and thus intensify the struggle for the distribution of scarce resources in welfare states.

The choice of what to do and the prioritization of scarce resources is becoming, to a greater extent than before, a task for welfare states, including ensuring that those who already have power do not benefit from the resources and/or that the resources do not go to those who shout the loudest and are the best at safeguarding their interests. It could increase the risk of more populist approaches at the same time as it does not provide assurance that groups with a weak position in society will also have a share in the progress of prosperity.

15.5 CONCLUSIONS

There is, perhaps there always has been, a strong and continued pressure for changes in public sector spending in order to fulfil the expectations of voters for continuous better and more welfare. At the same time, a number of pressures, especially as presented in Section 15.4, imply that new tasks (as well as options to deal with them) are there. These include demographic and technology changes, the impact of globalization, inequality, climate change, migration, etc.

Within these challenges, ideological and political positions – including struggles among different groups in a society – influence what is going to happen in different types of welfare states. In some, the universal approach will still prevail, with strong state intervention and an ambition to solve the many and varied challenges to keep the welfare state as the central answer. In others, a higher degree of using a market approach will be the central answer to find the solutions to the existing challenges.

Nevertheless, to end on a positive note, with an economic policy ensuring a climate-friendly growth there will also be resources available ensure the future of the welfare states in a solid way. State intervention in the market economy, without specifying the level hereof, to ensure socially cohesive societies will be important in order to cope with the constant changes and challenges to welfare states.

LITERATURE

Geiger, Ben Baumberg. 2018. "Benefit 'Myths'? The Accuracy and Inaccuracy of Public Beliefs about the Benefits System." *Social Policy & Administration* 52 (5): 998–1018.

Greve, B. 2017. *Handbook of Social Policy Evaluation*. Cheltenham, UK and Northampton, MA, USA: Edward Elgar Publishing. https://doi.org/10.4337/9781785363245.

Greve, B. 2020a. *Austerity, Retrenchment and the Welfare State: Truth of Fiction?* Cheltenham, UK and Northampton, MA, USA: Edward Elgar Publishing.

Greve, B. 2020b. *Myths, Narratives and Welfare States*. Cheltenham, UK and Northampton, MA, USA: Edward Elgar Publishing.

Greve, B. 2021. *Research Handbook of Austerity, Retrenchment and Populism*. Cheltenham, UK and Northampton, MA, USA: Edward Elgar Publishing.

Index

accountable care organizations (ACOs) 117
active labour market policies (ALMPs) 7, 22, 79, 180–91
    financial crisis 184–6
    Matthew effects 181, 189–90
    passive labour market policies 180–81
    post-COVID welfare 186–8
    social investment policies 181–4
        employment assistance 182
        incentive reinforcement 182, 183
        occupation schemes 182–3
        upskilling 182, 183
    technological change 189–90
    workfare 181–4, 186–8
affluent society 90
The Affluent Society (Galbraith) 89
Affordable Care Act (ACA) 7, 113, 117, 215–18, 221
Ageing and Health (Greer) 22
ageing process
    demand-side pressures 11, 13–15
    economic needs 12, 18–20
    financial needs 12, 18–20
    interventions
        employment rates 20–21
        labour market developments 22
        pension system characteristics 21
        retirement behaviour 21
        willingness to pay 22
    supply-side effects 11–12, 15–18
    working-age population 11–15
American Recovery and Reinvestment Act (ARRA) 213–14
American Rescue Plan (ARP) 220
American welfare state 210–21
    COVID-19 pandemic 218–20
    Earned Income Tax Credit 211–12, 214
    Food Stamp Program/SNAP 211, 214–15
    Great Recession 212–15
    health care reform 215–17
    liberal welfare regime 210
    Medicaid 211, 212, 216, 217, 219
    rugged individualism 217
anti-austerity movements 142, 145–7, 163, 164, 185
austerity 80, 144, 145, 148, 172, 181, 184–7
    to COVID crisis 104–8
    legacy of 48
    policy paradigm of 48

Biden, Joe 215, 216, 219
Buchanan, James 99, 103
budget balance rule 49, 51, 56, 59, 63, 64
budget consolidation 52–3
Build Back Better (BBB) plan 106

Carter, Jimmy 100
Centers for Medicare and Medicaid Services (CMS) 116
class 51, 146, 174
climate change 7, 84–95
    Galbrathian Affluent Postnational Oligarchy 92–3
    governance of welfare 84–5
    Jessop's governance of welfare framework 85–91
    Schumpeterian Workfare Postnational Regime 86, 91–2
climate crisis 5
climate migration 195–205
    critiques 201–3
    environmental degradation 203
    environmental migrants 203
    environmental refugees 196–8
    human mobility 195–6, 201–2

232

Index

new research agenda 203–4
Oxfam Study 195
securitization 198–201
   apocalyptic narratives 199
   destabilizing effects 200
   national and international security 199–200
   strategic threat of migration 201
   uncontrolled migration 200
   trapped populations concept 202
climate mobilities *see* climate migration
climate refugees 196–8
complex causation 52
conflicting perspectives 3–4
conjunctural causation 52
coordinated market economies (CMEs) 43
corona bonds 108
Coronavirus Aid, Relief, and Economic Security (CARES) Act 218, 219, 221
cost-effectiveness analysis (CEA) 116
costless health care interventions 119–21
country clusters 43–4
COVID-19 pandemic 1, 5, 7, 22, 80, 98, 118, 167, 169, 172–4, 176, 181, 191, 210, 211, 230
   active labour market policies 186–8
   American welfare state 218–21
   economic opportunities 227
   health care challenges 113–15
   Keynesian economic policy 104–9

debt-financed economic stimulus 99
DeLong, Brad 103
demand-side pressures 11, 13–15
demography *see* ageing process
deservingness 3, 71, 79, 215
Digital Economy and Society Index (DESI) 31–2
digitalization 31–2, 35–7, 42
Digital Platform Economy Index (DPEI) 31
discursive coalition 204
distributive profiles 138, 139

Earned Income Tax Credit (EITC) 211–12, 214
economic needs 12, 18–20
economic opportunities 227
Edin, Kathryn 220
Emanuel, Rahm 213, 215
employee relations 41–2
employment assistance 182
employment-based insurance 114
environmental degradation 203
environmental migrants 203
environmental refugees 196–8
episodic mass mobilizations 145, 146
European Commission 31–2, 105, 184
European Company Survey (ECS) 32, 41
European Economic Area (EEA) 49, 52
European Financial Stability Facility (EFSF) 105
European Pillar of Social Rights (EPSR) 180, 185
European Social Survey (ESS) 72, 73, 75, 148
European Value Survey (EVS) 72, 73
Eurostat demographic projection 13
Eurozone 51, 56, 59, 63, 64, 104, 105, 107, 184
evidence-based knowledge 228

Feldstein, Martin 103
financial crisis
   active labour market policies 184–6
   Keynesian economic policy 5–6, 101–4
financial needs 12, 18–20
fiscal consolidation
   case selection 52–3
   causal conditions 55–7
   expenditure reductions mechanism 49
   operationalisation 53
   outcomes 53–5
   revenue increases mechanism 49
   set-theoretical expectations 50–52
   socio-economic conditions 51
flexicurity 86, 180
flexploitation 86, 180
Food Stamp Program 211
Friedman, Milton 99
The Future of the Capitalist State (Jessop) 86
fuzzy-set qualitative comparative analysis (fsQCA) 5, 49
   necessary conditions 57

sufficient conditions 58–63

Galbraith, J.K. 89, 103
Galbrathian Affluent Postnational Oligarchy 92–3
Glass–Steagall Act 102
Great Financial Crisis 181, 182, 184, 186–8, 191
Great Recession 212–15
Great Transformation 127, 134, 135, 137

Hayek, Friedrich August von 99
health care challenges 112–21
    American welfare state 215–17
    COVID-19 pandemic 114–15
    low-cost/costless interventions 119–21
    prevention 115
    technology support 118–19
    value/value for money 115–18
        accountable care organizations 117
        payer arrangements 116–18
        social determinants of health 118
    welfare state context 112–14
        employment-based insurance 114
        private health insurance 113–14
        social-welfare maximization 112–13
human mobility 195–6, 201–2

ideology reasoning 71
incentive reinforcement 182, 183
industrialization 31
institutional reasoning 71–2
International Labour Organization (ILO) 31
International Monetary Fund (IMF) 100
International Social Survey Programme (ISSP) 72, 73, 77–9

Jessop's governance of welfare framework 85–91
Jones, Daniel Stedman 100
Juncker Commission 185

Keynesian Bretton Woods system 99

Keynesian economic policy 5, 98–109
    from austerity to COVID-19 104–8
    financial crisis 101–4
    neoliberalism 99–101
        debt-financed economic stimulus 99
        employment 101
        monetarism 99
        social justice 100
    prospects 108–9
Keynesianism 87, 103, 105
knowledge economy 127–40
    definition of 127
    educational expansion 128–31
    growth regimes/strategies 137–8
    labor market changes 131–2
    occupational change across countries 131, 133
    welfare legacies 134–7
        social compensation 134–6
        social investments 134–6
        two-dimensional 136
    welfare reform scenarios 138–40
        basic income strategy 139
        distributive profiles 138, 139
        market liberalism 138, 139
        social investments 138–9
        social protectionism 138, 139
Krugman, Paul 103

labor relations *see* union density (UD)
labour market 2, 15, 21–2, 75, 79, 80–81, 90, 144, 180–90
left parties 51
left-wing protesters 142–64
    data and methods 148–9
    descriptive results 149–52
        perceived bad standard of living of unemployed 148, 152
        perceived underuse of benefits 148, 152
        support for redistribution 148, 151
    hypotheses 146–7
    under increasing pressure 143–4
    multilevel regression analyses 153–63
        on outcome variables 154–5

perceived bad standard of living
of unemployed 148, 156,
159–60
perceived underuse of benefits
148, 156, 161–2
support for redistribution 148,
156–8
overview of 142–3
social movement participants 145–6
episodic mass mobilizations
145, 146
membership activism 145, 146
radical mass activism 145, 146
social movement responses 145
legitimacy 1, 71, 75, 85, 102, 106,
142–3, 226
liberal market economies (LMEs) 43
Lisbon Agenda (2000) 101
long-term care (LTC) 16–18, 20, 22–3
low-cost health care interventions
119–21

Maastricht Treaty 100, 101
market liberalism 6, 128, 138, 139
Matthew effects 181, 189–90
membership activism 145, 146
middle class 1, 3, 139, 146, 167, 174
migration 2, 14, 77, 196–205
*Migration and Global Environmental
Change* (Foresight) 202
monetarism 99
multilevel regression analyses 153–63
on outcome variables 154–5
perceived bad standard of living of
unemployed 159–60
perceived underuse of benefits
161–2
support for redistribution 157–8
Myers, Norman 196

national-level technology *vs.* work
analysis
cross-sectional outcomes 33–6
longitudinal analyses 36–40
neoliberalism 99–101
debt-financed economic stimulus 99
employment 101
monetarism 99
social justice 100

non-routine cognitive jobs 131, 132
non-routine manual jobs 131, 132
non-working-age population 12, 14
Nordic model 189
nudges 119–21

Obama, Barack 102, 212
occupation schemes 182–3
opportunities for welfare states 226–8
organizational characteristics and
preferences 32
organizational level technology *vs.* work
analysis 40–44
country clusters 43–4
digitalization/platformization 42
national level relations 41
outcomes 42–3
self-employed/labor relations/
employee relations 41–2

passive labour market policies 180–81
Piggy Bank 8
platformization 31, 35, 38, 39, 42
Polanyi, Karl 127
policy-specific welfare attitudes 77–80
Pollack, Mark 100
populism 3, 218
Posner, Richard 103
Prescott, Edward C. 103
prioritization 228–9
private health insurance 113–14
public pension benefit ratio 20
public welfare attitudes 71–82
across countries 73–5
across policies 77–80
future research 80–82
ideology reasoning 71
institutional reasoning 71–2
self-interest reasoning 71
socioeconomic groups 75–7

Quality-Adjusted Life Year (QALY) 171
Quality Outcomes Framework (QOF)
116

radical mass activism 145, 146
Reagan, Ronald 100
right-wing protesters 147, 153, 163
Roosevelt, Franklin 212

rugged individualism 217
Ryan, Paul 218

Schumpeterianism 87–8
Schumpeterian Workfare Postnational Regime 86, 91–2
securitization in climate 198–201
　apocalyptic narratives 199
　destabilizing effects 200
　national and international security 199–200
　strategic threat of migration 201
　uncontrolled migration 200
self-employed indicators 30–31
self-employed share 31, 33, 36, 38
self-employed working hours 31, 34, 37, 39
self-interest reasoning 71
Sener, Yilmaz 7
Shaefer, Luke 220
Single European Act (1986) 101
Smith, Vernon L. 103
social compensation 134–6
social determinants of health (SDoH) 118
social investments 6
　active labour market policies 181–4
　　employment assistance 182
　　incentive reinforcement 182, 183
　　occupation schemes 182–3
　　upskilling 182, 183
　welfare legacies 134–6
　welfare reform scenarios 128, 138–9
social justice 100
social legitimacy 142
social movement participants 145–6
　episodic mass mobilizations 145, 146
　membership activism 145, 146
　radical mass activism 145, 146
social protectionism 6, 128, 138, 139
social retrenchment 185
social-welfare maximization 112–13
socioeconomic group based welfare attitudes 75–7
solo self-employed share 31, 34, 37, 38
strategic threat of migration 201
Supplemental Nutrition Assistance Program (SNAP) 211, 214–15
supply-side effects 11–12, 15–18

tax-based consolidation 49
technological support
　active labour market policies 189–90
　challenges 229–31
　health care 118–19
　transitions 12
technology vs. work
　data sources and measures 30–32
　　digitalization 31–2
　　industrialization 31
　　organizational characteristics and preferences 32
　　platformization 31
　　self-employed indicators 30–31
　national-level analyses 33–40
　　cross-sectional outcomes 33–6
　　longitudinal analyses 36–40
　organizational analyses 40–44
　　country clusters 43–4
　　digitalization/platformization 42
　　national level relations 41
　　outcomes 42–3
　　self-employed/labor relations/ employee relations 41–2
　overview of 28–30
　standard argumentation 29–30
telehealth 118
Thatcher, Margaret 100
Tooze, Adam 107
total-age-dependency ratio 13
trade balance 50, 51, 56
trapped populations concept 202
Treaty of Amsterdam (1998) 101
Trichet, Jean-Claude 104
two-dimensional welfare legacies 136

Ukrainian crisis 1, 230
uncontrolled migration 200
unemployment 50, 73, 86, 102, 109, 183–5, 187, 212, 213, 219
unemployment benefits 2, 78, 79–80, 134, 180–81, 184, 186
UN Environment Programme (UNEP) 196
union density (UD) 28, 29, 31, 33–41, 43–6
upgrading 132
upskilling 182, 183

US welfare state 7

value-based insurance design (VBID) 116
value/value for money 115–18
    accountable care organizations 117
    cost-effectiveness analysis 116
    payer arrangements 116–18
    Quality Outcomes Framework 116
    social determinants of health 118
Volcker Rule 102
voters' expectations 229

Wall Street Crisis 176
Washington Consensus 98
welfare legacies 134–7
    social compensation 134–6
    social investments 134–6
    two-dimensional 136
welfare reform scenarios 138–40
    basic income strategy 139
    distributive profiles 138, 139
    market liberalism 138, 139
    social investments 138–9
    social protectionism 138, 139
welfare spending 167–76
    conflicting demands 174–6
    evidence-based policies 169–72
    public sector financing 172–4
    voters expectations 168–9
willingness to pay (WTP) 22
workfare 181–4, 186–8
working-age population 11–15
World Bank 55, 56, 100
World Trade Organization 100